The Profound Impact of PRODUCT LINE STRATEGY

Your Guide to Highly Productive Innovation and Product Management

PAUL J. O'CONNOR

The Profound Impact of Product Line Strategy

Your Guide to Highly Productive Innovation and Product Management

By Paul O'Connor

Published by
Advantage NPD, an imprint of
ADEPT GROUP Publishing, LLC
Ponte Vedra Beach, FL 32082
www.advantagenpd.com

Cover by Radar Media Group, Inc.
Print ISBN: 978-0-9997381-0-8
eBook ISBN: 978-0-9997381-1-5

U.S. trade bookstores and wholesalers: Please contact Adept Group Publishing, LLC, visit www.advantagenpd.com, or email the publisher at Booksales at www.advantagenpd.com.

Printed in the United States of America
Publisher's Cataloging-in-Publication data

Categories:

Business

Product Line Strategy
Product Line Innovation
Product Line Management
Product Development
Product Management
Marketing
Technology Management

First Edition

Product Line Strategy

"A product line strategy lays out a coherent approach to improve competitiveness, increase customer satisfaction, and maximize income—in the near and long term. It does this by astute management of interrelated issues toward creating, selecting, designing, developing, producing, supporting, and retiring related products and services."

— Paul O'Connor

Product Line Strategies
Trounce
Single Product Strategies

Contents

Foreword:

From Product to Process to Strategy

MANY OF MY friends and colleagues don't associate me with "strategy" topics. To them, I'm a product development process guru, portfolio management expert, or roadmapping wonk.

That impression wouldn't be completely wrong. For decades, I've helped corporations around the world improve their product development workflows. I've helped strengthen many portfolio management approaches. I've also both taught and set up roadmapping practices.

While doing that, I realized that something was missing. Many companies overlook the importance of having a product line strategy. Yet a strong product line strategy can be the difference between success and failure for an entire business! Who cares how effective processes might be when they aim at a poor strategy. This simple insight changed my direction. My concern and focus shifted to figuring out the strategy side of products and coupling it to processes.

This book is for executives, managers, and contributors in medium and large organizations, not those in small companies or entrepreneurial startups. It deals with big-company issues. It explains why good product line strategies are so important. It also explains what makes a product line strategy good and effective—or not so good.

The framework I lay out fills the knowledge gap about product line strategies. I explain how innovation and product management converge into a powerful context that can drive enormous value for any medium- or large-sized organization. Organizations that embrace the framework and adapt it to suit their situations will use it to improve current product lines and build new ones. It is not so much about tossing aside current approaches as it is about advancing them.

The framework I share is not just a set of forms with blanks to be filled. Rather, it is an approach that demands analytical and creative thinking. In traditional innovation and product management, such "mind work" involves coming up with concepts and new products. In contrast, the framework focuses on creating and improving whole product line strategies, while embedding strong practices into an organization's day-to-day work. This can be powerful.

The job of a product line team is identifying the paths that increase the value of products for their business. They must spot and exploit changes outside their business, while expertly managing necessary change within. That is far easier said than done.

Product line strategy is a puzzle to be solved, one having an endless stream of puzzle pieces. The resulting picture—and its beauty—may seem to gradually wither away over time, or, for some product line strategies, to fragment in an instant. And the puzzle itself is ever-changing ... more like a movie with each picture constituting a frame in an evolving storyline. Sometimes the story can seem mundane and frustrating, while at other times exhilarating. But it's *always* a tough challenge.

Genius in strategy does not arise just from analyzing competitive threats, suppliers, and market influences. Nor do I see it coming only from thinking about the future, although these are important. True strategy genius comes from matching bundles of technologies with bundles of customer needs over time and repeatedly. And it's about organizations carrying this out skillfully. Getting this right demands sharp thinking toward product line strategies. This is crucial for today's large businesses.

Unfortunately, most companies are more likely to tackle the challenge only by generating a laundry list of new product opportunities without addressing the coordination of work and decisions. That approach results in poor product line strategy. But that's the purpose of sharing this knowledge: to help organizations create effective product line strategies and avoid poor ones.

Good product line strategies are a key to profitability and to the overall success of a business. They have become increasingly important over the past few decades. Consider how many formerly successful companies have missed important markets and then disappeared from the limelight. Good examples are Kodak, Polaroid, Bausch and Lomb, and Blackberry. These companies were once profitability giants that missed critical opportunities for growth.

Combined with the right roadmap and smart pivoting, an effective product line strategy could have enabled these companies to capture new markets. For Kodak, this could have been the digital imaging market. For Bausch and Lomb, it could have been the daily disposable contact lens market. For Polaroid, it may have been multiple "instant and fun" photo markets. And for Blackberry, it was the enormous opportunity to ride the smartphone market.

After reading this book, you'll be able to recognize other companies that went down the same path. Perhaps similar end-stories await businesses we read about today. It could be Harley-Davidson if they are unable to adjust to the rapid decline of their "HOG"[1] market. Or it could be General Electric's turbine business if it fails to adapt to core technology changes and better target new market segments. Then there is Campbell Soup, which is struggling with its large and nearly moribund red cans. Pick up *The Wall Street Journal* and you're bound to see a story about some large, well-known company besieged by changes in markets and technologies.

For students of business strategy, I'm not a strict advocate of any particular school. I acknowledge the design school that brought us SWOT analyses and the positioning school that encourages actions based on industry forces. I also recognize the learning school that emphasizes understanding and re-interpreting knowledge, the entrepreneurial school that focuses on the future, and the various other schools.[2] I believe it's important for product line strategy to take useful aspects from each of these thought-worlds, while setting aside those not helpful. A strong dose of operational excellence in practicing product development and management is also necessary. Coupling this to astute organizational change makes the impact of this approach profound.

Over my consulting career, product development has evolved beyond a focus on single products to managing portfolios and complex systems. Here, I add product line strategies to traditional approaches such as innovation strategy, agility, product planning, and business-model innovation. These are methods that connect to product line strategy. But they are neither the product line strategy,

---

1 HOG is an acronym of Harley Owners Group.

2 Professor Henry Mintzberg of McGill University defined the strategy schools in his book coauthored with Ahlstrand and Lampel entitled Strategy Safari: A Guided Tour Through the Wilds of Strategic Management. It was published by Simon and Schuster in 2005. For the nitpickers among us, the approach toward product line strategy set out here might best fit the Configuration school, which views strategy as a transformative process that incorporates elements from the other schools.

nor its multiple dimensions that change over time. It's the dynamics of these dimensions and their effective management that matter.

While this book is written to help practitioners, I also encourage consultants and academics to examine the topic closely. Many people have made significant contributions to its parts. But a notable gap exists in knowing how best to address the Product Line Strategy topic as a whole. Much work remains to flesh out greater benefits.

Let's be clear, though: Practitioners are leading this journey with consultants like me merely organizing and streamlining the path forward. And academics help by analyzing how different subjects and parts like engineering design and organization structure can influence each other to improve product line strategy.

Smart executive teams know how and when to use key influences intentionally in their product line strategies. Understanding this topic reveals how such choices are deliberate choices within dynamic conditions. That's where the real game of product lines and their respective strategies is played.

I wish to start readers off with a simple call to action—to move beyond the singular nature of project-based product development and management and into the pluralistic world of product line strategies and roadmaps. It's important to be aware right from the start that this is a leap and not a small step. This is particularly true for large organizations with practices, processes, and cultures focused on developing and managing one product at a time. But it is a necessary step to enable companies to compete more successfully in today's world.

The Book

I divide this book into six sections to help organize your journey through the topic. The approach introduces, and then builds on, the concepts key to good product line strategies.

SECTION 1: **DEFINING THE PROBLEM:**

The Least Understood Yet Most Impactful Contributor to Any Large Business.

SECTION 2: **FUNDAMENTALS AND BACKGROUND:**

Knowledge and Perspectives to Tackle the Problem

SECTION 3: **LAYING OUT THE SOLUTION:**

The Product Line Strategy Framework — Getting to Good

SECTION 4: **RAMPING UP THE SOLUTION:**

Strategizing and Roadmap Management — Orchestrating the Flow

SECTION 5: **IMPLEMENTING THE FRAMEWORK**

Realizing Profound Gains

SECTION 6: **RESOURCES AND SUPPORTS:**

Systems Thinking, Cases, Tools of the Trade, and Finding Help

The Lexicon

Throughout the book, you will see a growing list of words and terms needing definitions. Together, they make up the lexicon or language of product line strategies. In separate sidebars, I call out a "definition alert" for those critical to product line strategy concepts. This is to help you as needed.

Some sidebars complement definitions with examples. And some sidebars reference entire chapters that explore the concept. There is also a glossary of terms at the end of the book, plus an index for those seeking page attribution.

The Good Product Line Strategy Build

Good product line strategies can yield profound, positive results. In large companies, getting to "good" and staying there is a core responsibility for all managers who deal with product lines. Understanding and doing this is what this book is about. At the end of some chapters and each of the five sections, I track the journey of getting to good product line strategies. This is a list of those characteristics discussed that make strategies good. And, when helpful, I also call out notable hindrances that work against the journey of getting to good product line strategies.

I hope you embrace the full impact this book is intended to convey. Welcome to the world of product line strategies!

Paul O'Connor, President

The Adept Group Limited, Inc

Acknowledgments and Thanks

I've learned that writing a book is not the easiest job in the world. It takes deep thinking, much editing, and the freedom to spend time on the task. For each of these, I am in debt to many people.

Many academics have influenced me. Their work and their ability to challenge my ideas is the foundation for this book. But I am not an academic. My view has always been through a consultant's eyes. And my focus has been on getting a job done for clients. It's not research that matters as much as getting work done in large organizations.

I might be out-of-bounds saying that an academic could never write this book. But I must also say I could not have written it without them. Product Line Strategy cuts across many topics. Each topic needs foundational thinking and must also be extended further. For this, I am deeply indebted to several academics who created the foundation. They set the stage for me to think about issues and challenges, often taking me months if not years to apply it to clients and build an understanding.

At the top of my list is the late University of Michigan Professor Merle Crawford. I had read Merle's seminal paper on Product Innovation Charters. He showed how using charters directs and gives purpose to product development teams. But it took decades for me to recognize the importance of charters. It turns out charters are key to roadmapping, portfolio management, and product line strategy formation. None of this was in the vocabulary of product development when Professor Crawford introduced innovation charters. His work, though, stuck with me. That's because Merle was my mentor when I was President of the Product Development and Management Association (PDMA.) He took the time to sit with me and explain his research, why he did it, and why it was important. Thank you, Merle.

PDMA is a conduit of knowledge about product innovation. Indiana University Professor Thomas Hustad is another mentor I met through PDMA. Tom was the editor of the association's Journal of Product Innovation Management. He encouraged and guided me to write an article for the journal on best practices in implementing a stage-and-gate process. And while I thought this a giant task, it's only in retrospect I see how guiding me was such a huge job for Tom. For this, I am deeply indebted to you Tom.

I would not have delved into process implementation if it had not been for McMaster University Professor Robert Cooper. I met Bob because of a common client, Exxon Chemical. It wasn't Bob's famous Stage-Gate work that got us together at first. It was his NewProd research, a brilliant approach to screening concepts based on empirical research. This was an approach that never took off. But it taught me much. It led me to understand systemic risks in product development portfolios. This pointed to organizational challenges that rear their head when cutting across a business unit's functional strategies. Understanding such challenges is fundamental to good product line strategies. Thank you, Bob.

I am reminded by my friend, University of Utah Professor Abbie Griffin, how I tapped her to head PDMA's research. It's silly to think I deserve any credit for Abbie's deep intellect and hard work. Without her work on QFD, Voice of the Customer, and Serial Innovators, the product development community would fall short in our collective knowledge. Abbie was also a notable force pushing me on the manuscript for this book. I hope it's worthy of her effort.

Another academic who made me think differently, and probably not realizing he did, was Nelson Repenning, now Associate Dean at MIT Sloan School. He used my article on setting up processes to support his work on Systems Thinking in product development. This opened an entire world that influenced my thoughts about product line strategies. Thank you, Nelson. Without your thinking, this book would be shallow.

Along the way, many consultants also had great impact on how I think about innovation and product management. Years ago, my friend George Castellion encouraged me to learn MIT Professor Edgar Schein's approach called "facilitative consulting." Understanding the approach changed how I worked with clients. It enriched my career. Thank you, George. It was a small gesture that made a huge difference.

Stepping up to thinking through strategy topics can be a daunting task. True, unless you learn from my friend and fellow consultant Greg Githens. Greg is a world-class expert on how to think strategically. He is also an expert in both product development and project management. Fortunately for me, Greg has been a sounding board for many of my thoughts on product line strategy. I have enjoyed Greg's help. Thank you, Greg.

Learning with clients has been half the fun. The list is too long to share. But there are a few clients I must thank. DuPont, Dow and Procter & Gamble played major roles in helping me learn the real-world side of product development and innovation management. I must give a special thanks to John Hillenbrand, former Chief Innovation Officer at OwensCorning and now heading technology for Armstrong Flooring. John helped me see how internal politics is a key thread within an organization's culture. I learned from John how personalities, shared-understanding, and intelligent leadership matter. Thank you, John, for allowing me to see an intelligent leader at work.

Throughout the book you'll see many references to culture. To many people, culture is a difficult topic to get your arms around. I had the good fortune of working with an incredible consulting firm in Thailand that made culture much more tangible. The firm was the APM Group, now known as SEAC and lead by Khun Arinya Talerngsri. Here, strategy consultant William Malek and the APM consulting team opened a new door for me. It helped me experience organizational culture from a different perspective, one not common to US or European companies.

My work in helping SCG Chemicals move their product line from commodity offerings toward greater value was especially rewarding. A special thanks to SCG Chemical's president, Khun Cholanat Yanaranop, and vice presidents Khun Sakchai Patiprnpreenchavud and Dr. Suracha Udomsak. Seeing and experiencing organizational behavior rooted in the rich Thai culture elevated my awareness and sensitivity to how behavior and culture matter.

I'd be lax if I didn't call out my friends at Waters Corporation, a leading liquid chromatography, mass spectrometry, and software company. Here I learned the challenge of moving a product line from hardware to systems and the pressures of changing markets. I hope my contributions prove positive in the years to come. Thank you, Waters Corporation.

My biggest thanks no doubt go to my family. For years, my wife, Donna, has been my sounding board. Her tenure teaching leadership to McKinsey & Company consultants and leading organizational development for several large organizations gave her a world of understanding. And it helped me through many client engagements. Donna encouraged me to write this book and then tolerated me as I did. Thank you, My Love. I must also add our son, Bryan, our daughter, Kristy, and her husband, David Lingebach. Their support is never-ending. And to our granddaughter GG. You brought an enormous smile to my face as you sat on my lap helping me through much editing. Thank you, Bryan, Kristy, Dave and GG.

SECTION 1

DEFINING THE PROBLEM

The Least Understood Yet Most Impactful Contributor to Any Large Business

Why Product Line Strategies Matter More Than Any Single Product

- The Profound Impact & Lost Opportunity
- Sidestepping the Challenge

Chapter 1

The Profound Impact of Product Line Strategy, Yet Lost by So Many

PRODUCT LINE STRATEGY can be a difficult subject to discuss. That's because many managers think they know the topic. But instead, they confuse it with other related areas. Often, I begin a conversation about product line strategy and someone will respond to me with thoughts about strategy for a single product. Then too, other managers somehow think portfolio management is the same as product line strategy. You may also hear people confusing the topic with roadmapping, product planning, and even business strategy. These subjects relate to, but are not the same as, product line strategy.

Product line strategy is unique to itself but relates to many other subjects. It cuts across markets and extends over time. It is about advancing bundles of technologies to match changes in market needs. And it seeks strong interplay with nearly every function within an organization while seeking to satisfy customers and beat competition.

Much has been written about business strategy, and a lot has been written about developing and managing *individual* products. But little (if any) literature concerns product line strategies, whether about planning or execution. Nor are there sources that describe how to transform poor strategies into good ones and carry them out superbly.

When working with clients on product development and management, I've seen many approaches added to their practices. These range from gated processes to lean and agile methods, from the voice of the customer to empathic research. These have elements useful to product development and management. At the same time, many organizations miss the full development of their skills toward driving growth. Traditional practices fall short. This is due to poor approaches toward building and keeping *strong product line strategies.* But the strength I am referring to is not just towards the markets it serves. It is also towards the internal behaviors and decisions that teams must navigate.

Products and services are the lifeblood of most companies. They connect the organization directly with customers, and they are what brings in revenue. Yet many companies pay little attention to crafting superior product line strategies and thereby miss opportunities for greater growth and success.

No company can rest forever on the laurels of a single product or service. Somehow the firm needs to grow, and that growth may come in many forms. A company can reduce costs and push demand, it can dominate a growing market, it may improve attributes of existing products, or it can expand into new markets. And, of course, it can launch new products, maybe even radical innovations with enormous potential.

New or improved products are a large source of growth for many companies. For example, we all viewed with admiration the new

"Swiffer" line of cleaning tools that Procter and Gamble launched. But we also groan when we remember how "New Coke" bombed after being developed and launched with overzealous confidence by Coca-Cola in the mid-1980s.

Top managers know growth is about creating new offerings that succeed over the long term. But it's also clear that few succeed in continually doing that. Time and time again, companies miss their growth targets. What happens then? Sales stagnate or even shrink, the company's reputation suffers, and poor customer satisfaction leads to reduced market share.

Consider the quagmire Sony currently finds itself in. Its new offerings over the past few decades have been lame compared to those of competitors like Samsung. Yet Sony was aware of every major opportunity that Samsung exploited like high definition TVs, cell phones, and notepad devices. Sony has been so poor at product line strategies that I'd argue it may have irreparably damaged its brand. PlayStation and movie-making seem to be its only remaining lines.

When poor product line strategies take hold, executives may be puzzled. They might scratch their heads and wonder, "Why this?" even though they believe they have been devoting notable resources to their development processes. In recent years, all major corporations have made major investments in their product development and management talent pools—from DowDuPont to BASF, AT&T to Vodafone, Microsoft to Apple, General Electric to Emerson Electric, and Tesla to BMW, but results can still fall short.

I've seen underperformance time and time again. The problems may vary, but the common source of these problems is simple: a failure to create superb, well-thought-out product line strategies that are flexible enough to respond to changing conditions. All too often, companies make reactive strategy moves too late. This doesn't need to happen.

The content I lay out in the next fourteen chapters is guidance to avoid missed opportunities and prevent strategy moves made too late. Since the problem lies in poor or mediocre product line strategies, the key to better performance is transforming these strategies into great ones. You can do this by developing successful product lines with strong strategies from scratch or improving those that lag.

This is not just about just matching product attributes to customer needs. Neither is it only about cross-organizational execution or gaining leverage to boost the line. Each of these is important. But, as you'll see, how these influences come together in a full approach matters more. Smartly addressing all aspects of product line strategy is critical to ongoing success.

How to do this is the core of this book. It lays out a clear framework that can help companies analyze what's going wrong with an existing strategy and how to improve their approach. And, for companies that have not yet developed excellent product line strategies, the framework helps put the right one in place. This framework purposefully aids product line teams, those responsible for managing and growing the product line to drive greater cash flows, ensure better use of resources, and increase overall customer satisfaction.

I call this the *PLuS Framework*™, where "PLuS" is a simple shorthand for Product Line Strategy. As you'll see, it's flexible and adaptable, not a strict discipline or method. And it's not a software application to be loaded on a server. Rather, it's an approach toward thinking through creative, analytical, and strategic challenges. And it's a discipline of deliberate choices and actions. When fully implemented, the framework keeps product line contributions to business strategy at their best—to the benefit of customers, shareholders, and the organization.

Chapter 2

Sidestepping the Problem

Before I present the framework for creating good product line strategies, let's first discuss some ways companies try to stimulate growth or make up for less-than-stellar product line strategies. These rarely work well enough to hit desired growth goals for the business, but they are important to understand. Avoiding their shortcomings, it turns out, is a key to crafting good product line strategies.

Well-developed and well-managed product line strategies keep pace with the fluidity of market and technology change. These good strategies help companies achieve growth more consistently and identify and capture opportunities more quickly. But some leadership teams are so bogged down in fighting the fires of near-term challenges that they don't realize the importance of strategy at the product line level. Neither do they see the enormous gains to be made from a disciplined reevaluation of that strategy.

Let's be fair, though. Nearly all managers involved with product lines recognize that some form of strategy does matter. Unfortunately, they don't always have the tools, resources, thought processes, or customer understanding to create a realistic strategy that achieves the most from a product line and can be measured and adjusted over time.

Then too, the problem may not be lack of tools or knowledge. Rather, it is often culture,[3] the sum of behaviors across an organization. This is not a malicious or evil force; in fact, it's the opposite. Culture can exude a positive feeling of well-being, one that induces people to be strong contributors and collaborative team players. Yet at the same time, it may reinforce a heroic, single-product orientation to product development. Or, it may encourage doubling down on "the customer is always right" thinking. This unfortunately often leads to leaning out, not building strategies. Left unchecked, seemingly positive cultures can run counter to smart product line strategies. Somehow, product line strategies must win out over such influences.

Product line strategies and their execution are key to business success. Most managers realize strategies should address topics like innovation and market positioning. They recognize the need to coordinate work to achieve milestones. Plus, they know successful strategies can change their company's inner-workings.

But these same managers have a difficult challenge. It boils down to making this happen in their companies. This means getting the resources, commitment, and, most important, top management's involvement—not just blessing.

As you read, you'll first learn how to spot poor product line strategies. You'll also learn how to improve them significantly with both the elements of strategy and needed organizational change. The framework I lay out will help you think through approaches and take deliberate actions toward advancing your product lines on a bad-to-good continuum.[4] But it is also about embedding and

---

3 Culture, as discussed here, refers to the behaviors and norms within larger organizations. I provide a clear definition in the Glossary at the end of the book.

4 I encourage readers to read UCLA Professor Richard Rumelt's book entitled Good Strategy Bad Strategy: The Difference and Why It Matters. It was published in 2011 by Crown Publishing Group, a division of Random House. .

improving practices. It's about making good product line strategies part of the fabric of your organization and its full business strategy.

Growth Approach #1: The "Next Big Thing"—The Project Rather than Strategy Approach

Many companies approach the growth challenge by thinking they only need to innovate one product or service at a time, and so they concentrate on the *"next big thing."* What's surprising is that it seems like such a positive driver. Some company's history and culture tell them they succeeded with one innovation, and things turned out great. Now all they need to do is just create another genius innovation, and everything will be better. Think it up, and they will come. Why? Because they believe, *"we're really good at what we do,"* and that's all that's needed. This belief is at the core of the organization's culture.

Companies need a string of successes—tied together. The problem is that a forced approach toward the "next big thing" just doesn't work consistently. A series of product offerings needs to advance with markets, customer needs, technologies, and competitors. *This calls for a holistic and multi-generational (Definition Alert) approach to growth across all related products. And this more powerful way of thinking starts at the product line level.*

> **DEFINITION ALERT:**
> Multi-Generational
>
> The term "multi-generational" refers to an orderly approach toward designing and developing products and services in a series of generations. The Apple iPhone is a clear example. It started in 2007 and has had eleven generations as of this writing. For Apple, a new iOS generation (operating system) accompanied each iPhone generation.

Relying solely on the "next big thing" approach makes for bad strategy. Sure, every company wants a great new product. But just because your company wants the product doesn't mean enough customers will buy it, or that it will impact growth and earnings significantly. The challenge is not about developing a solitary product. Rather, it is in gaining a fluidity toward creating, developing, and carrying out a good strategy. It is this fluidity that enables product lines to evolve, to advance technologies, and to match changes in customer needs and wants.

Let's look at a simple example of what can happen even to a young company that didn't have a good product line strategy with the correct execution. That company is Keurig, the coffee brewer manufacturer. Keurig had a very strong and positive culture that emphasized entrepreneurial success. Most people who worked for Keurig were and continue to be very proud, and they cringe at discussing mistakes. But when Keurig tried to innovate using the "next big thing" approach, it worked against them.

BOX 2.1: How Keurig Missed the Boat

Keurig is the company that invented the single-serve coffee brewer, which it launched in 1998. The machine appeared in its target market—corporate offices—soon after launch and moved into the consumer market a few years later. For many years, Keurig dominated this fast-growing market, having a virtual monopoly on this new way to produce individual cups of coffee with less mess.

But the company knew that the patent on its single-serve K-cup pods (a key to its profitability) was due to run out in 2012. To continue its growth trajectory, Keurig needed to expand its product family. The onus was therefore placed on Keurig's designers to create something new—the company's next big thing. Sure enough, they delivered. It was the cool-looking Keurig 2.0—a hot beverage brewing system that included the additional ability to brew a large canister of coffee.

Keurig's CEO Brian Kelley thought they had hit a home run. "Our new Keurig 2.0 system is the next innovative step for our hot beverage brewing system," he stated in 2014.

Unfortunately, consumers disagreed. Sales were low. Complaints poured in. The market balked. What was happening? "Full pots … [were] … something we bought Keurig machines not to have to do in the first place," wrote Daniel Kline for *Motley Fool* in April 2015.

The next big thing turned out to be not so big!

Where did Keurig go wrong? Could this stumble on the road have been avoided? Yes, it could have. In fact, good product line strategy ensures the match between product attributes and what customers really want. The strategy and how it was being carried out should have spotted and measured the key job consumers wanted: *making a good cup of coffee.*

The discipline of defining the right product line strategy would have identified the mistake of forcing the "next big thing" in advance. It would have homed in on the critical nature of market segmentation and of carefully matching the nuances of the customer's true wants, needs, and most important, desired "outcomes[5]." This is what I refer to as "attribute positioning," *(Definition Alert)* and it is fundamental to good product line strategies.

Consider how the Keurig 1.0 focused on making "a good cup of fresh-brewed coffee." Their mistake with the 2.0 was when the development team homed in on the wrong attributes or misunderstood them. "Making a good cup" was the job customers wanted done. The 2.0 did not improve on that task. Instead, it added the attribute of making pots of coffee, not just the single cup. It wasn't faster, tastier,

5 Much more on "Outcomes" is discussed in chapter 7.2. It deals with attribute positioning and ties directly to "Job-to-be-Done" theory.

or cheaper. For many consumers, it offered a less convenient approach to the central task of making a single cup of coffee.

DEFINITION ALERT:
Attribute Positioning

This is the deliberate targeting, development, and delivery of product or service features. Doing this work sets up a market position in a segment. The work matches product attributes to customer needs, wants, and desired use outcomes. Attribute positioning is key to good product line strategies. I share more on this topic throughout the book.

A smarter approach toward product line strategy would have convinced both developers and marketers to work together to explore other options. Without this thinking, Keurig wasted a lot of time and money. Sure the 2.0 still exists. But instead of being a new offering, it's simply a rework or next generation of the 1.0 without the full pot feature.

Many people who hear the Keurig story immediately jump on the need for different or better customer research. Yes, this is true. And in later chapters I will discuss what makes for better research. But the other story lies with Keurig's very strong and positive culture. A very positive, can-do attitude was supported by their enormous success. And who's to argue with success? But the challenge was to change behaviors and judgments to enable smart product line strategies. It should not have been just to take a reactive "next big thing" move.

A famous quip attributed to Peter Drucker states "culture eats strategy for breakfast." In Keurig's case, I'd argue culture ate strategy in meal preparation. Somehow product lines must avoid this. And as you will see in later chapters, the *PLuS Framework* works to address this directly and purposely.

The "next big thing" is not the only errant approach companies use as they seek growth and greater impact from new products. Let's look at two others.

Growth Approach #2: "The Workaround"—Putting Innovation Outside the Mainstream of Business

Another way companies deal with the product growth challenge is to avoid key internal problems altogether! That's right. Managers look for end-runs. This happens often in large organizations.

The obstacles to doing something new, like creating and carrying out a new product line strategy, can seem large. So large, in fact, that rather than stamping out bad strategies, creating new points of leverage with new platform-levers, or figuring out how to move into new markets, some managers just try to avoid everything.

Why does this happen? Possibly because the company lacks the capabilities needed to develop, launch, and manage notable innovations. It may be short on the skills needed or not have adequate approaches to sufficiently alter a product line. Then again, its culture might focus on a different direction. Often a situation like this makes it hard to argue against going outside the norm. The company seems to have no choice. Perhaps they really are incapable of innovating. This leads to many managers looking for other solutions. The most popular scoot-around approaches have titles like skunk works, lean startups, venturing, ring-fencing, and intrapreneurship.

Each of these has virtues. They can be very helpful, and they should be used. But to rely on them on a regular basis rarely works. While these approaches can yield positive returns, they tend not to be large or fast enough to impact growth notably for large businesses. Nor do they confront the work practices and cultural norms of a business. You'll see that no matter how good your plans, making end-runs around the way your company does business can backfire.

How Intrapreneurship Failed at One Company

Let me take one concept that's becoming popular again—intrapreneurship. I want to show you what happened at one prominent company that tried this approach. Gifford Pinchot[6] first suggested the concept of encouraging "intrapreneurs" within a company, and clients of his firm, Pinchot & Company, were the first to use it. Gifford promoted his thinking through his book *Intrapreneuring: Why You Don't Have to Leave the Corporation to Become an Entrepreneur* (1985). His concept initially gained some popularity but died out in the 1990s. Interest in it is now reviving, but any company considering it today should be aware of what happened at DuPont when it implemented its $eeds program to support managers seeking to become intrapreneurs.

BOX 2.2: How Intrapreneurship Fared at DuPont

Top management in Dupont's Research and Development and Commercial Dupont was always passionate about innovation. Nearly everyone in marketing and R&D took training in innovation. To drive innovation further, Dupont also hired reputable consultants to help set up an initiative called the "$eeds" program. It stood for "Dollars to Encourage Entrepreneurial Development."

6 Both Gifford Pinchot and I worked at the small innovation consulting firm, Innotech, in the early 1980s, although I never worked on any projects directly with him. This firm was dedicated to finding and exploiting opportunities in much the same ways as "open innovation" does today. The frustration for Innotech consultants (both Gifford and me included) was that clients seldom brought their newly found innovations to successful fruition. Gifford's recourse was to go around organizational impediments using the approach he named "Intrapreneurship." I, on the other hand, began working with Professor Robert Cooper, using his NewProd statistical algorithm to model success and failure of new products and the initial rollout of his Stage-and-Gate process to carry out development.

The program provided funding for potential innovations. It targeted managers who had a concept they thought justified being developed. The notion was for intrapreneurial managers to pitch their ideas to their business unit's management. If their top management turned down the idea, the "intrapreneur" could go to the $eeds program to request independent funding.

Unfortunately, and not surprisingly, a serious problem arose. When business unit heads say "No" to an idea, they tend to mean it. They don't want "their resource" to sidestep them for funding. Instead, leaders want their staff members to focus on the projects that they consider important. That was a critical issue. It boiled down to different views about the importance of the concept. Guess who lost out?

As the $eeds initiative revealed, a business unit's inner-workings to carry out strategy may conflict with an intrapreneur's wish to move her idea forward. This conflict led to the death of intrapreneurship, not just at DuPont but also at every other firm at which it was tried.

By the early 1990s, intrapreneurs were nowhere to be found. Many managers used a cutting remark to sum it up: *"Intrapreneurs are merely entrepreneurs in training."* In other words, these individuals shouldn't expect to work within their companies for too much longer.

Intrapreneurship isn't wrong. But like the other "work around" approaches, it won't fix the fundamental barrier to innovation: the business unit's inner-workings. The inner-workings are a combination of what I call the **"Chain-Link Strategies"** *(Definition Alert)* and an organization's culture. The *PLuS Framework*, laid out in the next several chapters, tackles these inner-workings directly. It does not sidestep them.

Growth Approach #3: "Everything Goes"—Progress Without Leverage

Consider a third approach many companies take when seeking growth from new products. It's what I call "everything goes." This is when product line teams and their organizations conjure up or have functions like the sales force thinking up every new product concept they can. They then filter out what they believe will or won't sell in sufficient volumes. If the idea has potential to yield positive financial returns, the thinking goes, then, by all means, continue with its development.

DEFINITION ALERT:
Chain-link Strategies

This is a way of thinking about business strategy in which many functional sub strategies are links in a whole chain. For example, a business strategy may comprise separate strategies for supply chain, finance, and human resources. Product line strategy is just one link within the chain-link business strategy. Good product line strategies will align with or gain alignment from other chain-link strategies.

UCLA Professor Richard Rumelt receives credit for the notion of chain-link strategy. He describes business strategy as a chain-link system in which the whole strategy is only as strong as its weakest link. This implies that strong product line strategies will fail when other links are weak. To succeed, good product line strategies need other chain-links to be aligned and equally strong.

The everything-goes approach is pervasive in product development, especially among those seeking to be progressively open in their thinking. It seems certain that organizations should support new product development projects that have a good likelihood of yielding positive financial returns. This always means there is some confidence that someone will buy the new product or service. And as long as the filter or screening method seems reasonably sound, the resultant project should also be sound.

Unfortunately, the everything-goes approach never ends well. It's not that one project may not succeed financially. It's that, over time, an accumulation of many such projects squanders the potential gains for the product line as a whole. When seeking to deliver customer satisfaction and fend off competition at the same time, this is a problem. Because of processes, methods, and culture, it's a problem that has deep roots within a business.

Sometimes organization don't have strong agreement across management to focus on the right parts of a product line and its offerings. Instead, they keep marching forward with the everything-goes approach. This can make it impossible to gain leverage, and leverage is the key to driving advantage in strategy. Consider Lucent Technologies, bought by the French company, Alcatel, which was then bought by Nokia.

BOX 2.3: Gaining Leverage at Lucent

After telephone industry deregulation in 1996, AT&T spun off the famous Bell Laboratories. It became Lucent Technologies. For several years, Lucent performed the same as Bell Labs and continued to provide technology to the other companies spun off. After deregulation, though, Lucent served many customers and dealt with several competitors. I consulted to Lucent about becoming customer-oriented during this change.

Product development at the time stressed staged development and cross-functional teaming. The approaches worked to build a market orientation each step of the way. In one of my engagements with Lucent, it was necessary to roll out a market-oriented product development training course to team leaders. When I asked how many leaders would be going through the course, I received a reply "we're not sure." After a few weeks, the answer came in. The Lucent team believed there would be roughly 2,600 project leaders needing training. How could that be? This was 50 to 100 times what

I would normally see, even in big companies. What in the world was I missing?

What I didn't understand was that nearly every sale became a product development project. For example, if Lucent sold a new switching station to PacTel, it became a project. Or, if it sold a full phone system to the country of Vietnam, it was a program and within it were many projects. And teams considered each project a new and unique development. Why? Because there was always something new in each project. Each was unique. Each required new software and ingenuity.

The real insight for me was about the design-to-order nature of Lucent's business. Each sale required the customized integration of software and multiple telephony components.

In effect, Lucent was perhaps the largest job shop in the world. Yet not once did anyone suggest they were in a service business—delivering customized integration of telephony components. Instead, management hammered home a focus on each telephony component and driving customer satisfaction. And they defined markets by customer types, not by integration needs or the outcomes desired by customers from complete systems.

The project managers had a different view of the development world. They focused on one customer at a time, each having unique integration needs. To them, hardware items were building blocks, not the core offering. Guess which view won—top management's focus on hardware or project managers' focus on integration services?

How could you think through strategy at any level without having an answer to this question? All eyes were fixed on the demands of Wall Street to become market-oriented. Yet the "market orientation" challenge seemed to blur everything. In hindsight, it is impossible to say whether a shift in focus from hardware components to integration services would have been more powerful for Lucent. But what is clear is that this confusion squandered Lucent's opportunity to gain leverage in its product line.

In product line strategy, there's need for intense focus on what I refer to as **platform-levers** *(Definition Alert).* If you can't agree what they are, leverage is unlikely. You're left only with the everything-goes approach.

For Lucent, the sales force brought in the projects. So long as the sale of a system would deliver a positive contribution margin and they could use their components, Lucent would go ahead with the system development. Every sale entered the everything-goes approach. The integration type or complexity did not matter. The everything-goes approach sought to deliver whatever the customer wanted.

DEFINITION ALERT:
Platform-lever

A platform-lever is a common factor that cuts across multiple products in the product line. It enables leverage — faster development and lower cost of delivering features and performance. Platform-levers impact throughout the creation, production, sale, and customer's use of related product offerings.

There are several types of platform-levers used in product line strategies. Product line strategy employs platform-levers singularly or in combination with other platform-levers. An example of a design platform-lever is a common motherboard used in multiple computers, or an automobile engine used in multiple cars. I share more about platform-levers throughout the book.

To Lucent's management, the customer was always right. But by neglecting product line strategy, their troubles mounted. They had little advantage in any market. Blaming Lucent's downfall on poor product line strategy may be like blaming the Titanic's sinking on poor training. Many reasons contributed. But like for others using the everything-goes approach, the results were not good.

Avoiding Mistakes and Driving Gains

I call out the three errant approaches (The Next Big Thing, The Workaround, and Everything-Goes) because they are common mistakes. The *PLuS Framework* works to build strong product line strategy that avoids them. In fact, the first pillar of the framework lays out the core of a product line strategy and tackles these three issues directly. I call this the **"Strategy-Essence."** *(Definition Alert)*

I explain the Strategy-Essence pillar in chapters 7 through 7.3. Through discussion and examples, I share how to turn these drawbacks into notable strengths. For product line strategies, this means greater gains and contribution to business strategy. But good product line strategy needs more than just a smart Strategy-Essence and avoiding these mistakes. It also demands continuous execution and calls for measurements and adjustments. It also needs incorporation into business strategy, and, most important, the organization's culture. These topics make up the *PLuS Framework's* other parts.

DEFINITION ALERT:
Strategy-essence

This is the core of a product line strategy. The Strategy-Essence has three parts: 1) Attribute positioning, 2) Chain-link alignment, and 3), Platform-lever leverage. A great Strategy-Essence will have notable contributions from each part plus unison across all three parts to boost their total impact. The Strategy-Essence is the first Pillar of the PLuS Framework.

TABLE 2.1 Spotting Problem Approaches

The Problem Approach	Why	Results of Approach	Recourse
Next Big Thing	Seeks to a create a single product to drive growth. Good product line strategy seeks success through a string of connected products. Good product line strategy is continuous.	Can have growth impact. But for large companies is seldom enough or enduring over long time periods.	Embrace an approach to relate multiple products as a coherent set. Use the right techniques to ensure matching product attributes to customer needs (customer desired outcomes.)
The Workaround	Seeks to avoid the internal workings of an organization. Good product line strategy works with the organization and induces change when needed.	Can produce positive results. Seldom counters the core challenges to existing product lines.	Openly influence organizational change to benefit the product line strategy or change the strategy to match the organization.
Everything Goes	Seeks to develop any products customers request when development seems financially sound.	Is guaranteed to lose advantage in the market.	Gain focus on building and sustaining "leverage" through well-defined platform-levers.

In the next few chapters, you'll read about the importance of product line strategies for gaining and keeping a company's competitive advantage. Then you'll see how products and strategies interact in the pluralistic world of product lines. Understanding the interaction sets the stage for what makes a product line strategy good and how companies carry them out. The discussion then leads to how to measure and adjust product lines and fully embed them in business strategy.

The Least Understood Yet Most Impactful Contributor to Any Large Business

Defining the Problem

PRODUCT LINE STRATEGY: GETTING TO GOOD

Seek to:

Use a holistic and multi-generational approach across all related products.

- ▶ Do not focus on just one product at a time. Exercising the whole product line is always more fruitful than going after just one product.

Avoid pitfalls and bad strategy moves.

- ▶ Stop hoping to win with a single "next big thing" product development.
- ▶ Avoid sidestepping organizational challenges to smart strategy moves.
- ▶ Don't use the "everything goes" approach. It does nothing to gain leverage.

Build awareness across your organization about how critical product line strategies are to business growth and survival.

Avoid your organization's "Kodak moment " by creating and executing good product line strategies to help growth and ensure survival.

Focus on the continuing work of good product line strategies while creating a discipline to influence an organization's behaviors and decisions. The task of getting to good product line strategies is more than just creating or forming the strategy. It's also about changing and advancing the organization and its culture.

SECTION 2

FUNDAMENTALS AND BACKGROUND

Knowledge and Perspectives to Tackle the Problem

Understand the Basics Before Taking the Dive

- Advantage: The Value of an "Economic Moat"
- Creating Bigger, Better Bubbles
- Product and Strategy Hierarchies

Chapter 3

Advantage: The Value of an "Economic Moat"

One way that companies drive shareholder value is by creating "economic moats" around their businesses. The term, popularized by famed investor Warren Buffett, describes a defendable competitive advantage that enables a firm to protect its long-term profits. The analogy is that the moat protects the business fortress and its shareholders from outside threats.

Good economic moats are always associated with a strong product line strategy. Good economic moats also need other non-product-related strategies to work with a product line strategy. As you'll see, Apple provides an excellent example of a company that has been protected by an economic moat. Although many companies have challenged Apple, Samsung for instance, none have so far been able to topple Steve Jobs' creation.

An economic moat places your company in a very strong position. Your business grows, your customers remain satisfied, and your competitors struggle. Because an economic moat insulates your company from competition, it's a positive for investors in your company, and rating agencies award it higher market ratings.[7] This translates into higher price-earnings ratios.

DEFINITION ALERT:
Economic Moat

Warren Buffett coined the term "economic moat." Buffet argues that investing in companies with wide economic moats is best. An economic moat is an advantage against which competition struggles. Companies only gain benefit from economic moats through smart execution of a deliberate business strategy. Often, good product line strategies strive to build economic moats.

How is an economic moat created? It's done through a collection of the right strategies. These are the chain-link strategies mentioned earlier. Depending on the business strategy, for instance, they include a sales strategy, a supply chain strategy, a branding strategy, and an intellectual property strategy. Most notably, a good economic moat always includes at least one product line strategy.

But having an economic moat does not mean it will last forever. Things change and so will the effectiveness of each chain-link strategy. You'll also see that companies can assume their moat remains intact, when instead the market has drained the water or a disruptive competitor has built a crossing bridge. Most often these failures deal with less-than-stellar product line strategies.

That's why it's critical for companies to constantly reexamine each strategy and to understand the divide between good and bad ones. Bad product line strategies can eliminate economic moats and leave companies vulnerable to competition, causing customers to look elsewhere. This is why bad product line strategies can foreshadow total business failure. Let's look at what happened to some giant U.S.

7 As evaluated by a shareholder-rating model created and used by Morningstar, an independent investment research and management firm.

corporations that unknowingly took their eye off their economic moats and let their product line strategies slip.

Sustained Advantage and Changing Needs

You'll see many companies treat product line management as a means to promote and manipulate individual products that already exist. That's fine, but strategy can and should go farther.

To develop and sustain an economic moat, it's important to manage product lines as a whole, not just the sum of individual products. Don't diminish product line strategy to a management guide focused only on products after their launch. Good product line strategies use the whole set of products to drive cash flow, beat competition, and increase customer satisfaction.

The challenge, though, is to keep strategies good when markets and technologies change. This requires a thoughtful approach toward change and renewal. It's also where many companies fall short.

Consider the sad stories of Kodak, Polaroid, and Bausch and Lomb. Each company employed many smart and talented people. I know. I consulted to each company. All had many innovation projects underway and had strong cultures. And each knew the threats from market and technology changes. But each failed.

BOX 3.1: Three Stories of Failure in Product Line Strategy

Kodak was eventually forced to downsize, file for bankruptcy, and nearly disappear. This is because it missed the digital market—a market it was well aware of from the very beginning of the digital age. But it didn't pursue this market quickly or hard enough. In addition, Kodak failed to sufficiently modify its inner-workings to enable it to win. Interestingly, it's worth noting that this happened despite some analysts crediting Kodak with creating the first digital camera! They were first, but never in the lead.

Polaroid is another example of a powerhouse of innovation that has largely disappeared. It hired the best and brightest, and people bragged endlessly about working for Polaroid. The company had a New-Age type brand image of "fun with instant images" and could have translated this to the value proposition "fun with almost anything." But Polaroid failed to do so, perhaps because it simply couldn't make the move.

Bausch and Lomb was a key player in the soft contact lens market in the 1980s. But they missed the shift to daily disposable lenses even though they had the same information on new technologies as their competitor, Johnson and Johnson (J&J). The difference was J&J figured out how to disrupt the market with one of the technologies. J&J drove contact lens cost so low they created the single-wear market. Customers could discard at the end of each day. Bausch and Lomb looked at things differently. They were the dominant player. Why would they risk that for a totally different technology? Unfortunately for Bausch and Lomb, the J&J induced disruption forced the market leader into bankruptcy.

Sometimes even very smart people working in seemingly positive cultures don't have the right insights, knowledge, or wherewithal to avoid closing shop

These cases make clear the importance of a smart, adaptable strategy at the product line level. Such a strategy plays a key role in creating and sustaining strong product lines. In turn, good product line strategies help build, reinforce, or totally remodel a company's economic moat.

Creating the right product line strategy using the *PLuS Framework* will help you recognize challenges and opportunities early on. You can use the approach to develop good strategy from the start, or turn a lackluster strategy into a successful one.

Culture, Moats and Product Lines

The importance of product line strategies to an economic moat is lost in many organizations. This is a critical problem. It happens because top management doesn't recognize the importance of product line strategies. Or they don't see how product line changes can help business strategy.

Most often, top managers are so consumed with firefighting they don't recognize how product line strategy moves and pivots are best carried out before the fires start. And sometimes they are so happy to put out fires that they don't see how reacting after the fact reflects poor strategy.

Unfortunately, the common response to a failing moat is to push on sales and marketing and to lean-out all operations. This approach doubles down on current product line strategies. It's the same as saying we're cutting costs and pushing harder on sales because we didn't advance our product line strategies earlier.

But how are we supposed to know about product line strategy moves and pivots so much earlier? Simple. It's the combination of discipline and insights. This is about busting through the culture – the sum of behaviors – that keeps organizations moving forward, often oblivious to changes in markets, technologies, and their industry.

To build and keep economic moats, product lines must aggressively get in front of key influences. The needed discipline is toward spotting and reacting to these influences. Good insights about those influences then set the reason and rationale for deliberate decisions that drive a product line's advancement.

Warren Buffett Was Right

When Warren Buffett discussed the positive value of an economic moat, he was right. I'd further argue that an economic moat gains its value by including strong product lines — those with good strategies that deliver ongoing value creation and can put a company in an enviable position.

Companies create such a moat by setting up a collection of functional and cross-functional strategies that are linked and so form a chain. More importantly, these strategy links align with and amplify one another. This makes the chain powerful in business strategy. Companies create an economic moat when competitors can't replicate or break the strategy chain. And, while a product line strategy forms just one link in this chain, it is a crucial one.

They key to an economic moat is having strong individual links that align with and amplify one another. This is done through the inner-workings of a business. In Chapter 7.1, I highlight how the inner-workings of a business come together, a matter of enormous importance.

Product line strategies form just one link in the chain. Clearly, good economic moats need good product line strategies. If you want to do your shareholders a favor, make your product line strategies as good as they can be while aligning them with the other functional and cross-functional strategies. The resulting chain-link is what matters.

Chapter 4

Creating Bigger, Better Bubbles

The goal of product line management is simple: *to expand opportunities and increase gains through better foresight.* These results are achieved through coordination of work, as well as by making both good decisions and wise investments. You'll find, though, that carrying out such work and decisions coherently needs guidance from a product line strategy.

Good product line strategies demand good insights and foresights. Being able to develop them sooner than the competition will make or break product line strategies. The *PLuS Framework* recognizes this, and it differs from traditional practices. You will see that most companies stress the speed of product development once concepts are in-hand. Instead, the framework seeks to minimize time lost well before a product concept is formulated. In the framework, then, speed in targeting strategically smart products and strategy moves becomes more important. The traditional focus on development speed is then a measure to aid strategy execution.

When concepts have been fully vetted, most companies then focus project teams on reducing time-to-market and minimizing risk. The notion of vetting is important, though. And it is why the *PLuS Framework* stresses vetting work *before or earlier than* typical development practices. Who cares about speeding development if concepts lack strategic purpose or impact? Measures such as revenue, profitability, market share, and customer satisfaction are what really matter. That's what organizations should care about, not just development speed.

A focus on reducing risk while speeding products to market is effective only if all competitors' products are roughly equivalent. And for those firms that are not the lowest cost producer, likeness of products in a market makes for poor strategy.

Up-front strategic thinking helps ensure sufficient time to create and thoroughly evaluate new projects. In addition, it allows time to adjust these concepts, should this be necessary. Consider the fictional example I give below. This is a company that gets into trouble with its portfolio of product development projects.

The case in Box 4.1 lays out the problem inherent in traditional portfolio management. And I'll explain how good product line strategy works to solve the problem.

BOX 4.1: SkinProtect Struggles to Meet its Portfolio's Financial Goals

SkinProtect, Inc., makes creams and lotions that protect against UVA and UVB rays. As shown in Figure 4.1 below, the company has four new products in development, represented by the four bubbles shown in Chart 1 on the left. The percentile within each project's bubble is that project's likelihood of success. Chart 1's x-axis is the distance or progress each project has made through each stage in its stage-and-gate process. The y-axis is the time remaining, in months, until each project is ready to launch.

The financial goal of the entire portfolio is $46 million to be reached three years following the launch of all four products. Here we see that BelleSilk is about two years away from launch. Thus, this goal should be reached five years in the future.

However, as Chart 2 shows, this goal is not currently achievable. Chart 2's bars represent the combined value of the four projects in each of the five years. The line running along the top of Chart 2 is the value of the portfolio that would yield the targeted $46 million in Year 5. Note that in all five years, the portfolio value falls well short of the value necessary to achieve the $46 million goal. Year 5's cumulative launch value is roughly $33 million, $13 million short of the portfolio goal. This gap presents the portfolio management challenge for this medium-sized business and raises the question of what to do.

Figure 4.1: SkinProtect's Product Development Portfolio

Chart 1 shows four product development projects in the SkinProtect portfolio, each progressing through their development stages (the X-axis). Each project has different development time remaining until launch (the Y-axis). The percent value next to each project's name represents the risk levels for the project. Chart 2 shows the portfolio's expected launch value for each of the next five years. The value is the risk-adjusted revenue for all products launched that year.

Chart 1: SkinProtect Products in Development

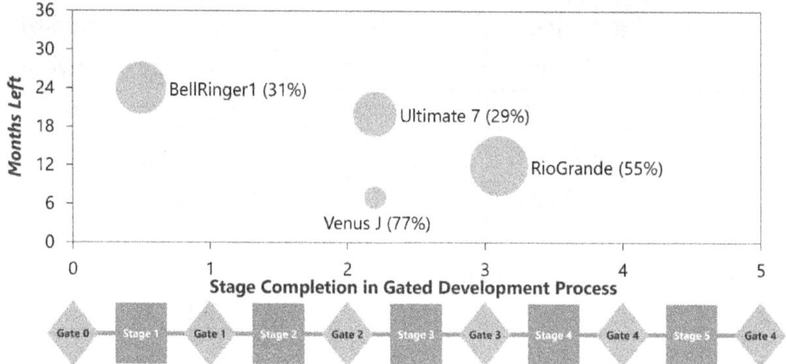

Chart 2: SkinProtect Cumulative Expect Launch Value

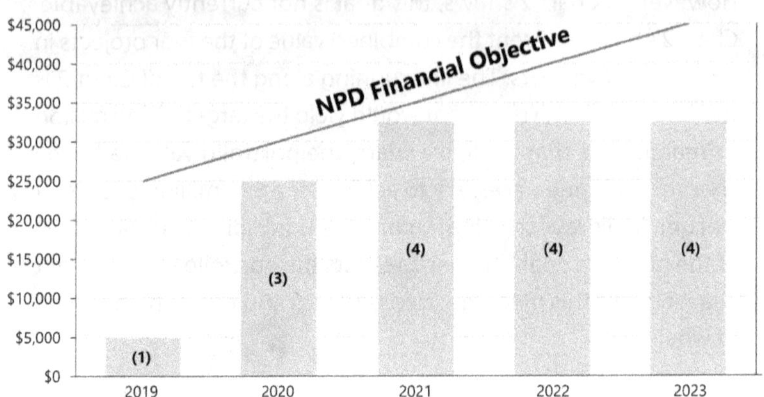

Portfolio Management Falls Short

In solving the SkinProtect case, most people home-in on each project's risk value, size, and months to launch. Venus-J, with a 77% success probability, seems to be the only near-certain project, but it's also the smallest. So, what then? Here are the two tactics managers typically try when they want to push their portfolios harder and solve the problem.

Option #1—Shed a project. The most common response is to shed a project (likely BelleSilk and Ultimate 7) and shift resources to the remaining projects (likely Rio Grand and Venus J). That's the common reason for having portfolio management—shifting resources across projects to get the most from the full set. However, in the SkinProtect case, stopping a project and shifting resources will cause the bars in the second chart to decrease. The bars shrink because of the smaller cumulative value of three projects as opposed to four. Under this option, the financial results still fall short.

Option #2—Add more projects. The thinking here is "If you need more out, put more in." Although this *may* improve the portfolio, adding new projects will inevitably slow down existing projects because they must share the limited set of organizational resources. The bars in Chart 2 in the SkinProtect example would shift to the right to reflect this product development delay, and the portfolio will continue to miss its financial objectives.

Creating Bigger, Better Bubbles

Both tactics try to deal with the situation by thinking about the trade-off of risk, speed, and resulting impact. Yet both fall short.

Traditional approaches leave managers in a quandary. What can they do? The answer may be surprising. It's to both shed poor projects *and* add new projects! The key to making this work, though, is to ensure that new projects are bigger, better bubbles. If the new bubbles have the same properties as the old bubbles (risk, size/impact, and development time), the company will continue to miss its objectives.

Flaws in Traditional Portfolio Management

Creating good concepts is the most important task in improving a portfolio. But it's also where traditional portfolio management falls short. Without introducing projects that bring better products to market, the portfolio will have less potential. Since finding bigger, better bubbles pushes product line strategies for greater gains, it's also the most important task for advancing a product line.

Both approaches try to fix the situation with some semblance of strategic thought. Option #1 above prioritizes projects with some combination of strategic importance and expected value, and then sheds those low on the list. Option #2 incorporates other projects that might fit the portfolio, arguably based on some notion of strategy. The problem is that both approaches fall short if adopted alone with only a vague idea about strategy.

Traditional portfolio management seeks to improve results from projects already underway but does nothing to introduce better, more significant projects into development. *The PLuS Framework* offers a different approach. In it, managers adopt strategic thinking in project creation, not just for vetting projects through selection and prioritization. As a result, new projects (as a set) have a better chance to deliver greater impact, lower risk, and quicker development times. And most important, it greatly increases the odds of meeting the financial goals.

The message is simple: *To improve a portfolio, find bigger, better opportunities sooner.* This is more impactful than improving work efficiencies or lowering development costs on existing products. When businesses use the framework, they gain an ability to find these bigger, better opportunities. The framework helps set guidelines and principles for what makes for "bigger" and "better." For those who choose other approaches, these adjectives remain vague and unhelpful.

Including bigger, better bubbles (projects) in the portfolio has another important implication for product line strategy: *If the value of a product line's development portfolio is in decline, its strategy is also most likely in trouble.* Let's say you take a snapshot of the "expected value"[8] of all the product developments underway in your organization for each of the last twelve quarters. If the portfolio's expected value is increasing, things are likely to be going well for the product line and its strategy. If this figure is trending downward, however, a pivot or major change to the product line and its strategy is likely necessary.

Remember this, because as you'll see in later chapters, the expected value of a product line's development portfolio is an important

8 This is the risk-adjusted value of a project. An example would be a project's net present value discounted by its technical and commercial risk (likelihood of success).

strategy metric *(Definition Alert).* Declining expected value should set off alarms about the product line strategy. New thinking will be needed to reverse this trend. For those in that situation, I advise you to keep reading.

DEFINITION ALERT:
Strategy Metric

A strategy metric is a measure of a product line strategy's change, impact, or results. Employing strategy metrics is fundamental to improving product lines. Using metrics with objectives is one of the four pillars within the PLuS Framework. I address strategy metrics in Chapters 9 through 9.2.

Product lines need new products if they are to flourish. Without improved offerings (bigger, better projects) added to a product line's development portfolio, the line will likely struggle. The message here is clear: Smartly creating and successfully commercializing new offerings are key to increasing the value of the development portfolio. They are also core purposes of product line strategies that move toward advancing the line.

Chapter 5

Product and Strategy Hierarchies

THE POWER OF a product line is greater than the sum of its products. One product can boost the impact of another product. Leverage can be gained from combined product design, production, and sales. And proper attribute positioning can drive customer satisfaction while blocking competitors. A focus on doing one product at a time squanders the power of the product line. But to gain this power, we need a basic understanding about what makes products lines and how there are different levels of strategy in large organizations.

Most large- and medium-sized corporations have product hierarchies. Even a company with just one main product may have enough variations to have a product line—and a product hierarchy. The definitions and relationships are important in developing a good product line strategy. But it's almost impossible to communicate effectively when product line team members don't use common definitions. (See Figure 5.1.)

Figure 5.1: Product Hierarchy

A simple product hierarchy divides items into four levels. The levels are the products, the platform-lever, the product line, and the product family. A product family may include multiple product lines.

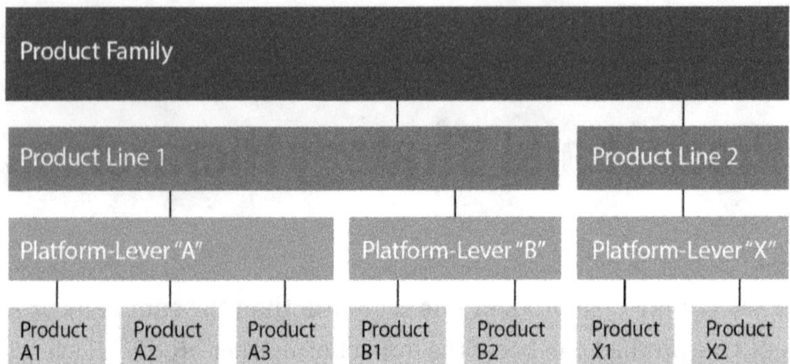

For our purposes, addressing only the basic product hierarchy is necessary. However, not all companies are the same, and, for some, other layers or combinations may be helpful.[9]

A product is a single offering with features that enable customer satisfaction. In Figure 5.1, the bottom row contains products—specifically, Products A1 through X2. Products are the foundation of the product line. In the second row up, **platform-levers** (*Definition Alert*) fall under product lines, which form the third row up in the product hierarchy. A *product line* is a group of products having at least one common platform-lever.

As Figure 5.1 suggests, a product line that lacks a platform-lever is a major void. Without a platform-lever, a product line's impact on overall business strategy is not ideal. To make a larger contribution, product lines need at least one well-thought-out platform-lever. They give leverage to product lines in driving stronger cash flows, faster product

9 Some teams also need to set up hierarchies to include "solutions" or "systems." Readers interested in this can find out more at https://adept-plm.com/plus-resources/ You'll see both solutions and systems defined by quality, economics, and functionality.

development, and greater customer satisfaction. They are so important, in fact, that I dedicate Chapter 7.3 to explain platform-levers in great detail.

The fourth and highest level in a product hierarchy is the *product family*. Here, multiple product lines come together to create the full offering of the business. A product family will have shared supports wrapping around the products, regardless of lines or platform-levers. Among these shared supports are contributions from such functions as branding, sales, distribution, and marketing.

The product family is often synonymous with a business unit. Specifically, each business unit has at least one product family. And, each product family may include one or more product lines. Therefore, when discussing "*business unit product strategy*," managers are usually referring to a roll-up of all the product line strategies within a business unit.

DEFINITION ALERT:
Platform-lever

In Chapter 2, I gave a simple definition of a platform-lever. In the hierarchy described in this chapter, you will see how a platform-lever cuts across multiple products. It enables faster development and economic delivery of each product. For example, the same circuitry and software may be used across many Samsung TVs. In consumer packaged goods, the same production process (a production-asset-type platform-lever) may produce a wide variety of packages, even for different brands. At an extraordinary level, consider VW Group's multi-billion-dollar design platform-levers for engines, frames, and bodies that cut across their Volkswagen, Porsche, Audi, and Bentley brands.

BOX 5.1: Samsung's Product Lines and Families

Let's look at Samsung, the Korean conglomerate, with business divisions focused on construction, consumer electronics, financial services, chemicals and materials, shipbuilding, and medical services. All use the Samsung brand. Each unit also has *at least* one product family. For instance, Samsung Consumer Electronics has several product families. Most people around the world are familiar with those families of products, which include communications, home and office, entertainment, and brown goods like TVs and appliances.

Product lines then fall within product families within business units. For example, Samsung's "Smart TV" product line falls under the brown goods family. Within the Smart TV line, the company would likely consider the circuitry–a single board–for its 4K UHD (ultrahigh definition) as a platform-lever. This same circuitry is included in multiple TVs, each of different sizes and with different attributes.

Why Product Lines Are Critical

The key challenge for both profitability and innovation lies at the *product line* level—not the corporate or business unit level, or at the individual product level. This is very different thinking from the single-product orientation pushed by many academics and consulting gurus. Rather than a focus on the single "next big thing," the more important challenge is to learn how best to exploit multiple generations of multiple products. And it's to do this in the context of changing customer needs while creating or reinforcing an economic moat.

Also, at some point, all product lines experience several forces that push against their advancement. For example, they may face negative forces from maturing products or changing consumer preferences. There are many ways to deal with these forces. Yes, striking back with approaches like lean startups, venturing, intrapreneuring, and open innovation are among these alternatives, but these help only to a limited extent.

As discussed in Chapter 2, the sidestepping approaches rarely address the real problem, and usually take longer to get done than the negative fallout allows. Instead, the best path is to explore, create, amend, and carry out effective strategies to consistently drive product lines forward, and do this better and sooner than competitors. This is proactive work, not a reactive response. The next chapter lays this out as a principle of the *PLuS Framework*. This approach aids business units in evaluating and improving existing product lines while spotting the need for and setting up new, more powerful product lines.

The Hierarchy of Company Strategies

Every business entity has a hierarchy of strategies. Each strategy will have its own purpose, objectives, and form. For some companies, this hierarchy is obvious, while for others, it's not. The corporate level sits at the top. Corporate strategy focuses on gaining advantage through shared back-office and financial support. Or they focus on objectives that cut across their portfolio of business entities. (See Figure 5.2.)

Figure 5.2: Strategy Hierarchy Within Large Companies

Within a corporation, different business units have different strategies. The business unit strategy focuses on creating a "moat" against the competition. Business units create the moat with a set of strategies called chain-link strategies.[10] Each should align and link with the others. These strategies then work in unison to support the business unit strategy. Product line strategy is just one of the linked strategies within the business unit.

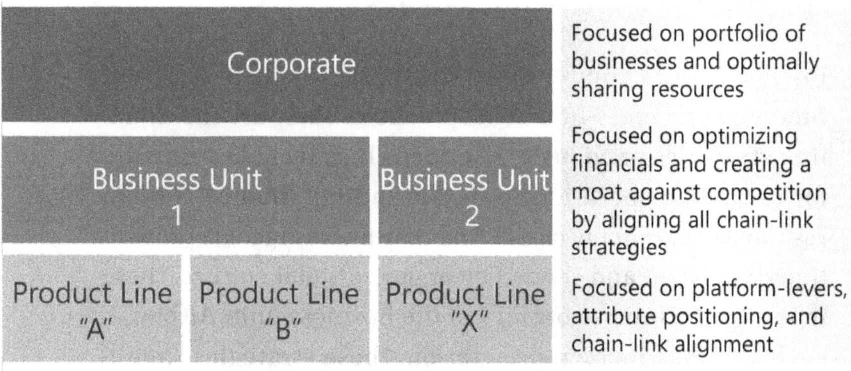

10 I explain chain-link strategy in chapter 7.1.

Strategy at the Corporate Level

In large companies, corporate strategies only reflect top management's values and aspirational goals. You'll find corporate strategies don't highlight specific product offerings. They also don't spell out advantages or the need to achieve milestones. Divisions in large corporations act much the same. They communicate only ambitions, not specifics in terms of products or services needed to realize those ambitions.

Strategy at the Business Unit Level

Business unit strategies differ from corporate strategies because business units deliver goods and services to customers. The *what, how, when,* and *why* of products are critical elements of business unit strategy. Business unit strategists also typically address customer satisfaction, competitive positions, and cash flows—also the three key objectives highlighted in product line strategies. But for business units, it's about the aggregate view of all its product lines.

A business unit strategy is always unique to the business. Those developing business strategy will quickly recognize that fact, though they will also be deeply sensitive to the effectiveness of all chain-link strategies, with particular emphasis on the unit's product lines.

Business units combine the strategies for their different functions and cross-functional practices. These are the chain-link strategies previously described. They include strategies for areas like operations, sales, branding, finance, human resources, and supply chain. And they always include product lines. Together, and shaped by organizational culture, these make up the inner-workings of the business unit. Although each area has its own orientation, these strategies should also align and connect. Once again, the notion is they work as one—like a chain—to support the business strategy and its execution.

A Strong Link

Product line strategies are a critical link in the business strategy chain. The goal of the remainder of the book is to share what makes for good product line strategies—what makes them strong links within a business unit's chain-link strategy.

Knowledge and Perspectives to Tackle the Problem

Fundamentals

PRODUCT LINE STRATEGY: GETTING TO GOOD

Seek to:

Understand and recognize the advantage businesses gain from creating an economic moat.

- ▶ However, consider how creating an economic moat is near impossible without a good product line strategy.

Create great product offerings using a product line strategy.

- ▶ Don't diminish product line strategy to be a management guide focused only on products after their creation.

Recognize that good product line strategies organize products and platform-levers into full product lines, and multiple product lines in product families.

Product line strategies are just one of several chain-links within a business unit's overall strategy. For a product line to succeed, there must be alignment across all chain-links.

SECTION 3

LAYING OUT THE SOLUTION:

The Product Line Strategy Framework – Getting to Good

Organizing and Relating the Elements of Good Product Line Strategy

---

The PLuS Framework

- Pillar 1: The Strategy-Essence and its Three Critical Parts
- Pillar 2: The Product Line Roadmap–Visualizing Strategy
- Pillar 3: Measuring and Guiding Strategy Performance
- Pillar 4: The Union with Business Strategy

CHAPTER 6

The *PLuS Framework*™

FORTUNATELY, ORGANIZATIONS IN recent years have moved away from strategy thinking only at the top or corporate level. Now, most recognize the importance of business performance. The emphasis is on how well chain-links (e.g., sales, operations, branding, and product lines) work by themselves and with one another to carry out the business unit strategy. Managers commonly call this "operational excellence.[11]" Within the chain, the product line strategy link is central to how well all links mesh. Having clarity about product line strategy can have a great impact on operational excellence.

The increasing dynamism and complexity of today's markets and technologies is causing the growing importance of product lines and their strategies. Product life cycles have grown shorter, and technologies evolve and converge at an increasingly rapid rate. As a result, competition among product lines is tougher than ever before. If product line strategies fail to keep up with this dynamic, the whole business unit chain-link strategy is likely to falter.

---

11 Operational Excellence is the effective, consistent, and reliable execution of strategy. It originated in Lean Thinking and Six Sigma. Operational Excellence stresses managing business processes and carrying out work systematically and doing so better than competitors can.

Top managers recognize the importance of product line strategies to the overall success of a business. Companies that develop effective product line strategies compete better. But to do so, they must also carry out their strategies well—continuously updating and adjusting them. Over time, it's strategy execution that leads to increased profitability and customer satisfaction. That's why the term "Operational Excellence" refers to how well a company carries out strategy.

DEFINITION ALERT:
Product Line Strategy Objectives

All product line strategies will, to different degrees, seek to improve in three orientations: 1-Cash flow, 2- Market share, and 3-Customer satisfaction. Good product line strategies highlight at least one, if not all three orientations.

Continually reexamining product line strategies to distinguish good ones from bad ones is also critical. In fact, this is an important reason for laying out a robust, understandable product line strategy framework. Why? Because conditions change, and a good product line strategy may not hold up over time, causing companies to lose their "economic moat" and possibly even experience total business failure. What was great operational excellence yesterday may not be so tomorrow. The framework aids in spotting what's good and what's not about a product line's strategy, and what's good or not about its execution.

Product line strategies can best address several important goals and objectives. The most critical are those that move toward gaining market share, satisfying customers, and driving positive cash flows (see Explanation sidebar). Strategies based just on innovation, technology,[12] or business model changes may not be as critical. Sure,

12 Gary P. Pisano, "You Need an Innovation Strategy," *Harvard Business Review* (June 2015) 93, no. 6: 44–54.

these approaches help, but it's at the product line level that bundles of technologies form product attributes to satisfy customer needs. And that's where companies make or break their futures.

Development of the *PLuS Framework*™

During work with dozens of companies around the globe, I developed the *PLuS Framework* for evaluating, creating, and improving product line strategy. When doing so, I sought to achieve several key goals. (See table 6.1.) This framework helps managers identify the weaknesses needing to be addressed. It also helps spot hurdles that need to be overcome, both in terms of strategy and an organization's culture. It ensures that managers develop a realistic strategy—responsive enough to change when needed and powerful enough to make a difference.

Table 6.1 Goals of *PLuS Framework*

Goal	Why goal is important
Identify product line weaknesses.	Weaknesses can be exploited by competitors; weakness manifest in less-than-stellar performance.
Define hurdles and obstacles to overcome.	Clearly defined hurdles and obstacles enable managers to better form solutions and recourse.
Form aggressive yet doable strategies.	Non-aggressive doable strategies always underperform. Aggressive but undoable strategies never perform.
Gain flexibilities to react to changes.	Things change (like technologies, competitors, customers, and regulations). Strategies must also change. Built-in flexibility is like health insurance, not needed until it's needed.
Measure achievement or lack thereof.	To paraphrase many consulting gurus, "What gets measured, gets improved." All product line strategies should seek improvement.
Develop meaningful impact on business strategy.	You might think product line strategy is good, but if it is irrelevant to business strategy, it is more likely to fail. Why? Because it either is or will be irrelevant to the business's chain-links.

The framework consists of four pillars, supported by cross-functional processes and focused on making smart, deliberate choices and decisions. (See Figure 6.1.) The pillars are the Strategy-Essence, Execution and Roadmap Management, the Objectives and Metrics, and the Rationale and Roll-up. Good product line strategies require all four pillars. The pillars are supported by a well-thought-out process that directs a workflow, information flow, and a decision flow. But the *PLuS Framework* isn't a rigid methodology. Rather, it's flexible and adaptable. It provides guidelines to help teams advance their product line in productive and effective directions.

Figure 6.1: The *PLuS Framework*

The *PLuS Framework* for creating, evaluating, and improving product line strategies has four pillars. Each pillar adds to the product line strategy. Each pillar ties to the three other pillars through a work, information, and decision flow. Together, the framework parts drive deliberate decisions and choices to carry out product line strategy.

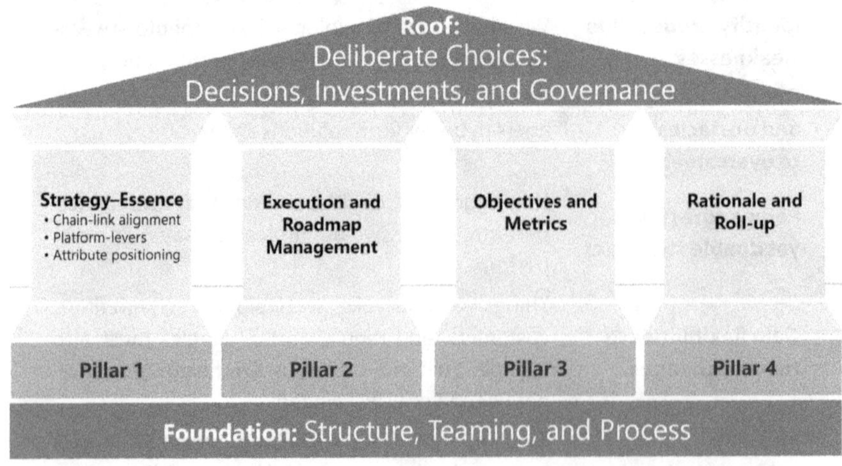

Teams can address each pillar within the framework in a general, nonspecific way. But it is very important, both to the strategy and the inner-workings of a company, that cross-functional teams tackle the tasks. Strong teams have contributors with deep knowledge about the product line, its technologies, and its markets, plus how work gets done and decisions get made. Within each pillar of the *PLuS Framework*, team members work to identify problems, opportunities, threats, key changes, and obstacles associated with that pillar. These are the pieces of the strategy puzzle to be assembled. The depth of insights and foresight that a product line team gains from this analysis is critical to developing a good strategy. The pillars ensure the analysis is complete.

Below I define each pillar and explain the process foundation and deliberate decision-making roof. I discuss each in depth over the next few chapters. After exploring each, I then address the requisite process foundation for carrying out the process of strategizing, then move on to deliberate decision-making that provides the framework's roof.

Pillar #1—Strategy-Essence

Strategy-Essence forms the core of product line strategy. I intentionally use this awkward sounding amalgam with the word "essence" to stress that it is specific to product lines. A Strategy-Essence has three parts, and all three matter. These are chain-link alignment, attribute positioning within market segments, and platform-levers. As shown in Figure 6.2, each part should build on and add value the others. I explore each part in several chapters.

Figure 6.2: Three-Part Strategy-Essence

The Strategy-Essence is the core of a product line strategy. It's made up of three parts. The first is chain-link alignment. The second is platform-levers (and their fulcrums). The third is product attribute positioning within market segments. Powerful product line strategies have all three working in unison.

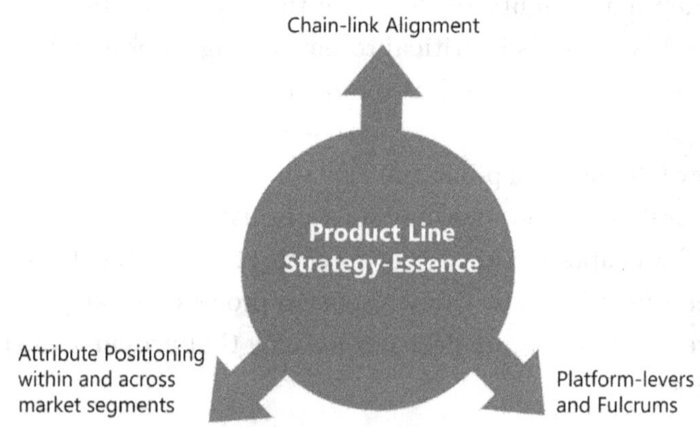

Pillar #2–Strategy Execution and Roadmap Management

The product line roadmap helps managers oversee and carry out their strategy. It's much more than a simple "timeline" or roll-up of product line project plans. Instead, it shows relationships between technologies, platform-levers, market segments, and product offerings. Well-crafted roadmaps clearly communicate both actions and intents.

Figure 6.3: Execution Roadmap

The Execution Roadmap portrays the work to carry out product line strategy. It uses a timeline to represent a platform-lever. It then relates technology building blocks to products coming from the platform-lever and seeking to satisfy customer needs in specific market segments. There are also graphic items labeled as "New Product to be Launched" and Product Innovation Charters (targets for innovation, not yet development projects.) Their locations on the platform-lever timeline suggest their planned launch date.

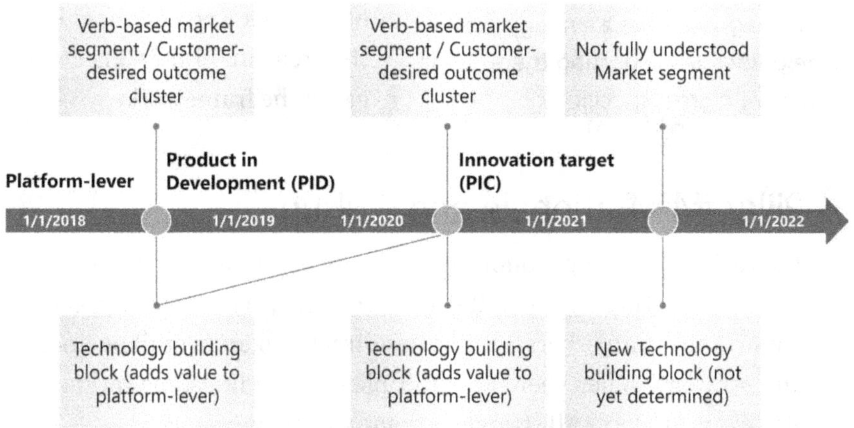

Pillar #3—Objectives and Metrics

Roadmaps lay out milestones for projects and innovation efforts. They don't capture financial, organizational, or strategic measures. Therefore, Pillar #3 is critical.

Product line strategy **goals and objectives** (*Explanation*) for product lines always reflect at least one of three orientations. These are cash flow, customer satisfaction, or competitive position. Chapter 9 explains this in much greater detail. In the trenches of product line strategy, the *PLuS Framework also* uses metrics to guide team efforts. I share much more about product line strategy metrics in Chapter 9.1.

Embedding and using objectives and metrics goes far in changing organizations and how they handle product line strategies. These are as much about improving the strategy as they are about making organizations and their cultures adaptive to smart moves. Indeed, the smart work embodied in Pillars #1 and #2 can go for naught without embracing objectives and metrics. For that reason, Pillar #3 is critical to the framework.

EXPLANATION:
Goals and Objectives

Good goals and objectives are key to guiding product line strategy work and decisions. "Objectives" differ from "strategy." An objective is where you want to go whereas a strategy provides the guideline for getting there, sometimes with great specificity.

Pillar #4—Rationale and Roll-up

The rationale for a product line strategy explains why one direction is better than another. It shows why certain tasks have greater importance than others. Plus, it ties directly to an overall business unit strategy. When there are multiple product lines, the rationale also examines how all strategies come together.

Pillar #4 provides an understanding of why strategy moves, pivots, and/or changes to the chain-links might be necessary. The rationale addresses the context of what is happening in markets with customers, competitors, and technologies. It also provides the context of what's happening within the company across all product lines. In addition, this fourth pillar combines all product line strategies within the business strategy. The approach highlights how each product line will play out relative to key business, industry, and market forces.

The rationale and roll-up help business units to clearly spot potential opportunities for new product lines. Product line teams and their organization's top management need this clarity to vet each product line's strategy. It also enables the team to communicate effectively about the product line strategy.

The aim of the rationale and roll-up is threefold:

1. To engage key contributors and business unit leaders in a deep review of all product line strategies.
2. To gain commitment from top management in carrying out each roadmap, while also encouraging cross-organizational involvement.
3. To embed into an organization's culture the work, decisions, and information flows required for strong product line strategies.

The lack of a rationale may make it impossible for any product line strategy to succeed. This fourth pillar is fundamental to a business's continual growth. I discuss this in great detail in chapters 10 through 10.2.

The Foundation & Roof—Process Flow and Deliberate Decisions

Every product line strategy must advance as customers, competitors, and technologies change. Working across an organization, product line teams must work, create, and think through how they will carry out these advancements. The *PLuS Framework* tackles this directly by building a coordinated and iterative process supporting the four pillars. The framework works to keep a focus on making and carrying out deliberate decisions and choices that tie together. Most important, it does so by entrusting key responsibilities to product line teams and specifically designated managers and executives.

As product lines advance, so too must organizations. The framework, when fully implemented, supports such changes. And, as you will read, this needs commitment and involvement by senior managers.

EXPLANATION: Product Line Responsibility— The Dual Mission

Product line teams are much different than a business unit's executive team. They are also much different than single-product development teams. They need to cut across core functions purposely to gain alignment with the business unit's other chain-links.

The unique challenge for product line teams is that they have two different, yet complementary missions. Their first mission is to formulate and improve strategy. Their second mission is to carry out the strategy and manage the product line. While it's likely the core team for each mission will be the same, other contributors may not be the same. This teaming dynamic comes into play when we take a deeper look at the process for creating good product line strategies.

The *PLuS Framework* diagram in Figure 6.1 depicts process as the foundation below the pillars, and deliberate decisions as the roof above the pillars. I address these important framework parts in Chapters 11, 12, and 13.

The *PLuS Framework*, described in the chapters that follow is not merely a set of forms and spreadsheets with blanks to be filled in. Yes, tools aid managers in carrying out different parts of the framework. But on the whole, it's much more. It's a framework for analyzing, thinking, and acting. It works by helping organizations gain coherency and synchronization of actions and decisions. And it does this while driving greater performance from a discipline embedded in a company's culture.

Product Line Teams, Roles, and Responsibilities—It's a Big Deal!

Throughout the next several chapters, I will discuss evaluating, forming, and carrying out product line strategies using the *PLuS Framework*. Such work cuts across many roles and functions. In most companies, there is a core set of managers on whom these responsibilities fall. Without these managers, the product would wither and die.

The question top management faces is whether to dedicate managers to the tasks. Should those responsible work within a function dedicated to a product line? Or, should they remain within functions and contribute as part-time members of a team? Or, should there be a combination of the two?

Exploring what constitutes the best organizational structure or team composition in an open-ended theoretical manner is a heady proposition. It looks much different for those in "the trenches" of a specific product line. This is because an organization's top management must consider so many factors. The real world narrows the considerations by handing out many of the factors. For example, only certain people can do the job. And, the size of the job and how it relates to the rest of the organization matters greatly.

Consider the product line team composition or functional position for a highly complex line with sales over $1 billion a year. Compare that to a simple line with perhaps $50 million in sales. These teams or functions will be different. Decisions about organizational structure or cross-functional team composition will be unique to the line, the organization, and members' skills and knowledge. See Table 6.2 for a list of some factors affecting product line teaming.

Table 6.2 Factors Affecting Team Structure

Some Factors Affecting Teams or Function	Concerns to Consider
Number of product lines in the business unit (single line versus many)	When there is only one line or one line is dominant, that line is the business. Product line leadership must be at the top of the organization. This is best done by a dedicated function, not a cross-functional team.
Size (revenue and contribution) of the product line	If a product line is small, it may be difficult to justify dedicating an organizational function to its oversight.
Growth or decline of the line	When a line is experiencing growth, many people may wish to join a team. When the line is in decline, it may be hard to keep people on the team.
Industry technologies, market behaviors, or regulations change	If an industry's core technologies or market behaviors change, as with many products associated with the internet, the specific skills of team members may also need to change.
Number of platform-levers in the line	When a line has many platform-levers, let say ten, it may be impossible to have each platform-lever represented on the product line team. This is not the case when there are just two platform-levers.
Diversity and complexity of technologies employed and markets served	When platform-levers and technology building blocks serve many market segments, team members may need both broad and deep skills. This is a common challenge.

There are many factors that affect teaming beyond what is on the list in Table 6.2. All of them, though, are highly situational. Each product line has a unique set of factors influencing the team or the function's creation. As you read through the book, you'll see more.

A key principle in the *PLuS Framework* is that product line leadership and its contributors greatly affect their line's performance. In several chapters, I build in roles and responsibilities for product line teams alongside the work and decisions needing to be addressed. You'll see, though, I first recommend forming a core group of managers into a function dedicated to the task. Only after bumping into organizational issues related to product line strategy formation and execution should management explore part-time teaming as a resolution. This is a key topic when I discuss processes, work flows, and decision-making—the foundation and roof of the *PLuS Framework.*

EXPLANATION:
Function vs Teaming

In large companies with notable product lines, product line leadership should not be a part-time job. Good product line strategies are more likely managed by a full-time function. The job of strategy formation, improvement, and execution is simply too important to rely on part-time roles and responsibilities. Product line teams often augment dedicated roles with specific skills and knowledge when developing strategy.

I lay out guidelines for structuring a function versus part-time teaming in chapter 11. This discussion explores process flow and its tie-in with other organizational activities.

Now, let's take a deeper dive into each of the *PLuS Framework's* four pillars.

Chapter 7

The Strategy-Essence *PLuS Framework* Pillar 1

THE STRATEGY-ESSENCE,[13] one of the four pillars of the *PLuS Framework*, has three elements:

1. **Element #1**: Chain-link alignment
2. **Element #2**: Market segmentation and attribute positioning
3. **Element #3**: Platform-levers and their fulcrums

A product line team need not address these in any specific order, even though I start with chain-link alignment. However, addressing all three will move teams toward the right Strategy-Essence for their product line.

13 The term Strategy-Essence is unique to the *PLuS Framework*. I define and explain the term throughout the book.

As you read about the three elements, you'll recognize the importance of each. In good product line strategies, you'll also see that each element builds on and boosts the other two.

Another way to say this is the three Strategy-Essence elements resonate with each other. When one falls out of harmony, the effectiveness of the strategy declines. Put more bluntly, disharmony across the elements results in poor product line strategy. Developing and carrying out good strategy demands the elements of the Strategy-Essence work as one.

The interaction of the three strategy elements is important. When one changes, it is best to determine if and how the other two should also change. For example, if attribute positioning demands a high variety of products, the platform-levers may need to be reformed. In turn, the change may place different demands on the sales and operations chain-links.

The interplay across the three Strategy-Essence elements is fundamental to all product line strategies. Good strategies come from clearly defining the impact from each element separately, and then superbly managing their interaction. Let's take a look.

7.1: Chain-Link Alignment— *PLuS Framework* Pillar 1, Element 1

Chain-link[14] alignment refers to seamless coordination among functional and cross-functional strategies. Each chain-link contributes to the business unit's overall strategy. Product line strategy is just one of the chain-links. But other chain-links can make or break a product line's success. Therefore, aligning them and the product line strategy is essential. (Examples of other primary links in the chain are shared in Table 7.1.1.) You'll see how the links form the whole chain-link business unit strategy in Figure 7.1.1. Let's explore this a bit.

Table 7.1.1: Non-Product Line Chain-Links

Chain-links are functions that contribute to an organization's business strategy. Each chain-link has its own strategy. Together, they form a business unit's strategy. They include:

- Operations/ manufacturing
- Branding
- Technology
- Human Resources
- Sales
- Engineering
- Marketing
- Supply chain
- IT
- Customer care and service
- Any other functions in the company's business model

14 The term "chain-link" builds on Harvard Professor Michael Porter's "value chain model" and UCLA Professor Richard Rumelt's work invoking "chain-link logic" in strategy, where one link adds to another. Porter introduced the value chain in his 1985 book *Competitive Advantage* published by Free Press. Rumelt wrote about chain-link logic in his book *Good Strategy Bad Strategy: The Difference and Why It Matters*, published in 2011 by Crown Publishing Group. Neither work associates the single word "chain" to the other. Also, neither Porter nor Rumelt reference product line strategies within their separate thinking. You may blame this book's author for using the chain-link system plus culture to address the inner-workings of organizations.

Figure 7.1.1: Chain-Link Alignment

Alignment across chain-links can influence product line strategy effectiveness. Gaining alignment across chain-links is key to the success of the product line strategy and the business unit strategy.

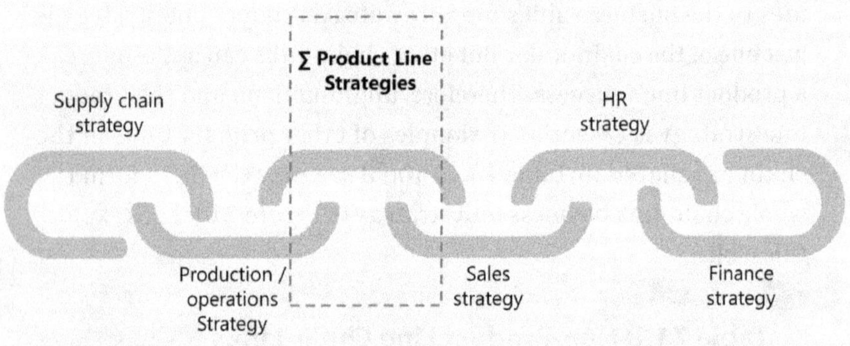

For every business unit, the links uniquely combine to form a chain-link strategy. And every business unit will stress each chain-link to different degrees. Many factors will determine whether the combination is satisfactory, good, or great. Chief among them are the specifics of each chain-link's strategy, the organization's internal operational excellence, and the alignment across the links. Apple is an example of a company that has used its chain-links very effectively.

BOX 7.1.1: How Apple's Chain-Links Have Created Success

Steve Jobs would be proud. His firm is arguably one of the most successful companies of all time. Apple is the first company to pass the one trillion dollar valuation mark.

Many articles have been published extolling the prowess of each of Apple's chain-links. One article might praise the virtues of its retail strategy, applauding how the company leads all retailers in sales per square foot, while another gives credit to Apple's supply-chain skills. Still other articles heap praise on the company's superb "i" branding or give kudos to its intellectual property strategy. And most pundits would admit that Apple's product line strategies are stellar and contribute to its success.

Each of these chain-links is powerful. However, as much as we like Apple's products, its success is attributable to the unique combinations of all its chain-links. It is not solely because of its product line strategy.

The synergy Apple gains across its chain-links makes it nearly impossible for competitors to copy them. In its overall business strategy, Apple's chain-link synergy creates an economic moat insulating it from competitors. The company's competitors may match or exceed one or two of Apple's strategy links, but these competitors find copying all of Apple's links, all the time, impossible. For example, Apple may see a major competitor such as Samsung match or even exceed its iPhone product line strategy. But because Samsung continues to fall short on other chain-links, Apple remains the market leader.

The biggest threat to Apple's chain-link prowess comes from the Chinese market. In China, Apple's functional chain-links don't drive synergy to the degree seen in the West. Its retail, supply chain, content delivery, and intellectual property links don't hold up as well there as they do in the West. As a result, stock rating firm Morningstar lowered Apple's economic moat[15] rating (as discussed in chapter 3). This downgrade, no doubt, is a major concern for Apple because of the size of the Chinese market and its influence across Asia.

Table 7.1.2 provides examples of large corporations (including Apple) with strong non-product line chain-links that have contributed to their success.

---

15 In Chapter 3, I discussed Warren Buffet's economic moat as an advantage that insulates a business from competitors. Morningstar is a stock evaluation firm that operationalized the notion into an empirical rating assigned to companies and their equity.

Table 7.1.2: Non-Product Line Chain-Link Strategies Within Large Corporations

The way chain-links combine affects a business unit's strategy. Product line strategies form just one link in the chain. However, alignment across all chain-links will affect a product line strategy. Consider how these companies' chain-links align.

Business Entity	Key Non-Product Line Chain-Links
Apple	Brand, intellectual property, cross-product family strategy, supply chain, content delivery, advertising, and retail store
The Coca-Cola Company	Brand, packaging, dispensing and equipment, bottling network, advertising, and multiple product lines
General Electric Engineering Plastics	Technology, sales, engineering, supply chain, and service
Comcast	Capital investment/scale, service (perhaps not stellar in the eyes of the consumer, but cost-effective), product line (TV, Internet, phone, security), and content
Georgia Pacific	Supply chain (backward integration), sales, and distribution
USAA	Market (military segmentation), customer service, operations, and fulfillment

Non-Product Line Chain-Links and Product Line Management

The degree to which non-product line chain-links either support or detract from a product line strategy always affects product line results. For example, consider how a commodity producer may struggle to be successful with a specialty product. Without the correct sales and service capabilities, the attractiveness of the high margins associated with specialty products will be lost. Or, consider the electronic hardware company innovating software to extend its offering into a profitable medical instrument market. This would require new quality management and deeper regulatory oversight. Without these chain-link abilities, the innovation may prove valuable only by licensing it to others. For the product line to gain value from the innovation, other chain-links often need to change.

You'll see the best product lines will fall short when other chain-link strategies do not align with them. Even great products developed using superb methods and genius technologies will struggle to overcome poor chain-link alignment. Therefore, product line teams should purposely and continuously seek to gain alignment and synergy across the business unit's chain-links. The idea is to craft product line strategy deliberately to gain amplification from other chain-links, and to avoid misalignment that might dampen the product line. This analysis should cut across the full set of a business's chain-links.

Gaining alignment with non-product line strategies is critical to a product line's effectiveness. Therefore, chain-link alignment is central to the Strategy-Essence pillar. Failing to align the chain-links creates negative internal forces that most product teams don't want to fight.

When addressing the alignment challenge, teams inevitably run into challenges. The problem is that gaining alignment might demand changes to other functions and their strategies. But the change may not be what another chain-link's management wants. What's good for a product line might not seem or be as good for other chain-links.

We can't ignore that product lines are not the only chain-links in an organization's strategy. And companies shouldn't rely solely on side-stepping techniques like lean startups, intrapreneurship, and ring-fencing. What's critical is for product line teams to define and communicate to all players the chain-link changes they need as part of their Strategy-Essence. They should then reflect on the work to carry out chain-link changes within the other pillars: execution and roadmap management, the objectives and metrics, and the rationale and roll-up.

Business Models and Chain-Links

It should be clear how chain-link alignment affects a business unit's strategy. As I've shared, that's what's referred to as operational excellence. But there is more to it than just alignment. The manner in which the chain-links combine creates what most commonly refer to as the **Business Model** *(Definition Alert).* It is the means or manner through which customers gain satisfaction toward "Jobs-to-be-Done," and companies bring in revenue or renumeration.

DEFINITION ALERT:
Business Model

A business model describes how an organization creates, delivers, and captures value. This may be in economic, social, cultural, or other contexts. Constructing and changing a business model is called business model innovation. Business models are a cornerstone of business strategy. The business model relates directly to the manner in which chain-links work as a whole.

Product line strategies always contribute to a business model. Product line teams should recognize how the Strategy-Essence always changes when business models change. Of course this is true. The business model change is, by definition, a change to each element within the chain-link. One can only expect alignment will change. The questions are how the business model change affects segmentation and attribute positioning and how it might affect platform-lever effectiveness.

Consider how Gillette's razor product line needs to deal with a new business model invading its industry. The new model is known as "Shaving as a Subscription." This is where companies like Harry's and Dollar Shave Club offer blades to be delivered to the consumers door. Consumers merely select the blade, of which there is a limited variety, and the delivery frequency. This has become a major threat to the once ingenious model of "giving the razor away and making money on blades" so well executed by Gillette.

The Strategy-Essence in the new models is completely different from that which drove Gillette's growth. A streamlined service becomes the platform-lever, not the scaled production process relied on by Gillette. Then too, attribute positioning and chain-link strategies look very different. Because the new business model matches a customer need (some customers' job-to-be-done) this is an obvious threat to Gillette.

Gillette's response was to create a similar offering. They call it the "Gillette Shave Club." The challenge, however, is that Gillette chose to embed the new line into their existing organization, using the same chain-links as their traditional business. The chain-links are supposed to serve both the new line and the traditional line. While forcing the fit is possible, gaining alignment and optimal amplification of each product line's strategy may not be possible.[16]

The Gillette case has yet to play out. Yet it's easy to recognize that it is a case to be solved. The Strategy-Essence is different for each line and the demands on chain-links are also different. For these reasons, I'd argue that the new business model should be split from the traditional shaving business as soon as its scale might allow, and perhaps even earlier.

---

16 Value chains clearly look different for different business models. When a single organization carries out two business models concurrently, conflict will arise within portions of the value chain. Then too, business models tie directly to core assumptions and behaviors (culture) that guides work and decisions. Should assumptions and behaviors differ for the different business models, notable conflict can arise. These conflicts make it difficult and improbable for product line strategies to gain optimal amplification across chain-links when organizations seek two business models to coexist..

Culture and Chain-Links

Culture also influences chain-link alignment, sometimes not for the better. For example, the folklore of a company may praise the heroics of individuals conducting product development as an independent activity. Other cultures might emphasize being lean and resourceful, encouraging behaviors that "make-do" without resources. In such cases, gaining collaboration across chain-links can be challenging.

Simply put, some managers not in the product line strategy chain-link may behave to carry out their own job as well as they can, at least from their perspective. They believe they should leave all product line actions to others. Similarly, when culture drives inclusion and consensus, making bold strategy moves—those outside the norms of the company—may turn out to be difficult. My experience suggests the first place such misalignment shows up is at connection points between chain-links. It's in meetings, discussions, and decisions that cut across everyday work.

Here, I want to call out a reoccurring principle of the *PLuS Framework. Good product line strategy takes more than just recognizing the parts of the strategy. It also requires setting up continuing work and adding discipline into your organization's behaviors and decisions.* It's about continuous change, not just a change event.

While product line teams may be working to change strategy purposely to match markets and technology, the inner-workings of the organization may not be so fluid. Good execution requires chain-links and culture also to change. Without such change, strategy moves meet with internal friction. This does not make for good product line strategy.

You'll see the *PLuS Framework's* Pillar #3, Pillar #4, foundation, and roof work with the organizational dynamic. Each interfaces with behaviors to influence better outcomes.

Product Line Teams and Chain-Link Alignment

Inducing change across chain-links and behaviors is a major task for any manager. The *PLuS Framework* helps by offering process approaches and practices to facilitate reviews and decisions regarding such change. However, most experienced managers recognize that product line team members have the responsibility for inducing chain-link changes, but have no authority to do so. This is a classic matrix management issue—being given responsibility without authority to carry it out. The key to unlocking this problem is gaining the key skill of influence.[17]

Influence skills are necessary to product line team membership. They are an absolute necessity for team leadership. It works best to bring skilled and knowledgeable managers from key functions onto the product line team. The preference is for these individuals to be dedicated to the product line. This means creating roles that report to the product line leader. They then should have dotted line relationships back to the chain-link function.

The rationale for this is simple. It keeps the product line strategy and its execution as a central focus. Here, the team's objective is to gain the most from the product line. It is also to influence needed chain-link changes to do so. The first objective is not to change the product strategy to maximize the chain-link strategies. The latter is usually a function of leaning out practices, not seeking growth.

Now, let's examine the next element of Pillar #1 (the Strategy-Essence,) what I call "market segmentation and attribute positioning."

---

17 Cohen, A.R., Bradford, D.L. (2017). Influence Without Authority. Hoboken NJ: Wiley & Sons

7.2: Market Segmentation and Product Attribute Positioning *PluS Framework* Pillar 1, Element 2

Every manager who has taken an introductory course in marketing knows the importance of product positioning. But those courses usually focus on communicating the advantages of a *single* product to potential customers of that product. They don't address positioning *across a product line*. Nor do those courses teach teams to conceive and develop multiple generations of products. And they do not teach how to use platform-levers and technologies to deliver attributes that position a stream of products to match evolving needs, jobs, or outcomes customers seek.

It's not surprising that the positioning across most product lines doesn't gain an advantage to the degree it could. Typically, products, each with certain attributes, simply fall into segments as they will. Marketing teams then use traditional analysis to conjure up positioning statements. Often, other competing products and their lines have the same positioning message. In strategy, this isn't helpful. However, it creates opportunities for smart strategy moves through better positioning.

Product line positioning is about advancing product attributes. This happens only when attributes match customers' evolving needs, wants, and desires—continuously. Only after developing the right attributes is it about crafting a marketing message. Because customer needs and competitor responses constantly change, attribute positioning is more like a game of multi-dimensional chess than simple checkers. My goal here is to describe and explain these dimensions and how to win the game.

Product Line Positioning–A Very Different Mindset

Positioning a line of products across multiple customer needs can yield powerful results. This is one way that leverage from a platform-lever plays out. It implies, though, that attributes supported by one platform-lever can address multiple needs. In product line strategy, it's each team's responsibility to figure out the needs set that best exploits a platform-lever. Or, conversely, they may work to create a platform-lever that matches sets or clusters of customer needs.

Figuring out positioning alternatives within markets is both a creative and analytical task, wrapped in strategic thinking. It demands a deep knowledge of customers, competitors, industry dynamics, and organizational capabilities. Perhaps the most crucial factor deals with customer needs. This goes beyond the traditional voice of the customer mindset. It embraces the actions or work needed to solve the jobs and outcomes customers are seeking, regardless of whether in consumer or business-to-business markets. In addition, such knowledge should reflect both the current state of things and an insightful view of the future. Later, in Chapter 12, I address placing

DEFINITION ALERT:
Verb-based Segmentation

Verb-based segmentation is dividing a market using application of the Jobs-to-be-Done theory. This is different than using Jobs-to-be-Done to improve attribute selection for a single product.

Traditional segmentation is based on noun titles like geography, product types, industries and price points. A verb-based segment may cut across multiple noun-based segments.

Product line strategies gain advantage from market research that details customer-desired outcomes within Jobs-to-be-Done segments. Such research is more comprehensive than that for single-product development.

methods that relate to product line positioning into a fluid process as part of the *PLuS Framework.*

Before diving into product line positioning, I want to set the stage by discussing a few underlying concepts. The first is market segmentation. This is the grouping of customer needs. It plays a key role in the framework's first two pillars (Strategy-Essence and Roadmap Management).

Attribute Positioning based on delivering product features always ties directly to segmentation. When working with my clients, however, I often see them jump to defining target markets even before figuring out a segmentation scheme. Typically, the targeting and segmentation merely reflect the products they already sell. Or some companies use industry groupings to define segments. Even many off-the-shelf research studies address things this way. Unfortunately, that approach isn't helpful for thinking through product line strategies and product attribute positioning.

A better way to view market segmentation is to distinguish between "noun-oriented" and "verb-oriented" segments. Noun-oriented is based on widgets, geographies, or industry slices. Verb-oriented divides the market by *how* customers gain value, what tasks or jobs they want to complete, and what outcomes they desire. These jobs could be anything from carrying out complex tasks and workflows in a business-to-business setting, to satisfying a food craving with a tasty snack in the consumer world. Verb-based segmentation is key to forming good product line strategy. Therefore it is also important to the *PLuS Framework.*

Market segmentation is part of good product line strategies' logical groupings of tasks customers want executed. This is segmentation by what some experts call the customer's "Job-to-be-Done."[18,19] Going one step further, we see that customers in each Job-to-be-Done segment have a desire to attain a set of outcomes related to their jobs or tasks. Smart positioning delivers products (through their attributes) specific to these sets of desired outcomes.

Figure 7.2.1

The relationship between segments and customer-desired outcomes is important to good product line strategies. They set up the target for concept generation and setting design specifications. Clusters of outcomes desired by customers are key to product attribute positioning. These are determined by quantitative market of all possible desired outcomes and across all verb-based (Jobs-to-be-Done) market segments.

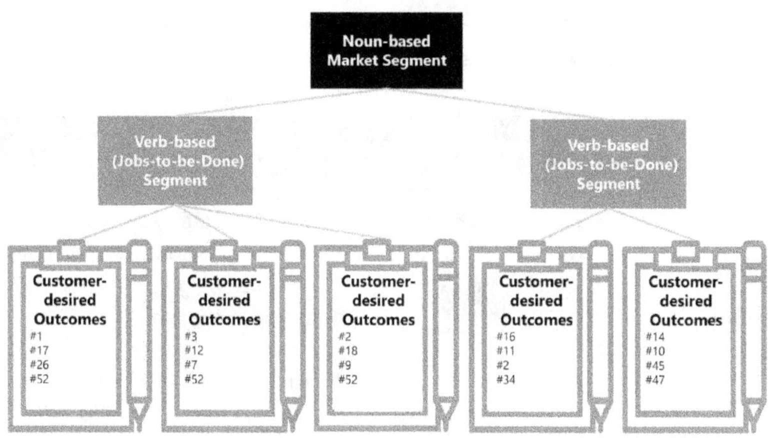

---

18 "Jobs-to-be-Done" theory is laid out by Harvard Business School Professor Clayton Christensen with Karen Dillon, Taddy Hall, and David S. Duncan in their book *Competing Against Luck: The Story of Innovation and Customer Choice,* HarperCollins 2016. Christensen and his coauthors were also published on the topic in the September 2016 issue of *Harvard Business* in the article: *Know Your Customers' "Jobs to Be Done."*

19 The Jobs-to-be-Done theory builds on "customer-desired outcomes." The customer-outcome approach was developed and is promoted by Tony Ulwick and his consulting firm Strategyn. See https://strategyn.com/. Ulwick details this in his book, *What Customers Want: Using Outcome-Driven Innovation to Create Breakthrough Products and Services,* McGraw-Hilll 2005. Ulwick's more recent book, *Jobs to be Done: Theory to Practice,* Idea Bite Press 2016, details how to gain benefit from the Jobs-to-be-Done theory.

In product line strategy, verb-based segmenting is not enough by itself to lay out a full marketing approach. Other influences and characteristics like growth rates, regulatory demands, and competition should also be considered. Nor does verb-based segmentation get ahead of competition or technology changes, or align with other parts of a business unit strategy such as sales or manufacturing. Reconciling these shortcomings is important. And therefore, the full four-pillar *PLuS Framework* becomes so important. You will read about this in Chapter 10.

Table 7.2.1

Example of noun-based and verb-based segments with listing of qualitatively defined customer-desired outcomes ready for quantitative clustering. Notice the word minimize in front of each customer desired outcome. This is to standardize questions within a quantitative survey.

Noun-based Segments	Verb-based Segments (Job-to-be-Done)	Customer-desired Outcomes across all segments
Tablet Computer	■ Creating Presentation Graphics on the go ■ Viewing Media on the go ■ Reading eBooks anywhere	■ Minimize battery outage ■ Minimize operating system crashes ■ Minimize weight ■ Minimize eye strain ■ Minimize thickness ■ Minimize muffled sound
Portable Computers	■ Gaming ■ Creating Media ■ Manipulating Data ■ Running Major Programs	■ Minimize internet to CPU lags ■ Minimize data slowness ■ Minimize thread overload ■ Minimize screen glare ■ Minimize screen reflection ■ Minimize lost wi-fi signal ■ Minimize touch screen sensitivity ■ Minimize fragility ■ Minimize cost ■ Minimize down time ■ ...n, this may be 100+ statements

To underscore the value of the *Strategy-Essence as a whole, not just its parts,* I want to point out a frequent issue that arises. Although a product line team may make the needed leap to define verb- or task-orientated market segments, other chain-links may not. For example, a sales force may still segment the market by noun-based geography, an approach that supports their chain-link strategy. Here, the sales force approach may not be best for the product line strategy, and vice versa.

The chain-link alignment component of the Strategy-Essence helps address this conflict. To be effective, these two parts of the Strategy-Essence must work in unison. And as we will see, similar conflict can arise involving platform-levers, the third Strategy-Essence component. That's the purpose of keeping the three components of the Strategy Essence as one pillar in the framework. Later, Chapter 10.1, you'll also read how the Rationale and Roll-up Pillar (#4) of the framework tackles issues like this but does so alongside other product lines and across the whole business unit.

Matching product features to verb-oriented segments is also fraught with uncertainty. This is especially true when looking to the future. In some manner, every product line team deals with this. The *PLuS Framework* purposely guides product line teams to match attributes and features to verb-oriented segment needs by embedding the match into "innovation charters." These are targets for innovation that have purpose in strategy and include the targeted needs, or, more specifically on the customers' desired outcome set. Innovation charters are <u>not</u> development projects or concepts to be developed. Let me explain why that matters.

The Product Innovation Charters

A product innovation charter is a target or focal point for innovation. It is not a concept or a product idea. At its root, the innovation charter captures strategic intent, both in terms of objectives and purpose. To drive good product line strategies, teams should embed smart attribute positioning into targets for innovation. Hoping for ideation to produce a fit with customer needs is simply not good practice. Indeed, that's the whole basis of the Jobs-to-be-Done theory. And its product innovation charters that put the theory to work for whole product lines.

Product line teams need a means to focus on innovation and where the strategy is headed. That's why product innovation charters (PICs) matter. Yet many managers are less familiar with PICs than with products already in the market (PIMs) and products in development (PIDs). PICs capture where and how specific offerings intend to take a product line. This makes them critical to strategy. Without PICs, product line strategies wander in the world of chance, hoping for the next great product.

The notion of PICs was first introduced in the 1980s by the late Professor C. Merle Crawford,[20] an outstanding innovation pioneer, and, I'm proud to state, a good friend. His research showed that having a defined focus on finding an innovation markedly increases the odds of finding something notable and being able to develop and commercialize it successfully.

Figure 7.2.2: Example Product Innovation Charter with Attribute Positioning

The simple example of an innovation charter on the next page shows attribute positioning highlighted in gray. Most product line strategies demand more information than shown here. More on customer-desired outcomes may be needed. Notice how the charter calls out getting perfect sleep as a Job-to-be-Done, verb-based market segment.

---

20 C. Merle Crawford, Professor Emeritus of Marketing at the University of Michigan, co-authored the seminal textbook on new product management with Professor Anthony DiBenedetto of Temple University. Crawford was also a founder of the internationally acclaimed Product Development and Management Association (PDMA). The Association has recognized Professor Crawford by placing his name on its highest academic achievement award.

Product Innovation Charter ID QRN-7267

Objective

To gain greater market share in the fast-growing, high-end, long-wear "getting perfect sleep" market segment via noise-cancelling + masking wireless earbud

Purpose in Product Line Strategy

- *Fend off competitors and gain greater leverage from QRZ micro-power platform-lever.*

Grand Business Strategy Guidelines

- *Do not diminish any company brand.*
- *Do not position as low cost.*
- *Achieve perception of superior quality compared to alternatives.*
- *Achieve best-in-class noise-cancelling parameters.*
- *Achieve buying intent.*

Target Noun-based Segment(s)

- *High-end, sleep market—long-wear noise-cancelling earbud market segment.*

Target Verb-based (Jobs-to-be-Done) Segments

- *Sleeping deeply, comfortably, and free of noise disturbances*

Highly Ranked Customer-Desired Outcomes

- *Pillow-to-ear comfort level—minimize discomfort*
- *Enduring sleep—minimize sleep physical- and noise-based disturbances*
- *Sweat-free use—minimize sweat and heat buildup*
- *Long wear power without wires—minimize power loss at less than 14 hour use*
- *Ambient noise elimination—minimize < 8,000 Hz seepage*

Platform-Lever Parameters

- *Leverage existing QRN micro-power platform-lever with new third-degree material finite modeling for micro battery density and S/N optimization.*

Timing Parameters

- *Ready for Consumer Electronics Show, Spring 2020*

Cost Parameters

- *Not to exceed fully absorbed costing of $115 per headphone with accessories and case— based on 2nd-year production.*

The *PLuS Framework* uses Crawford's Innovation Charter but adds key directives to it from attribute positioning based on desired customer outcomes. (See Figure 7.2.1.) The charter sets a sharp and purposeful strategy focus for generating concepts and detailing product requirements. We'll also see that smart analysis of desired outcomes can go far in determining requirements for new platform-levers and that such definition may cut across noun-based market segments.

An upfront strategy focus using innovation charters shaped by clear attribute positioning all but eliminates the role of product screening. It differs greatly from traditional product development and management.

The framework sets up another notable change by using innovation charters. Once you move an innovation charter onto a product line roadmap, the charter becomes set for investment of money and people's time. In other words, you are adding the innovation charter, as a project, into the product line's project portfolio. From this point forward, the charter's project should be managed in trade-off with all development projects. See Figure 7.2.3 to see how the innovation charter plays a critical role in connecting market segments to product requirements.

The new approach differs from the traditional portfolio management practices. Now, portfolio management expands to include strategy-oriented innovation charters. It no longer only oversees those projects in a staged and/or agile development process. The framework extends portfolio management to include front-end work—the specific portfolio management shortcoming I call out in chapter 5.

Figure 7.2.3: Noun-based Segmentation to Product Specifications

The picture below displays the "Segmentation to Specification" breakdown structure. Here, a building materials product line is an example. The three middle layers are critical. Here you'll see customer-desired outcome clusters within verb-based segments. You'll also see innovation charters that target customer-desired outcome clusters.

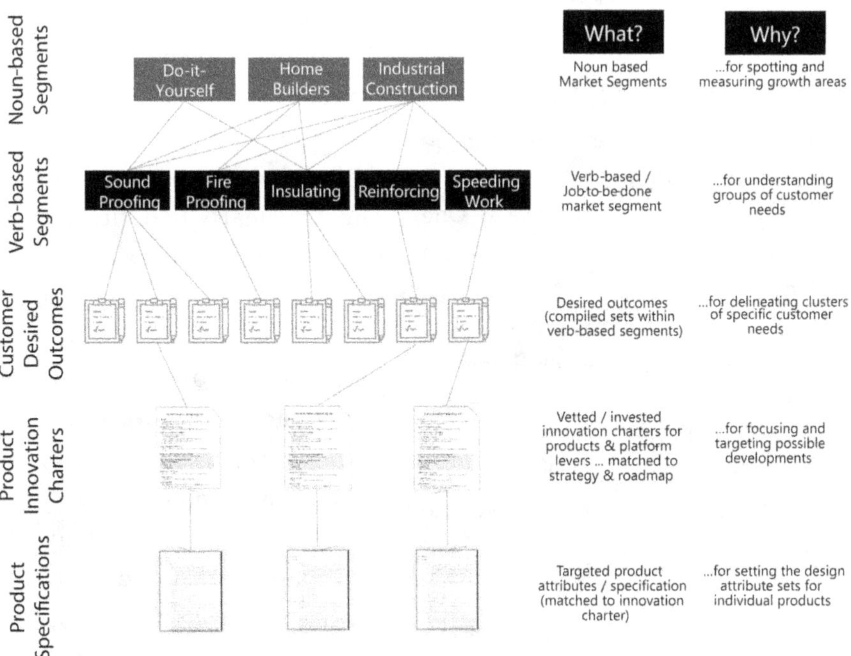

Innovation Charters and Positioning

A core tenet of the *PLuS Framework* is to "*never jump ahead with a concept.*" Just because someone conjures up a product idea does not mean it should become part of the strategy, no matter how important the person or people doing the conjuring. Instead, teams should work to create innovation charters designed deliberately to advance the product line. That is, teams first "deconstruct" such concepts into innovation charters. They then shape the charter by using relevant Strategy-Essence directives. This also means teams should conduct in-depth customer-desired outcome research to target proper attribute positioning.[21]

DEFINITION ALERT:
Execution Roadmap

An Execution Roadmap is a diagram that communicates key milestones in carrying out a product line's strategy. It typically includes three swim lanes. One for market segments that includes both noun- and verb-oriented segments. One for platform-levers portrayed as timelines. On platform-lever timelines, current and future products are represented. The third swim lane includes technologies (called building blocks) that add value to platform-levers by enabling unique attributes for each product.

Creating and using product line roadmaps are the PLuS Framework's second pillar. I discuss roadmaps in great detail in Chapters 8 through 8.2.

At initial stages, the most important directives clearly articulated are attribute positioning goals and platform-lever relationships.

Only when the innovation charter clearly benefits the product line strategy should the team set it up for further development. I refer to this as placing it on the strategy **Execution Roadmap** (*Definition Alert*), a visual map of how teams intend to carry out the product line strategy. By doing so, teams declare the charter ready for investment of time and resources. The goal of the investment is to generate concepts that resolve their charter and then translate positioning goals into requirements and product specifications.

21 Such customer-desired outcome delineation requires quantitative (not qualitative) research.

Each charter should link to at least one verb-based segment on the roadmap. If the segment is not clear or is vaguely defined, further work may be needed to describe the segment and customer -desired outcomes. Clear definitions for each segment and its cluster of customer needs are necessary for good product line strategy. In the pluralistic nature of product lines, then, teams should lay out and rationalize the full set of segments before using each in their strategy.

The framework also recognizes that good product line strategies employ exploratory and scouting work. This is about finding and shaping new technologies to help advance the product line. For some, the approach might violate everything they've learned in their marketing courses—always lead with known customer needs. But innovation charters can target unknown markets the same as they target unknown technologies. Charters then give a project team a focus for addressing the future and the uncertainties that come with it. Most important, though, is for charters to guide teams in positioning future products with the correct attributes.

Positioning and Branding

There is one last point I wish to make before discussing positioning dimensions. It is that positioning *always* relates to branding. The brand image and message should work with (not against) each product's positioning. But brand management is a separate chain-link. Don't assume that a brand and a product line are the same.

A product line can cut across multiple brands, and a brand can have multiple product lines. This enables positioning moves independent of brand image. For example, consider a branded laundry detergent coming from a product line. The product line can also serve store brands. This can be especially helpful for gaining greater leverage from one of the line's platform-levers. In setting up attribute-based positioning, there is more flexibility and opportunity when lines associate with more than one brand.

We've addressed verb-oriented segmentation, innovation charters, and brand management flexibility. Now let's look at the dimensions to consider in product line positioning.

Position for Purpose (A Key to Good PICs)

Teams should consider four strategy purposes when positioning their line's products in different verb-based segments.

1. **Driving demand.** Good positioning happens when one or more products in a line positively influence the demand for other products in the line. Consider how the Mercedes high-priced luxury S-550 model affects demand for its low-priced C-250. Although branding affects the C-250's demand, customer satisfaction with the product itself also drives demand. All products should be designed, developed, and placed in their positions to take advantage of this effect. Platform-levers often play an important role in enabling improved cost structures.
2. **Beating competitors.** Good positioning blocks competitors from gaining the critical mass to gain leverage from their platform-levers. This ties directly to fulfilling customer needs with specific attributes in task-related segments. You block competitors by selectively satisfying customers. Smart positioning calls for teams to think through verb-based segmentation schemes in terms of both customers and competitors. Johnson & Johnson's Vistakon business did just this when it introduced the first disposable contact lens. J&J scaled its production platform-level so large that its capacity exceeded 75% of the total market. Competitors could not scale sufficiently to match J&J's leverage.

3. **Exploiting capabilities.** There are many moving targets in product line positioning, and hitting these targets consists of more than just price-setting and communicating the benefits of the line's products. Teams also create, design, and engineer product features that fit each segment. Simultaneously, teams need to get the most from platform-levers and keep strong chain-link alignment. This requires the team to either have (or be able to get) the right skills in marketing, technologies, design, and idea-generation to gain the best results. Without the right skills, some positioning moves may be impossible. Consider how Dow Chemical exploited its capability when it raced its competitor Exxon Chemical to market with a new polymer (plastic). Dow shifted its focus from leveraging a production reactor as its platform-lever. Instead, Dow built a simulation model and used it as a platform-lever. To make this effective, the company then had to change its sales force's orientation and align operations with the new approach. You may read this full case in Chapter 14 A.
4. **Timing dynamics.** Forward-looking positioning, beyond today's competitive status quo, can also achieve notable gains. For most product lines, this approach demands more than a continuous focus on segmentation and technologies. It's about constantly advancing the whole strategy with an eye on the future. This is the role of innovation charters. Teams can purposely set innovation charters to target evolving or future customer needs. It often involves the multi-generational planning of platform-levers, each tied to evolving market-segment positioning. Consider the planned advancement of Amazon's Kindle product line. The Kindle product line has several platform-levers—Paperwhite, Fire, Voyage, and Oasis. Each progresses and renews over successive generations. Amazon targets each generation with new user requirements. In turn, these requirements translate into engineering design specifications. The timing of each platform-lever generation is key to product line strategy

effectiveness. This also must tie to successive generations of its operating systems; customized Linux for Paperwhite, Voyage, and Oasis, and Android for Fire.

The One-off Positioning Disaster

While all teams should employ attribute-based positioning in their strategies, not everyone does so to their product line's full advantage. For example, some managers find themselves in reactive, one-off planning sessions following a competitor's move. When this happens, it suggests the team is adjusting its strategy late. And being late can be a problem. Positioning ahead of competitors—making moves first—is far better. This is called the "first-mover advantage."[22]

To enable fast and timely moves, teams need a total view of the product line. This includes all potential offerings to all possible segments, as attribute possibilities change and customer clusters may morph. For many product lines, this is a large, complex playing field. And it's especially true because customers in each segment have unique wants and needs and desired-outcomes. At the same time, competitors keep advancing their products and internal behaviors may be pushing in the wrong direction. But that's the game. You can either play it to win or face the consequences.

Positioning Tactics for Products and the Line

Figure 7.2.4 shows the four orientations for positioning products. Remember, this is positioning with product attributes, not messaging. The tactics are:

1. **Price or value**. A team can focus on providing an *economic advantage* to the customer by having lower cost structures

22 The term "first-mover advantage" was popularized by Michael Spence in his 1981 article "The learning curve and competition," published in the Bell Journal of Economics. Spence is a Nobel Laureate and past Dean of the Stanford Graduate School of Business.

than competitors. There are a few ways to do this. It can be done through the direct cost of the product or service. This may also involve payment timing or methods. Or it can be done indirectly, over time, through the "total cost of use" of the product or service.

2. **Quality and delivered performance.** A team can focus on delivering product features with superior performance compared to competitive alternatives within specific segments. This may also mean that some segments and customers might not be targeted.
3. **Speed of benefits/timeliness.** Speed and timing may be very important to success in the marketplace. A team may focus on delivering benefits more quickly than their competitors can, or at specific times. Speed determines how quickly customers gain satisfaction from a product or offering. Timing refers to the delivery of product attributes over the life of the product or service, and of multiple generations of a line.
4. **Offering variety.** Providing choice (or not) for the customer can be very important to the success of a product line. Different approaches may call for different levels of product variety. By extending variety, more customers in more segments may be satisfied, and competitors might be kept at bay. Variety within the line is measured by both length (the number of uniquely different products) and width (small variants on products, like size and color).

Figure 7.2.4: Positioning Tactics

Product line teams can position their products within a market segment by using one or more of four tactics.

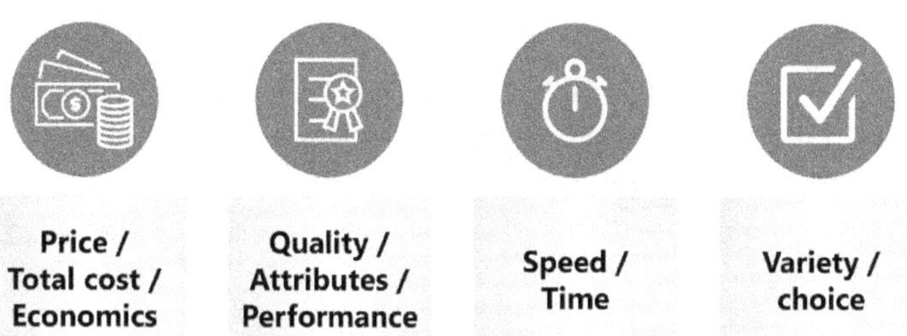

Striving for leadership with one, two, or three positioning tactics can be a worthy goal. Doing so could drive greater customer satisfaction plus fend off the competition. However, simultaneously striving for leadership with all four may lead to undesirable trade-offs. This is because at least one will likely be sub-optimal. Competitors may then exploit that weakness by focusing their products with new features directly against the weak option.

BOX 7.2.1: The Exception to the Rule: Blue, Red, and Purple Oceans

In a special case, when organizations introduce a new platform-lever into a new market, all four positioning strategies come together nicely. Strategists commonly call this a "blue ocean strategy." This distinguishes it from a "red ocean strategy," one entailing competition. This market (ocean) is called red because competition may become bloody.

In a blue ocean strategy, everything is open and new. There is no competition, and product line teams can work all four positioning tactics without provoking a competitive response. Gaining an advantage by using all four tactics can make it especially difficult for competitors to catch up if/and/or when they enter the market.

A blue ocean approach often conflicts with an organization's existing chain-link of strategies because blue ocean strategies inherently have a high degree of newness. However, strategists seeking a blue ocean positioning can't allow the constraints of existing chain-links to limit them. Blue ocean opportunities are obvious candidates for ring-fencing their development and rollout efforts (i.e., separating them from existing chain-links).

Note that, while blue ocean positions are enviable, they aren't common. Most product line strategies, however, must deal with competition. Some experts, therefore, argue that organizations should orient themselves toward competing in "purple oceans," a blend of red (competitive) and blue (non-competitive) oceans. The strategy discussion throughout this book deals with purple oceans.

Using attributes to position products is one part in the *PLuS Framework's* Strategy-Essence pillar. A key principle in this pillar is that each part of the Strategy-Essence works with the other two to boost the results of the whole. Effective attribute positioning, therefore, demands unity with the other two contributors: chain-links and the platform-lever. This unity matters and contributes greatly to the strength of a product line strategy.

Driving Value

Seeing the need for verb-based segmentation is fundamental to good product line strategy. The same is true for understanding the desired customer outcomes in each segment. Without these, positioning can easily go astray. But knowing this is of little value if a product line team cannot act on it. What matters is doing it. This demands an investment of money and time, and it must couple to both market analytics and creative exploration.

My experience and that of other experts is that companies can woefully underinvest in this fundamental aspect of product line strategies. Instead, they seek luck and serendipity to lead the way.[23] It is not uncommon to see companies invest several magnitudes less than the value such information and insights would bring.

The issue here tends to be the single-product mindset some top managers continue to embrace. **Top management** *(Explanation)* will not invest much money or assign notable resources if the result affects only one product. But in smart product line strategy, good positioning is not about one product; it's about the whole line. This is

23 This is the premise of Professor Clayton Christensen's book *Competing Against Luck: The Story of Innovation and Customer Choice*, HarperCollins 2016.

notably more valuable. And the research, time, and work to achieve good positioning are also more costly than for single products.

Building such thinking into the fabric of the organization can be slow. Some top managers are likely to push back, and that's to be expected. But it is also part of the challenge. Here, you'll see Pillar #4 and a well-thought-out implementation of the *PLuS Framework* discussed in Chapter 13, tackling this challenge directly.

Now, let's look at the third very important contributor to the product line's Strategy-Essence: Platform-Levers and their Fulcrums.

EXPLANATION:
Top Management

Who is "Top management?" Top management refers to a business unit's most senior executives. Top management includes those in a governance roles, or members of the business unit's governance body. Such top managers have oversight and authority across functions. Top managers have the power to assign resources to product line strategizing and execution work.

7.3: Platform-Levers and Fulcrums

PLuS Framework Pillar 1, Element 3

Platform-levers are a part of the Strategy-Essence and critical to good product line strategy. Understanding what they are and how to use them is foundational to understanding good product line strategies. I encourage you to not assume you know this before learning more.

Platform-levers create a means for product lines to deliver multiple products that increase customer satisfaction, improve cash flows, and beat the competition. But what makes them so important is they are doing this quickly and efficiently. They enable <u>speed</u> and <u>efficiency</u>, what I refer to as "leverage."

"Leverage" is central to product line strategy. For each dollar invested, a platform-lever enables the strategy to yield a greater return. The more leverage applied, the greater the value. For example, consider the core design of Samsung's 4K UHD TV, which combines complex circuitry for handling and processing TV signals. Along with software, the same circuitry finds its way into each of Samsung's TVs across their 4K UHD product line, from top-end to low-end, from large to small. This circuitry is a platform-lever. It enables faster development speeds and greater production efficiencies. Specifically, it is a design platform-lever and is uniquely different from other platform-lever types. I discuss the types of platform-levers later in this chapter.

I use the term "platform-lever," not just "platform," for a reason. Platform-levers are deliberately defined focal points. Their selection and definition are critical to creating a superior product line strategy. Managers, however, will use the single word "platform" in many contexts other than about product lines or their strategies. As I use it, the term "platform-lever" relates only to product line strategies.

Many people confuse product line strategy platform-levers and whole business-strategy ecosystem platforms. These are different. Platform-levers, as we'll see, gain leverage within the organization and the product line. Ecosystem platforms[24] gain leverage outside the company. It accrues from partners, cooperators, and developers who add value as part of the "ecosystems." Sometimes customers themselves add value. Easy-to-spot examples of ecosystem platforms include Apple, Facebook, and Google. Our focus on platform-levers, however, is internal to the company and product line-specific.

Platform-levers

When they first hear the term, some managers mistakenly think platform-lever refers to some entity that is a "given," such as a market or technology. It is not. Like positioning and chain-link alignment, in good strategy, teams deliberately choose or create their platform-lever (or levers) and then focus on it (them) to the product line's advantage. The choice also means other potential platform-levers will not receive the same intense attention. This is the most important aspect of platform-levers: *Their effectiveness stems from the deliberate choice to focus on them intensely.*

In product line strategy, advantage should stem directly from one or more platform-levers. Each platform-lever enables the gains to accrue to products sharing a "common factor." The degree of leverage gained then depends on how well and how clearly the company defines and focuses on the common factor. In addition, an organization's ability to scale the common factor and apply it to the value chain of creating and delivering goods and services becomes crucial.

24 The ecosystem platform is discussed in Phil Simon's book entitled *The Age of the Platform: How Amazon, Apple, Facebook, and Google Have Redefined Business*, Motion Publishing 2011 and 2013.

Not all potential platform-levers are good for a product line. And product lines often suffer from ineffective (or not as effective) platform-levers. A poor platform-lever lessens the competitive advantage of a product line, reducing cash flow. The line can also struggle to grow or maintain customer satisfaction. Without a good platform-lever, the overall business unit strategy would need to count on other chain-links, not the product line chain-link, to drive success.

Platform-levers always play a key role in good product line strategies. A word of warning, though. Not all potential platform-levers are equally effective. Some possible platform-levers may have problems. This may happen when the way they produce leverage conflicts with other parts of the Strategy-Essence. For example, a production asset type platform-lever (see below) may be geared toward high volume and limited variety. At the same time, a positioning move may call for high variety, i.e., many features for many markets. These orientations conflict. This is why it's important that teams explore all platform-lever possibilities and review them within the Strategy-Essence and the four-pillar framework.

Now, let's examine the types of platform-levers in greater depth.

What's the Common Factor?

Previously, I defined a platform-lever as a common factor across a set of offerings or products belonging to a line. Although a product-lever need not be common to all products, the business unit must *invest* in it. However, more important, organizations need to realize positive *returns* from the investment. Otherwise, the platform-lever is ineffectual.

Two key characteristics affect receiving a notable return from using a platform-lever. First, it should aid in developing new offerings and introducing them to the market more quickly. Second, it should produce superior products at less cost than otherwise. I realize this is still fairly broad, and so let's look at some examples.

Table 7.3.1 below shows common factors for platform-levers. I classify platform-levers by their common factor.

Table 7.3.1: Platform-Levers Types

This list is ever-expanding. You may notice that some platform-lever types did not exist a few decades ago. No doubt, there will be new-type platform-levers a few decades into the future. When thinking through product line strategies, understanding the platform-lever types is enormously helpful. In strategy, it's often rewarding to use different platform-lever types before competitors catch on.

Common Factor Type	Platform-Lever Example	Leverage Source
Production Asset	A chemical reactor, paper-making machine, just-in-time automation	Scale or flexibility
Hardware Design	A computer motherboard	Design reuse
Service	An automated bank teller	Automation, speed
Software Systems	A software operating system	Versatility within the intended domain
Proprietary Technology	A unique pharmaceutical, molecular structure, formula, complex system	Uniqueness
Embedded Infrastructure	An optical fiber network, social network	Connectivity
Modular Systems	A roofing system, integrated automation equipment	Adaptability in use
Algorithms and Artificial Intelligence	Bank loan screening models, search engines	Rules, judgment, and decision acceleration

Common Factor Type	Platform-Lever Example	Leverage Source
Connected Integration (IoT)	Intelligent and integrated HVAC (heating, ventilation, and air-conditioning) controls	The data structure, stack, queues
Hybrid and Combination Platform-Levers	An automotive assembly (with engine and frames as separate platform-levers)	Multiple

Thinking through how well platform-levers deliver leverage is a key task for all product line teams. They also need to consider how well each potential platform-lever matches the other two parts of the Strategy-Essence. In a good product line strategy, platform-levers work with, not against, chain-links and attribute positioning. The reverse is also true. Chain-link strategies and positioning should work in unison with the platform-levers.

Platform-levers create advantages when extended over a portion, if not all, of the product line. The example in Box 7.3.1 below shares how important platform-levers can be. This example recounts how Johnson & Johnson created a platform-lever using a *technology-driven production asset.* This enabled them to capture and dominate a new market.

Box 7.3.1: How J & J Created and Captured a New Contact Lens Market

In the early to mid-1980s, Bausch & Lomb and Ciba Vision, a division of Ciba-Geigy, were the key players in the contact lens market. Johnson & Johnson was a relatively small player. The properties of the polymers used to produce lenses were important. These polymers gave lenses their needed attributes such as oxygen permeability, rigidity, fit, and comfort. Each company's proprietary polymer formula was its platform-lever. Each company also stressed quality and performance in its market and brand positioning.

Over time, soft lenses replaced hard lenses, with price points from about $300 to $500 a pair. Soft lens wearers had to buy special solutions to clean and store their lenses overnight. Wearing soft lenses for over 18 to 20 hours wasn't within FDA prescriptions.

To make soft lenses, competitors could use either molds or high-precision lathes, and each lens's specific shape and thickness entailed high manufacturing demands. The polymer's weight was a mere fraction of an ounce, and water was a lens' major component. As a result, the variable cost for producing a soft lens was nearly zero.

By the mid-1980s, J&J had established only a toehold in the industry. However, at around that same time, a small firm was shopping a technology known as "Danlens" to each industry player. The J&J annual report described this technology:

"A unique multi-patented process which enabled a company to mold lenses in a continuous soft state. This provided an entirely new standard of precision, eliminating the hydration distortions common to traditional hard-state manufacturing. The result was a high-quality lens that was virtually 100% repeatable and reproducible, combining excellent vision with comfort and convenience."

From among the firms in the soft lens market, only J&J expressed an interest in Danlens. With its minuscule market share, J&J knew it needed something significant to beat the dominant players.

Therefore, in 1987, J&J bought Danlens and announced how it intended to use the technology. They sought to take advantage of another feature that became crucial to J&J's eventual success in this market—it was easily scalable. This enabled J&J to lower manufacturing costs with high-volume production. Recognizing the potential of this new technology, J&J was determined to exploit it. The company committed almost $1 billion to scale the technology to a level not before seen in the industry; it increased the company's manufacturing capacity by several magnitudes.

Indeed, the production volume far exceeded the total capacities of all soft lens competitors combined.

J&J recognized that it could drive down manufacturing costs to levels never before seen in the industry. Costs were so low that lens wearers could throw away their J&J contacts after just one day. They need not bother with cleaning and storing them overnight.

According to J&J's calculations, the capacity it envisaged would supply over 70% of the market. Its dominant share of the market would leave inadequate volumes for its competitors to scale-up and offer disposable lenses at comparable price points. So long as lens wearers would throw away their lenses at the end of each day, J&J's approach would succeed.

J&J's product line strategy using a unique production asset type platform-lever was both brave and brilliant. J&J flipped its platform-lever from the industry norm based on chemical materials to a large-scale molding production method, and so changed everything. The change was so great it literally shut down the contact lens cleaning solution industry and forced competitors to engage in a frantic search for alternative platform-levers, a search doomed to fail. Bausch & Lomb entered bankruptcy, and CibaVision was saved only by its parent company (Ciba-Geigy), which transitioned it into pharmacological eye products.

Fulcrums Enable Leverage

Leverage doesn't happen just because something is declared to be a platform-lever. Rather, it comes from an organization focusing deliberately and intensely on the platform-levers. The deliberateness and intensity of focus are central to success. The focus matters. Product line strategies gain deliberateness and intensity of focus by employing what I call the platform-lever's fulcrum. Without a fulcrum, a lever is simply a flat plank that adds no great advantage to the product line or its strategy.

In the visual model in Figure 7.3.1 below, the pyramid's top represents the fulcrum of the product line's platform-lever. This top layer of the pyramid is the product line's strategy—a statement of its objectives, intent, and how certain platform-levers will play important roles. It highlights the role a deliberately chosen platform-lever plays in driving the line's strategy.

This fulcrum also supports the actions to gain alignment with the other, non-product-related chain-link strategies. Plus, it spells out the cross-segment positioning of the line's products. The Strategy-Essence is at the top. It sets the purpose and intent of the platform-lever. It places the platform-lever at the core of strategy. Everyone in the organization should recognize it and focus on it intensely.

The next level down in the pyramid is organizational structure. This is specific to the platform-lever, including the roles, responsibilities, and dedication of managers driving leverage and advancing each platform-lever. The intense focus on the platform-lever comes directly from those managers assigned this role. Their job is to drive leverage from the platform-lever through work, decisions, and investments—in both current and future timeframes.

Figure 7.3.1: The Fulcrum Enables Leverage

Fulcrums create an organizational focus on platform-levers. Without deliberately formed fulcrums, platform-levers won't deliver leverage to the degree they could. Platform-levers without well-formed fulcrums yield less-than-stellar product line strategy.

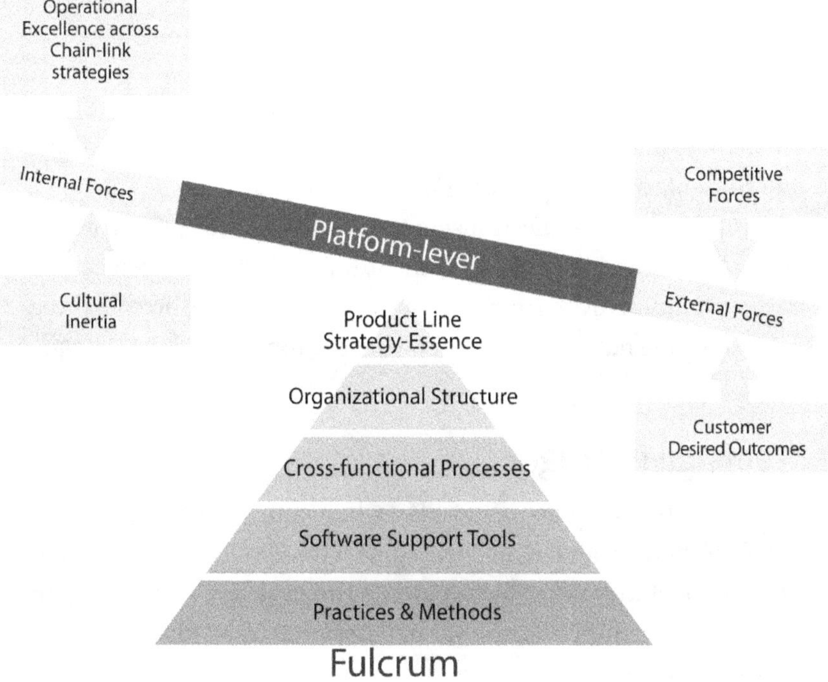

The focus of the pyramid's middle is on streamlining work practices and processes that cut across the organization. These processes support developing products, scouting technologies, tracking finances and cost, and marketing. The fulcrum should also tailor these processes, making them specific to the platform-lever. Good fulcrums ensure the approach toward work and decision-making helps and does not hinder leverage gained from the platform-lever. Note, however, that product lines having different platform-lever types may require different processes to support them.

At the bottom of the fulcrum are systems, tools, and specific practices. Tailoring or configuring software and other tools to match the platform-lever will also drive leverage. For example, customized financial and cost metrics about a platform-lever could enable teams to make fact-based judgments about its leverage. Here, too, different platform-lever types may require different support systems, tools, and practices.

Always start at the top of the fulcrum pyramid when setting up a fulcrum to gain intense focus on a platform-lever. After you see a fulcrum–platform-lever combination in use, this becomes obvious. The top level of the fulcrum sets the platform-lever into strategy, while the second level down dedicates people, through roles and responsibilities, to assuring that leverage happens. The bottom three levels become natural builds following the top two.

Gaining Leverage

There can be much genius at play when companies deliberately amplify their product line strategies with good platform-levers. Don't expect an expert from outside the organization to step in and identify your platform-lever or determine what should be best. Figuring it out often requires a deep understanding of markets, technologies, competition, and customers.

Decision-makers, in particular, need deep knowledge of the inner-workings of their organizations. And, once a management team defines a platform-lever, it should shift focus to creating and investing in its fulcrum. Merely declaring a platform-lever exists does not yield the intense focus needed to gain leverage. In practice it's difficult, if not impossible, to think of product lines with outstanding platform-levers yet without seeing that organization focusing on the lever intensely.

Trying to gain leverage from too many platform-levers can be as big a problem as not having any. This happens when a product line has so many focal points there is no intense focus on any. The recourse is to choose which to focus on with deliberate fulcrums. This also means choosing which to relegate to **technology building block** status *(Definition Alert.)* A technology building block adds value to a platform-lever, and does not perform in strategy as the platform-lever. This is exactly the approach Dow Chemical took when introducing its new polymer line. Their product asset platform-lever was relegated to being a building block to the new service-oriented production modeling platform. (See Chapter 15A.)

DEFINITION ALERT:
Technology Building Blocks

Technology building blocks add to platform-levers to create products. Specifically, they create feature sets that embody as products. Combining platform-levers and technology building blocks enables attribute positioning within verb-based market segments.

Relegating a platform-lever to be a building block can be a tough decision. However, such decisions are necessary and fundamental to good product line strategy. It's how a product line team improves strategy when it has too many platform-levers. Remember the fundamental principle as you think through your product line strategy: *having too many platform-levers kills leverage.*

How many is too many? The answer is situational. But let me give you my rule of thumb. When product lines have five platform-levers, I grow uncomfortable. When product lines have ten platform-levers, I can't stand the discomfort. If forced to a number, I'd say seven. In other words, I think it unlikely that a product line could muster intense focus and gain cohesive planning and execution across more than seven platform-levers.

Some Advanced Thinking

Anyone involved in product lines and their strategies should be sensitive to changes in markets, customers, competition, and technologies. Nothing ever stands still, and platform-levers should evolve. In fact, even the common factors as outlined earlier in Table 7.3.1 also evolve.

The basics of platform-levers just laid out will help in understanding product line strategies. However, two more advanced topics should be recognizable to anyone involved in product line strategies. The first deals with a new platform-lever type. The second is about combining or matrixing multiple platform-levers to create new products or services.

The Internet of Things (IoT)

Production asset platform-levers used to be very common, and many industries grew up on production asset platform-levers. As a result, business management in many industries tends to focus on gaining leverage from scaling production assets. However, as software, connectivity, and analytics have advanced, a new platform-lever type has taken shape. Based on intelligent integrated systems, it is quickly becoming a systems type of platform-lever for many product lines. This is the "Internet of Things."

The impact of the Internet of Things (IoT) on product line strategy is vast. Imagine that every bit of data about your customers' use of your product or service is right at your fingertips. These data can easily be added to internal business and external environmental data. Combined with Enterprise Resource Planning and other information, product-use data then contribute to several strategy topic areas, including segmentation, competitive analyses, and positioning. These data may also reveal how customers realize satisfaction, and analysis may influence a product line team's thinking toward positioning and chain-link interplay. The data may even reveal insights about the business model being pursued.

Coca-Cola Freestyle® is a good example. Coke has a strong brand strategy and a powerful supply-chain strategy. It has a commanding carbonated drink product line strategy, and it also gains from a superb bottling strategy. And while the business strategy gains markedly from these chain-link contributions, it also gets a major boost from its dispenser line.

In 2009, Coke's dispenser product line took an exponential step forward with the Coca-Cola Freestyle® platform-lever. This touchscreen-capable platform-lever extended to several different dispenser designs. Each used the platform-lever's micro-dosing technology (originated by the medical industry) to serve up, sometimes, over 100 Coca-Cola drinks. This radically new dispenser platform-lever enables consumers to blend syrups to mix their own unique drink.

The platform-lever uses precision syrup delivery. It does this alongside RFID tracking technology while using the Internet to track inventory data. At the same time, Coke collects data on customer blend ratios, use time and volumes, and maintenance diagnostics. This gives Coca-Cola a large real-time data source on which to use analytics to support its strategy.

Intelligently integrated systems will not be a platform-lever for every product line. It's up to each product line team to shape this common factor as it wishes and as it is able. We're still trying to think through and model the impact of this new common factor in product line strategy. Labeling such systems as a single type of platform-lever might not be correct. Doing so now may merely reflect where we are in the evolution of such systems. My take is that, so far, we only have a basic understanding of the possibilities. It's up to product line teams to discover these possibilities and exploit them through stellar product line strategies.

Matrixing Platform-levers

The second topic that needs a brief exploration is multiple platform-levers that need to combine to create superior product line performance. This notion has been around for decades, but it has taken time to work out the practices that make combining platform-levers a success.

The automotive industry has done this and provides a good example of the multiple platform-lever approach. Take just two parts of a car: the frame and the engine. For car companies, each frame and engine platform-lever needs notable investment and must be able to scale production to succeed. Yet how well these platform-levers come together is what makes or breaks the strategy. This is because, in large product lines, a single frame and a single engine would not be dedicated to one another. Instead, each engine mounts onto different frames. And each frame can accept different engines. In a company like General Motors multiple engine platforms would need to match multiple car frames.

Now add other platform-levers that could come into play in the engine-frame combination. For example, transmissions, axles, brakes, wheels, and even lithium batteries. It's easy then to see that such product lines need a matrix of platform-levers. Each cuts across several brands and addresses multiple market segments. Think about what this means in terms of design engineering and possible conflicts with chain-links like each brand, production, and the supply chain.

Matrixing independent platform-levers is frequent practice for the product line strategies in many industries. For example, laptop computer motherboards need to combine with display screens and memory storage. Banking services need to combine online delivery with loan processing and investment handling. Equipment manufacturers will seek to combine data handling (software), sensors, and automation, each as a platform-lever with its own fulcrum. Moreover, the strategy needs different platform-levers to cut across each other to create some or all the line's products.

In product line strategy, the question is whether to treat these common factors as platform-levers with intensely focused fulcrums or as technology building blocks without dedicated focus. When platform-levers cut across one another, internal organizational challenges are heightened. In these cases, certain practices (sometime facilitated with certain libations) can help coordinate and facilitate work and decisions, both for managing existing products within product lines, new offerings, new platform-levers, and completely new product lines.

At issue in matrixed platform-lever strategies is whether the fulcrums act in unison or conflict with one another. Specifically, it is whether there is conflict at each pyramid level of the respective fulcrums. This issue comes into play mostly when platform-lever types differ. For example, a design platform-lever may use practices such as waterfall project management coupled to staged development. This may differ from the quick sprint, agile approach used by a matrixed service or software system platform-lever.

How should leadership for these platform-levers coordinate and collaborate cohesively? The answer is critical to carrying out good product line strategy. But the answer is straightforward. It boils down to setting up practices that are a hybrid of both agile and waterfall project management approach. Gate deliverables may be adjusted a bit, but strategy execution milestones (the roadmap) still hold true.

The challenge associated with matrixed platform-levers is that workflows, decision flows, and information flows must work together. Understanding this and resolving potential conflicts early in the life of a product line strategy is important. The reason is simple: It's much easier to avoid conflicts than to deal with such aftereffects as inferior product quality and project-schedule slippage.

Seeking Your Platform-lever

When companies step up to examine their product line strategies, a key task is to figure out what their platform-levers are or what they might be in the future. For mature companies, this is a tough challenge. Often what started years earlier as a specifically defined platform-lever has morphed to address ever-changing market needs. Over time, such changes can cause loss of leverage. I refer to this as normal "platform-lever entropy." Without control and management, platform-levers always move toward unfocused chaos—the very definition of entropy.

Here is where understanding platform-levers becomes so important. By developing a mutual understanding about the current state of platform-levers, product line teams can better determine and create a common vision of a future state.

It would seem that all you have to do to define current platform-levers is get in a room and hash it out. It sounds good. But my experience suggests otherwise. Most mature organizations do <u>not</u> have unanimous agreement among managers about their platform-levers. How do these companies gain the desired leverage without a common focus? The answer is simple: They don't. Or perhaps better stated, they don't get as much leverage as they wish.

The first challenge in figuring out platform-levers is to recognize the confusion that arises because the platform-lever changed, or is changing continuously. What platform-levers were, are, and should be are different. The next challenge is to recognize what's possible and what's not. Here, understanding platform-lever types is critical. In opinionated situations (yes, some managers can be opinionated), it's also helpful to understand what's not a platform-lever. Remember this, because later in Chapter 11.3, I discuss forming product line strategies. There, I lay out a smarter approach for defining future platform-levers.

What's Not a Platform-lever

A frequent mistake is to declare something a platform-lever when, in fact, it can't be. This is most troublesome when the mistake is made by senior executives or outside advisors. If errant declarations come from near the top, whole organizations can move errantly to support it.

Therefore, it's helpful to complement the list of possible platform-lever types (Table 7.3.1, above) with a list of common mistakes (Table 7.3.2, below). A key point of interest is how some mistakes come from various uses for the single word "platform."

Table 7.3.2: Common Mistakes About Platform-lever Types for Product Lines

Common Errant Types	Reason Why
Market Segments and Market Segment Clusters	Platform-levers enable products to fulfill common customer needs within market segments. Sometimes the common needs become names or titles for the segments. This may mistakenly sound like the name of a platform-lever. Market segments, however, do not deliver leverage.

Common Errant Types	Reason Why
Geographies	Geographies are a distinct market segment type, usually designated by sales or distribution. These can be powerful and meaningful in business strategy. They are also helpful for segmentation schemes on product line roadmaps. However, segments do not enable leverage in the product line. Therefore, they are not platform-levers.
Reusable Modules	In the design world, reusable configurations are commonly called "platforms." However, declaring each reusable configuration a "platform-lever" is a mistake. The confusion is that all reusable modules have potential to be platform-levers. Here, the distinguishing factor is whether the product line strategy has or should call one out to receive intense focus.
Skills and Competencies	The intense focus organizations place on platform-levers comes from deliberately set fulcrums. Each fulcrum includes organizational structure, roles and responsibilities, and managing competencies. When people use their skill and competencies on tasks related to a product line, it becomes a force on the platform-lever, not the lever itself. Therefore, skills and competencies are not a platform-lever.
Functions and Chain-Links	Some managers confuse business strategy and product line strategy. You hear this when they say a function or chain-link within a business is a "platform." For example, it might be wise to declare the sales force to be a powerful chain-link within the business unit strategy. However, this does not make the sales force the platform-lever in the product line strategy.
Intellectual Property	Intellectual property and trade secrets can be powerful in both business and product line strategies. However, intellectual property and trade secrets are best thought of as forces that drive or support platform-levers, not the levers themselves. Intellectual properties and trade secrets management is a chain-links strategy. It needs alignment with the product line chain-link.

Common Errant Types	Reason Why
Brands	Managers often confuse brands and platform-levers because, for some product lines, a one-to-one relationship may exist. This is an anomaly of business strategy. It is not because of product line strategy. When developing and improving product line strategies, the two should be separated. Product line strategy then seeks leverage from a recognizable platform-lever. Business units should seek to unite product line strategy with brand strategy. Each is a separate chain-link in the business unit strategy.

Understanding the current state of platform-levers sets a baseline from which a future state may originate. This is the starting point for change or transition. A notable change to platform-levers, not just next-generation advancements of an existing platform-lever, can be a big step in product line strategy. By definition, this is a "pivot." And all product line pivots cause change to how attributes position products within market segments. Plus, pivots demand a renewed view of gaining alignment and synergy across chain-links in the business unit strategy.

Product line strategy pivots led by platform-lever changes are as much about organizational change as they are about the lever itself. Pivots require changes to other chain-links in the business strategy like sales, operations, and marketing. They are also about changing the fulcrum and its parts. This is where some organizations, especially mature companies, miss the boat. They think they can merely change platform-levers and gain the benefits of a renewed product line strategy. Unfortunately, it does not work that way.

If advancing a product line strategy calls for changing platform-levers or adding new platform-lever types, it also calls for organizational change, both in structure and in behaviors. This makes an organization's agility as important as the genius behind its platform-levers. Chapter 12.1 lays out a specific method to advance current platform-levers to new generations, or pivot to completely new platform-levers.

Helpful Resources

To learn more about platform-levers, check out The Adept Group's website about the topic. There you'll find white papers, short blogs, and video discussions. There are also several case studies that show the critical role that certain platform-levers and their change have played in different circumstances. You'll find these resources at https://adept-plm.com/plus-resources/.

Laying out the Solution

The Strategy-Essence

PRODUCT LINE STRATEGY: GETTING TO GOOD

Seek to:

Align with and gain lift from all chain-link strategies that comprise a business unit strategy.

- ▶ Make sure no chain-link is working against the desired product line strategy.
- ▶ Use organizational change purposely to offset the normal cultural inertia across chain-links that hinders product line strategies.
- ▶ Work and build discipline toward influencing the full organization's behaviors and decisions.

Position products via their attributes within verb-oriented market segments. Let branding and advertising position for emotions.

- ▶ Use positioning across the full set of products coming from the product line. Don't just position one product at a time. Have product-attribute positions work as a set. Make sure they complement one another.
- ▶ Position for purpose — Drive demand, beat competition, exploit skills, meet timing.
- ▶ Focus on customer-desired outcomes. Do not use vague "needs."
- ▶ Use Product Innovation Charters to define product attributes and guide developments.

Use platform-levers to deliver multiple products faster and more economically.

- Focus deliberately and intensely on gaining development speed and delivering economical attribute performance from platform-levers.
- Use dedicated organizational fulcrums to gain intense focus on each platform-lever.
- Pivot to change platform-levers when the market, competitors, and technologies change.
- Recognize platform-lever pivots as a necessity for continual growth and long-term survival.

Gain unity and harmony across the three Strategy-Essence parts: Chain-Link Alignment, Attribute Positioning, Platform-Lever Leverage.

Chapter 8

Strategy Execution and Roadmap Management *PLuS Framework* Pillar 2

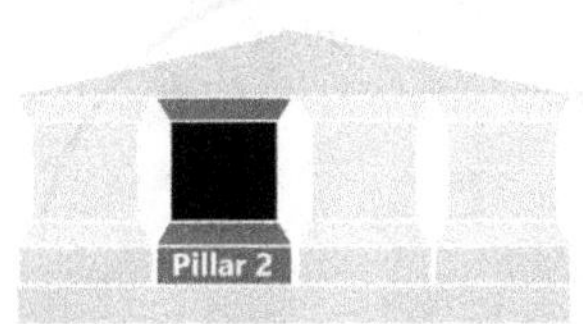

Most managers agree with a simple maxim: **How companies carry out strategy is as important as the strategy itself.** No doubt this holds true for product line strategies. A well-thought-out product line strategy needs great execution, or all is for naught. That's why managing strategy execution is the second pillar of the *PLuS Framework.*

Product line strategy execution is about rationalizing, prioritizing, synchronizing, and conducting work. Its goal is *to carry out a coherent work effort aligned with the Strategy-Essence.* Yet it presents a major challenge for many organizations. Good execution demands several approaches toward doing work to join as a whole. These approaches, shown in Figure 8.1, are portfolio, process, and project management working in unison with Roadmap Management. Today, most large companies are building skills and systems to drive these four approaches.

Figure 8.1: Strategy Execution Parts

Good strategy execution strengthens a smart Strategy-Essence. It comes from project, portfolio, and process management tied to well-thought-out roadmap milestones. When joined, these processes help product line teams and top managers oversee and guide work to achieve great execution.

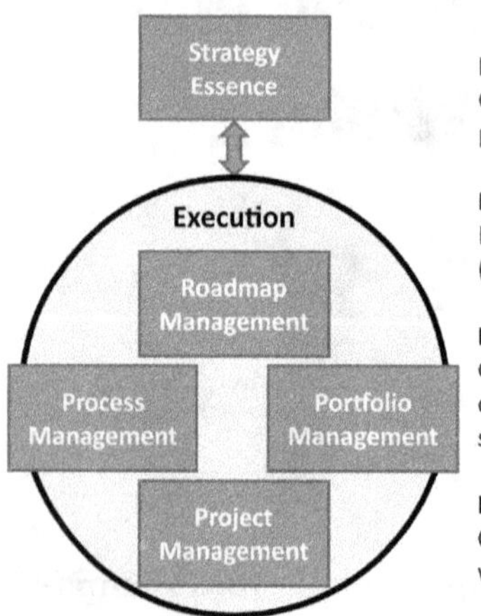

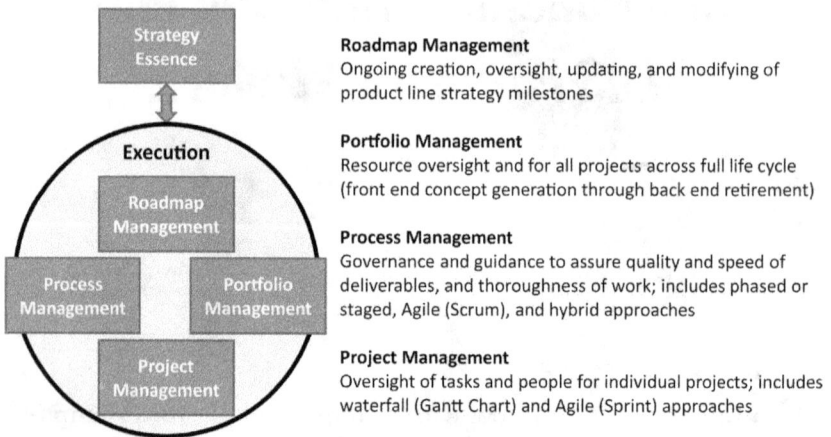

Roadmap Management
Ongoing creation, oversight, updating, and modifying of product line strategy milestones

Portfolio Management
Resource oversight and for all projects across full life cycle (front end concept generation through back end retirement)

Process Management
Governance and guidance to assure quality and speed of deliverables, and thoroughness of work; includes phased or staged, Agile (Scrum), and hybrid approaches

Project Management
Oversight of tasks and people for individual projects; includes waterfall (Gantt Chart) and Agile (Sprint) approaches

Roadmap Management Challenges

Before discussing how these approaches join with one another, let's first explore product line roadmapping, or what I call Roadmap Management. It's about creating and managing strategy milestones. Without it, good strategy execution is difficult, if not impossible.

As you dive into Roadmap Management, you'll see a few challenges. These pop up because many managers don't fully grasp product line strategy. For example, you may hear someone substitute "roadmap" for the word "plan." Or, you may see managers cling to the singular "product roadmap," not that for a product line and its strategy. These are simple disconnects. The problem is they confuse discussions about how best to carry out the strategy, a situation only made worse when the disconnect is with top managers or executives.

You may also see two other common errors. The first is when managers roll up several project Gantt Charts and call it the roadmap. A few product development software companies have even grabbed onto this thinking. Unfortunately, Gantt chart roll-ups presume the development projects, as a set, correctly focus on a strategy. Yet the approach falls short without showing milestones related to market segments, platform-levers, or chain-link changes. It doesn't connect with the Strategy-Essence.

EXPLANATION:
Good Roadmap Management

Well-crafted roadmaps build an understanding about the strategy. They also enable coordination and flexibility to carry it out. Donald Sull, Rebecca Homkes, and Charles Sull examined the topic in their article "Why Strategy Execution Unravels—and What to Do About It" (Harvard Business Review - March 2015). They point to three contributors—understanding, coordination, and flexibility—as critical to good-strategy execution. These contributors are fundamental to product line roadmaps. Good roadmap management, therefore, is a set of practices and supporting software that enable creation, oversight and modifcation of such roadmaps.

The second error is when organizations combine multiple product lines into the same project portfolio. They then seek to "balance and prioritize" their way to effective strategy. Unfortunately, the approach skips creating a Strategy-Essence and roadmapping the milestones to carry it out. The idea is to tie portfolio management direct to strategy. This approach is nonsensical without a well-vetted Strategy-Essence. It shifts focus away from driving each product line's strategy. In Chapter 10, you'll read how the framework's fourth pillar resolves trade-offs between product lines. But it does this related to business strategy, not portfolio management.

Understanding roadmapping mistakes is important in setting up good Roadmap Management practices. It's more than just declaring "I know how to draw a roadmap." It's about engaging the organization with a shared understanding of the strategy and what it takes to carry it out. It's also about facilitating and managing change throughout a product line's life.

Product Line Roadmap Management

The purpose of Roadmap Management is threefold.

1. To build a common understanding about what the strategy seeks to carry out.
2. To coordinate the "right" work on the "right" projects at the "right" time across all roles and chain-links.
3. To enable responsiveness and flexibility toward strategy changes across the organization.

Roadmaps lay out the milestones and work that teams envisage to carry out their strategy. Most important, roadmaps set the stage for middle management, not just those at the top, to lead the strategy. Such management is best done in the immediacy of everyday work and decisions, not by waiting for business unit leadership to resolve issues.

The key to middle management's leadership is gaining a shared understanding the *what, why,* and *how* of the product line strategy. This can be difficult. In project management, Peter Drucker pointed out how most Gantt charts tend not to survive "contact with reality."

The same can be true for poorly thought out roadmaps, those not set up or managed for change and adaptability.

Working through a roadmap helps teams spot where reality might collide with intentions. It also aids in deciding responses, whether through smart changes, milestone recasts, or major pivots. Good roadmaps lay out a basis for change, not a blind mandate to achieve milestones. They are living, dynamic documents. And they help organizations realize success by developing deep and shared understanding of the strategy coupled to its path forward. This understanding is vital in leading work efforts. It's also vital to following the lead.

EXPLANATION:
Roadmaps in Business

Roadmapping applies to many topics in business. Its early use began over a quarter century ago to visualize how technologies might change. Technology-centric roadmapping then extended to the customer, supply chain, and whole industries.

Technology-centric: lays out expected technology advances.

Supply Chain-centric: focuses on supplier readiness to match product development and launch.

Customer-centric: seeks to convince customers to stay dedicated to the company's products or platforms.

Industry-centric: coordinates the advancements to and with an industry's infrastructure.

Our focus is on the milestones to carry out a product line strategy.

Seeing Where You're Going

Creating good product line roadmaps refines and brings clarity to a strategy. Using and updating roadmaps then aids teams in coordinating work across chain-links, and it helps adjust actions because of constraints and opportunities. Therefore, this second pillar of the *PLuS Framework* is both an analysis tool and a guide for carrying out the strategy.

Over the next three chapters, I divide Roadmap Management into sections. First, I build understanding about roadmap variants. I then discuss and give examples of crafting the master roadmap. I wrap up Strategy Execution by showing how project, process, and portfolio management combine with roadmaps to enable the right work on the right projects at the right time.

8.1: Roadmaps and Their Management *PLuS Framework* Pillar 2

Our goal for Roadmap Management is to lay out specific work to be carried out at specific times —in line with the Strategy-Essence. But you'll see that a single roadmap diagram is rarely enough to do the job. Good execution needs different roadmap versions or variants. This helps in communicating with different audiences and assuring all milestones for the Strategy-Essence get laid out.

Sad to say, many managers want to jump to the tasks of roadmapping. They see a plain "timeline" of products and their development schedules as the deliverable. But doing this without thinking through the Strategy-Essence is a problem. These managers believe the quicker they get something down on paper, the better off they'll be. This sounds good, but it's a mistake. Without a Strategy-Essence and its three parts, roadmaps lack coherency. That's why Roadmap Management addresses execution with a master roadmap and with audience-specific roadmaps, called subordinate roadmaps or sub-maps. Let's explore these roadmaps to see why they are different and why we need them.

The Master Product Line Roadmap

The master roadmap is the parent document to which subordinate roadmaps synchronize. The master roadmap displays all objects related to carrying out the strategy. These **roadmap objects** (*Definition Alert*) include platform-levers, markets segments, technology building blocks, and product offerings.

The master roadmap shows the *what, when*, and *how* of many key parts of the strategy. If any part is a weak contributor, creating and refining the master roadmap help expose it. The analysis may then lead to changes in the execution, the strategy, or both.

In a master roadmap, timelines are laid horizontally to represent each platform-lever in the product line. Milestones on the platform-lever timelines include products in the market, products under development, and future targets for innovation. All current and targeted market segments (the verb-oriented segments discussed in Chapter 7.2) appear at the top of the diagram. Key technologies are placed at the bottom of the diagram. These are technology building blocks that add value to platform-levers. By combining with platform-levers, these technology building blocks form products or, better stated, embed attributes into each product.

DEFINITION ALERT:
Roadmap Objects

Roadmap objects are those shapes and figures placed on the roadmap diagram that represent key elements of the product line strategy. These include market segments, platform-levers, technologies adding value to platform-levers (called technology building blocks), and products/services. Roadmaps display products as products-in-the-market (PIMs), products-in-development (PIDs), and targets for product innovations, i.e., product innovation charters (PICs).

Figure 8.1.2 shows how the key objects in the master roadmap relate to one another. Technology building blocks relate to platform-levers to form new products. Products then relate to specific market segments. The platform-lever timeline also shows delivery milestones for development projects and product launches.

Figure 8.1.2: Basic Construct of a Master Roadmap

A product line roadmap displays platform-levers as timelines. Key objects then relate to the platform-lever timelines. These include market segments, technology building blocks, and products. PIMs are "products in the market," PIDs are "products in development," and PICs are "product innovation charters," specific targets for innovation. Each "object" connects to another. Together, they reflect how the product line will advance.

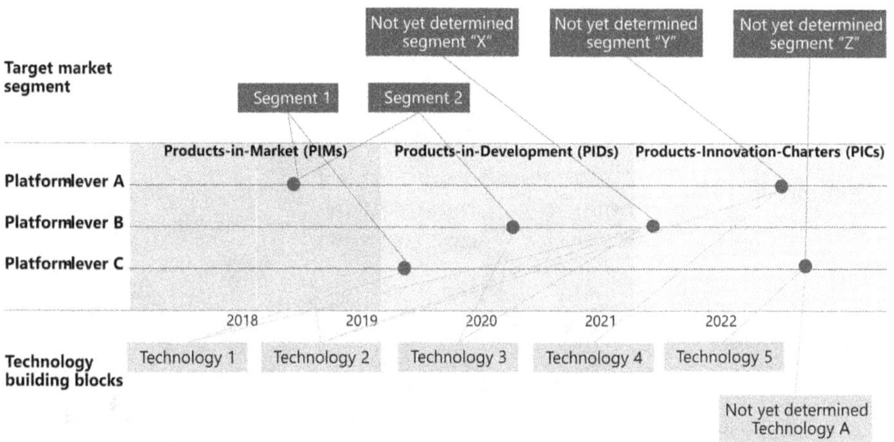

Tied to Strategy

Notice how platform-levers and attribute positioning toward verb-based market segments show up on the master roadmap. These are two parts of the Strategy-Essence. Changes and work related to chain-links, the Strategy-Essence's third part, are absent. This gap undermines good execution. Roadmap Management, however, fills the gap by creating and using chain-link-specific sub-maps.

You'll see that sub-maps lay out work that affects the strategy yet may not be related to specific development projects. This includes work across all chain-links. For example, sub-maps call out market research work, technology scouting efforts, manufacturing updates, and sales initiatives. Sub-maps also highlight investigative work to reform and advance platform-levers over multiple generations.

There may be many sub-maps, each with a unique purpose. Table 8.1.1 shows common sub-maps and their tie-in to the master roadmap and the Strategy-Essence. Sub-maps capture milestones for chain-link changes and non-product-related work that supports product line moves.

Sub-Map	Audience	Purpose	Tie to the master roadmap and Strategy-Essence
Critical-to-Success	Top Management, Governance Bodies	Key Item and Project Recognition	Highlights the product line strategy's key moves
Non-product Aggregate Roll-up	Top Management, Governance Bodies	Coordination and Synchronization across Chain-links	Ensures coordination of key activities
Segment & Positioning	Marketing	Research, Buyer behavior, Requirements Definition	Create a focus on product attribute positioning in noun-based and verb-based market segments
Technology Building Bock	Technology and Engineering	Technology Scouting, and Readiness	Lays out timing and readiness of technology building blocks
Market Communication	Marketing	Advertising, Promotion, Collateral	Ensures coordination of emotional positioning
Skills and Capacities	HR Planning	Planning, On-boarding Resources	Ensure correct long-term skills hiring and development
Chain-Link Changes	All Chain-links	Chain-link Alignment	Makes visible the need for key chain-link changes.
Sales Readiness	Sales	Sales Planning and Launch Readiness	Enables coordination of sales management with product management

Sub-map Graphics

Teams have much leeway in creating sub-maps. There's no specific format like I advise for the master roadmap. Sub-maps don't have to show market segments, platform-levers, or technology building blocks. Sub-maps need only show milestones or achievements relevant to the intended audience. But they must also synchronize with the master roadmap. How you display this may be as simple as a timeline or a Gantt chart. And, as you'd expect, it's best to create each sub-map with members of the audience with which it will be shared.

Two sub-maps need special attention because both should be shared with top management as part of governance.[25] The first is the "Critical to Success" sub-map. It shows only those projects that will unravel the strategy if they fail or become delayed notably. This view is both for near-term and long-term success. It's not just a display of projects needed in the next quarter or the current year; It's about the full life of the product line. Top management needs to review the status of critical-to-success projects either quarterly or semi-annually. If they fall off track, top management's job is to make decisions that shift resources and reorient these projects. Or, if that's not enough, to call for a change in the product line strategy and its execution.

The second sub-map needing special attention is the non-product Aggregate Roll-up sub-map. This is a view of projects and work key to strategy success but not product development-specific. See Figure 8.1.3. For example, it may include sales initiatives, market research work, and quality-improvement work. Some work may be conducted by the product line team, and other work may be done by other chain-links. What's important is whether the product line strategy is counting on the work. If so, it should be captured and displayed.

---

25 Governance is a critical part of the PLuS Framework's roof. I discuss this in chapter 12.

Figure 8.1.3: Aggregate Roll-up Sub-map

This sub-map summarizes all non-product-specific projects and work for successful strategy execution into a view that complements the master roadmap. Each bar represents work critical to advancing the product line and its strategy.

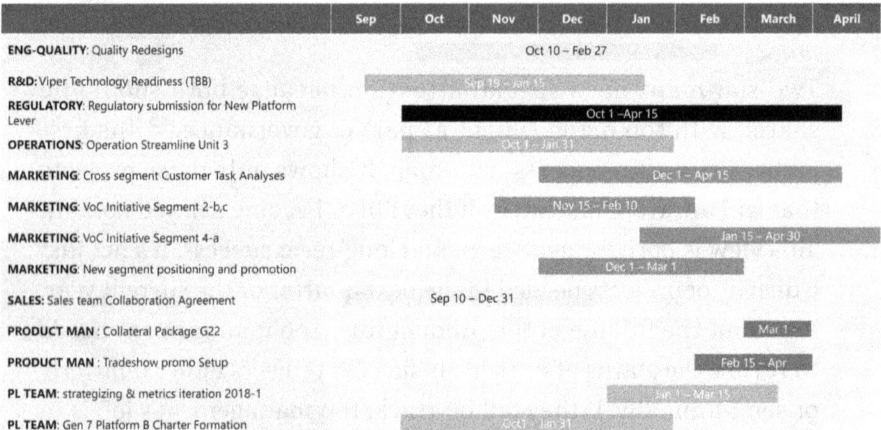

Top management's acceptance and oversight of the Aggregate Roll-up sub-map is integral to chain-link alignment. It shows that certain activities, some outside the product line, are needed for successful strategy.

EXPLANATION:
Strategies & Roadmaps

When you embark on creating product line roadmaps (master and subordinate), you'll see that doing so tests the strategy. You'll also see that good strategy sharpens the roadmap. This makes it important for contributors to understand how internal work might interplay with external market and technology changes. Knowledge and insights about the past and present are critical, especially for project durations and resource needs. So too are smart speculations and foresight about future possibilities.

Mastering the Master Roadmap

Smart Roadmap Management starts with creating a good master roadmap built from a well-thought-out Strategy-Essence. Sometimes, the master roadmap, like the product line itself, is complicated. There can be many parts, and all of them may be in motion. Graphing this may seem daunting, but I encourage teams to tackle the task. It's fundamental to good product line strategies.

The next chapter segment provides some help. I show how to lay out a Master Roadmap, using data tables and graphing tools.

8.2: Creating a Master Roadmap

The approach teams take to create a master roadmap is critical. It's so important that the task is part of the strategizing process, the *PLuS Framework*'s foundation. But to understand the master roadmap, it's helpful to see how teams create them. Instead of waiting to explore the topic in Section 4, I bring it forward, here, to our discussion on the master roadmap.

A good master product line roadmap includes more information and more insights than just launch dates and milestones. It also displays connections between contributing technologies, products, platform-levers, and market segments. Consider the basic master roadmap shown in Figure 8.2.1.

The connecting lines between objects are crucial in communicating the product line's strategy and its execution. The problem here, though, is that such diagrams can be difficult to understand. There can be so many items on some master roadmaps that only those who worked on it understand it. No matter, it's important to keep master roadmaps reflecting reality. If there is a need to present a slimmed down roadmap, good roadmap management does so with sub-maps that synchronize with the master roadmap.

Figure 8.2.1: Simple Roadmap

The product line roadmap shows how an organization will carry out its strategy. I recommend that product line roadmaps have three swim lanes: (1) market segments, (2) platform-levers (represented as timelines), and (3) technology building blocks (TBBs). Notice how PIMs, PIDs, and PICs are labeled on the platform-lever timeline. This roadmap also highlights new, not-yet-served market segments and new, not-yet-developed technology building blocks.

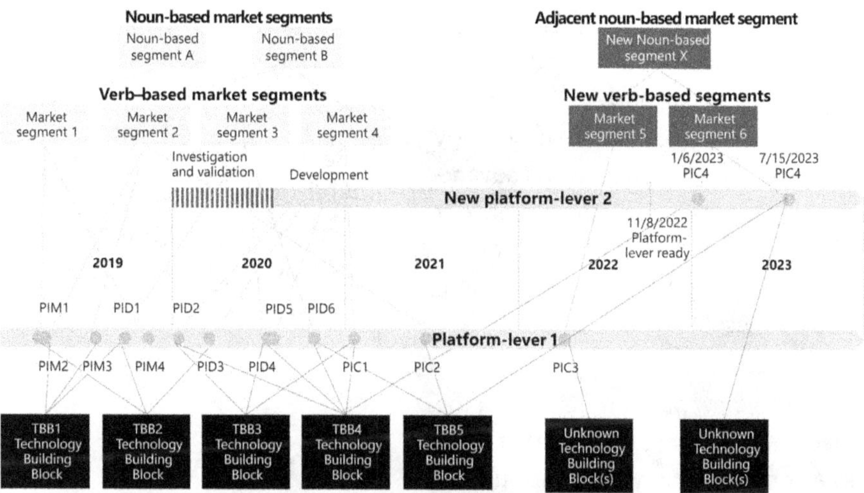

Tools for Robust Product Line Roadmapping

Many managers try to create product line roadmaps in MS Excel and PowerPoint. This is time-consuming, and the end graphic is difficult to edit and change. Instead, I recommend using Microsoft Visio, with its more sophisticated graphics, to create product line roadmaps.

Visio offers an easy-to-use timeline function that embeds within swim lanes, a useful combination. The tool aids users in formatting roadmaps with different shapes to represent different object types. Visio users may change, copy, update, or otherwise place these shapes on the timeline as needed. Plus, for the ambitious, Visio also enables users to use a customizable database engine to populate and format roadmaps.

It's also possible to configure product- and portfolio-management software to support product line roadmapping. Software that supports product development from firms like Atlassian, Planisware, Sopheon, and Planview can help you do this. They continue to build capabilities to support good roadmap management. Eventually, all businesses will likely use such software and automate roadmap graphics.

EXPLANATION:
Other Innovation Charter Types

Targeting innovations is not only about products. In 8.2.1 you'll notice the technology innovation charter and the market opportunity charter. These other charter types give purpose in strategy and guidelines for what fits and advances the product line. Such charters get placed on the roadmap when investments have been committed for projects that resolve each.

You'll see "new platform-levers" on the roadmap. These are projects that form, as a concept, a fully thought-out and vetted platform-lever. Once fully vetted, it becomes a platform-lever in development project.

Roadmap Swim Lanes

Good master roadmaps show how items in the strategy connect to one another. For instance, in the template I use to create master roadmaps, I start with a basic timeline. [26]

To that, I add "swim lanes" to show at least three major orientations.

1. Market segments (verb-oriented)
2. Platform-levers, products, development projects, and innovation targets

26 This is a Microsoft Visio template I created. It's available free for registered visitors on my firm's website at www.adept-plm.com/plus-resources/

3. Technologies (value-adding building blocks)

Adding and Connecting Objects

In a second overlay, each project (or product) is positioned on a platform-lever timeline reflecting its completion or launch date milestones. Again, see Figure 8.2.1 for an illustration. As I shared earlier, the acronyms I use for the three main project types are:

- PIMs—Product-in-Market, products already in the market; extension, cost reductions and repositioning
- PIDs—Product-in-Development, projects under way to develop new products (in staged or agile development)
- PICs—Product Innovation Charters, projects targeting future innovations and customer-desired outcomes

Objects, Data, and Information

The first step in creating a master roadmap is to compile data on all possible roadmap objects. This sounds easy. But it's common to discover that platform-levers, market segments, and technology building blocks are not defined or agreed upon. Deliberately embedding an object on the master roadmap also declares its importance in strategy. This is where the rubber hits the "roadmap" for product line strategies. What makes sense in the Strategy-Essence can collide with the master roadmap's reality.

EXPLANATION:
Roadmap Management
Roles and Responsibilities

I recommend the same managers who oversee projects assume responsibility for Roadmap Management on all product lines within a business unit. This is often the Project Management Office. By including Roadmap Management with Portfolio, Project, and Process Management, the role changes to be "The Office of Product Line Strategy Execution."

Those responsible for Roadmap Management must work with product line management to work out inconsistencies. This starts with the list of roadmap objects and expands to showing how the objects connect.

Most teams will use Excel to capture relationships or connections between roadmap objects. In an Excel sheet, place a list of platforms, technology building blocks, and market segments across the top rows. Then add the PIMs, PIDs, and PICs down the first column. (See Table 8.2.1.) An "X" within a cell represents an association between the objects in that row and column. Different values in the cell may show different relationships or dependencies. This leads to two questions product line teams must answer.

1. Is each roadmap object part of strategy and defined well enough to be on the roadmap?
2. Does the roadmap object relate to any others? Will these objects connect with one another in the master roadmap?

Table 8.2.1. Roadmap Object Relationships

An "X" shows an association between roadmap objects. On the master roadmap, the association appears as a line connecting the objects. Teams creating the master roadmap usually use two software tools to create graphics, one to collect data, and the other to make pictures.

A central data repository is most useful for capturing information about roadmap objects and the relationships among them. These data are the raw material to create the master roadmap.

		Product Line Platforms		Technology Building Blocks				Market Segments				
		Platform 1	Platform 2	TBB1	TBB2	TBB3	TBB4	MS1	MS2	MS3	MS4	MS5
Key Products in Market	PIM1	X		X				X				
	PIM2	X		X				X				
	PIM3		X		X				X			
	PIM4	X			X			X				
	PIM5	X			X				X			
	PIM6		X			X				X		
	PIM7		X				X			X		
Products In Development	PID1		X		X				X			
	PID2		X	X	X				X			
	PID3	X		X				X				
	PID4		X		X				X			
	PID5		X			X				X		
	PID6		X			X				X		
	PID7	X		X				X				
Product Innovation Charters	PIC1		X			X					X	
	PIC2	X	X			X	X		X		X	
	PIC3		X			X	X			X		
	PIC4		X		X	X					X	
	PIC5		X	X				X				
	PIC6		X				X					X

Your first tries at creating a master roadmap demand the data structure be flexible. Teams must be ready to add or subtract fields within the data to help characterize and confer relationships between the objects. This may be difficult when teams don't know what objects will be on the "in-use" master roadmap. Roadmapping teams often find Microsoft Excel as their tool of choice in early stages of creating master roadmaps.

The first task in creating a repository is to make a list of the different objects, with fields or data columns for characteristics of the objects. These fields may include values or descriptors for each roadmap object like:

- Titles and identifiers
- Object type
- Short descriptions
- Date ranges (begin and end dates)
- Milestone- or project-delivery dates
- Investment size, likely need for CAPEX
- Economic value
- Critical-to-Success status
- Risk or likelihood of success

When creating or updating the master and subordinate roadmaps, it's also helpful to use colors, highlights, or shapes. These visually signal major changes and the critical-to-success (CTS) status of projects and activities. When a company has multiple product lines, it's best that each roadmap uses the same standards to help senior managers, who will likely review them all, better understand them.

Figure 8.2.2: Master Product Line Roadmap

The master product line roadmap displays the work to carry out the product line strategy. The top swim lane in the roadmap shows market segments. The middle lane shows platform-lever timelines, PICs, PIDs, and PIMs. The bottom lane shows technology building blocks.

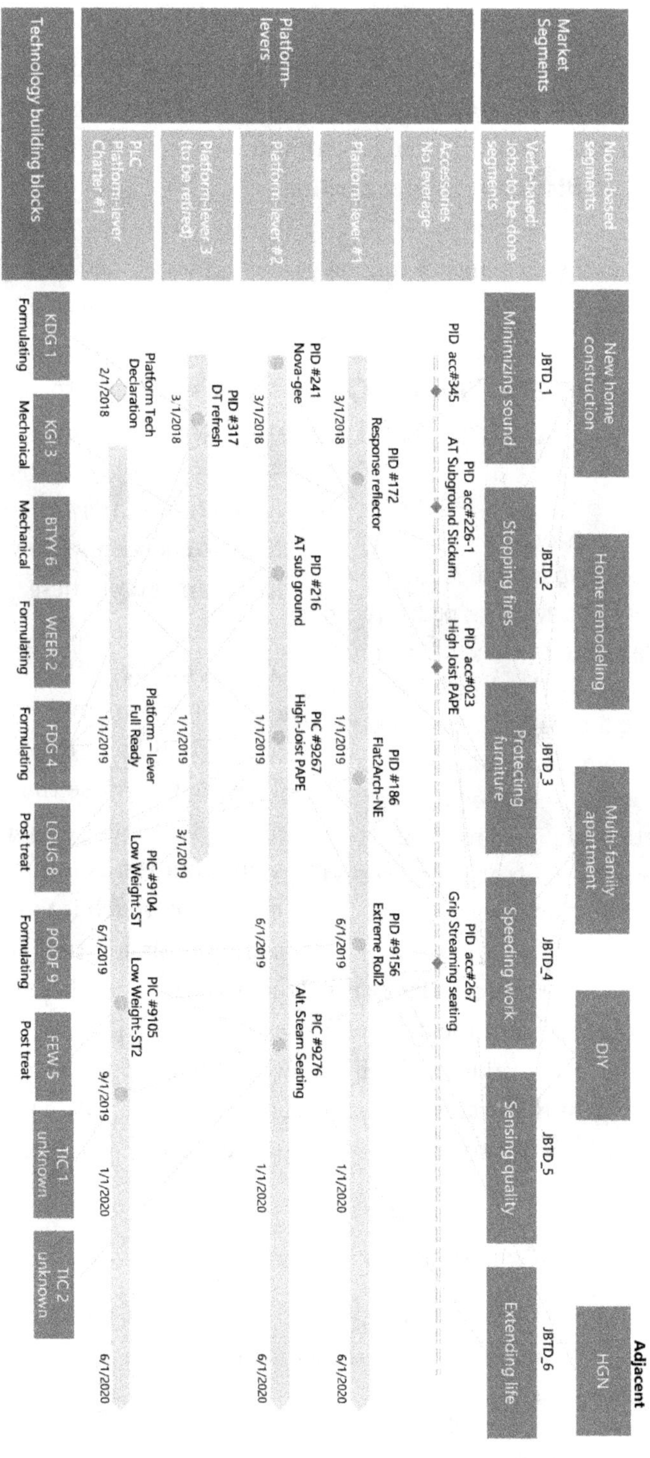
Adjacent
Market Segments
Noun-based segments
New home construction
Home remodeling
Multi-family apartment
DIY
HGN
Verb-based: Jobs-to-be-done segments
JBTD_1
Minimizing sound
JBTD_2
Stopping fires
JBTD_3
Protecting furniture
JBTD_4
Speeding work
JBTD_5
Sensing quality
JBTD_6
Extending life
Accessories No leverage
PID acc#345
PID acc#226-1 AT Subground Stickum
PID acc#023 High Joist PAPE
PID acc#267 Grip Streaming seating
Platform-levers
Platform-lever #1
3/1/2018
PID #172 Response reflector
1/1/2019
PID #186 Flat2Arch-NE
6/1/2019
PID #9156 Extreme Roll2
1/1/2020
6/1/2020
Platform-lever #2
PID #241 Nova-gee
3/1/2018
PID #216 AT sub ground
1/1/2019
PIC #9267 High-Joist PAPE
6/1/2019
PIC #9276 Alt. Steam Seating
1/1/2020
6/1/2020
Platform-lever 3 (to be retired)
PID #317 DT refresh
3/1/2018
1/1/2019
3/1/2019
PLC Platform-lever Charter #1
Platform Tech Declaration
2/1/2018
Platform – lever Full Ready
1/1/2019
PIC #9104 Low Weight-ST
6/1/2019
PIC #9105 Low Weight-ST2
9/1/2019
1/1/2020
6/1/2020
Technology building blocks
KDG 1
Formulating
KGI 3
Mechanical
BTYY 6
Mechanical
WEER 2
Formulating
FDG 4
Formulating
LOUG 8
Post treat
PODF 9
Formulating
FEW 5
Post treat
TIC 1 unknown
TIC 2 unknown

Using the Master Product Line Roadmap

For people not involved in the product line, master roadmaps first appear complicated and difficult to understand. Yet those involved can gain much from creating, communicating, and critiquing it. Figure 8.2.2 displays a master roadmap.

Anyone reviewing a master roadmap does so by studying the objects and their timeline placement. Objects may vary in size, shape, and color to suggest qualities like economic values, strategy roles, and importance. It's up to the team to choose how they wish to use and graph these.

EXPLANATION:
Roadmaps in Use

The master roadmap is a continuing project. Objects on it will change. The master roadmap becomes the team's declaration that says, "This path forward is how we intend to carry out the product line strategy." Updating and communicating the roadmap are vital tasks. Doing so helps maintain understanding of product line strategies across an organization. Stating a roadmap is "in use" means all objects on it are invested and their execution is underway.

The complexity of master roadmaps can make these graphics difficult to present. They may confuse the audience. So, when preparing a roadmap presentation, a helpful approach is to create a simple version that shares only critical-to-success (CTS) items. Remember, without these items, the strategy will fail. The debates and creative thinking that decide CTS status can be valuable. Drilling down to the project level like this often sharpens the strategy and its Execution Roadmap. It's a full-out review of what's important and where projects stack up in priority.

Roadmap Management Lexicon

Defining or labeling strategy changes tracked by Roadmap Management can be helpful. A lexicon helps teams communicate better and faster.

Here are a few terms that describe changes to strategies and roadmaps.

1. **Roadmap Recast**. These are changes to a project on the master roadmap. They may include changes in completion dates or feature sets, or they may help synchronize work. The main characteristic is that they do *not* alter the Strategy-Essence. They do not change attribute positioning, platform-levers, or chain-link alignment.
2. **Strategy Move**. This change affects the Strategy-Essence. This change will somehow affect platform-levers, positioning, or chain-link alignment. Strategy moves always show up on the master roadmap. But a strategy move causes no change in how functional chain-links interface with one another or the business model they carry out.
3. **Pivot**. This move is one step up from a strategy move. It's significant enough to change both the strategy and how the chain-links connect and work with one another. A pivot is a major change in a product line Strategy-Essence.
4. **Business Model Transformation**. The most significant change is when an organization purposely changes how a product line creates, delivers, or captures value—its business model. An example would be when the line changes from selling products outright to a subscription service where customers pay as they use each product.
5. **Critical-to-Success (CTS).** This project classification is a statement about its importance in strategy and on the master roadmap. These projects are significant enough that if one fails, it will compromise achieving one or more of the strategy objectives.

Strategy Execution and Roadmap Management, the second pillar of the *PLuS Framework*, ties directly to the Strategy-Essence, the first pillar.

8.3: Portfolio, Process, and Project Management

I am often asked how roadmaps and project plans connect. This is a great question. Both roadmaps and project management are about producing deliverables. The difference is that roadmaps lay out the milestone deliverables of the whole product line. Project management, whether by waterfall, agile, or hybrid practices, lays out the work and deliverables for individual projects.

A major issue arises when companies try to link project management for individual projects directly to business strategy. They unknowingly skip creating the product line's strategy and roadmaps. This works for startups where there's usually just one project underway, but it does not work for large companies, for whom I've written this book. It cannot, and let me explain why.

The challenge for large companies is there are always many projects underway. And within business units, there may also be multiple product lines. The issue highlights how product line plurality differs from project management singularity.

Think about this as an information technology (IT) challenge. Imagine you're given the IT task of rolling up all project-management plans and relating them to the business unit strategy. The first issue you'll bump into is figuring out how to codify projects and business unit strategy. There need to be fields or data values that enable a relationship between the two. Here the issue is figuring out the business unit strategy without understanding potential contributions from each product line and other chain-links.

The problem is you can't resolve this without deconstructing the strategy. Here is where we need product line strategies and their roadmaps.

Specifically, we need milestones, especially "Critical to Success" milestones, from the product line roadmap. Project management can tag deliverables and gates to these roadmap milestones. The milestones then link product line strategy to business unit's strategy.

Consider the diagram in Figure 8.3.1. In the center of the diagram, you'll see how product line work connects to project management on the bottom. It also connects to business strategy on the top. The dark upper-left boxes are for product line strategy. The gray lower-right boxes are for project management. Without the product line-strategy dark boxes, project management has no way to connect to business strategy.

It's fruitless for the IT group to force a connection between project management and business strategy. The only noticeable impact will be an increase in the number of frustrated project managers.

Figure 8.3.1: Connecting Project Management to Business Strategy

This flow diagram shows how development practices and business strategy relate. The dark blocks represent parts of product line strategy.

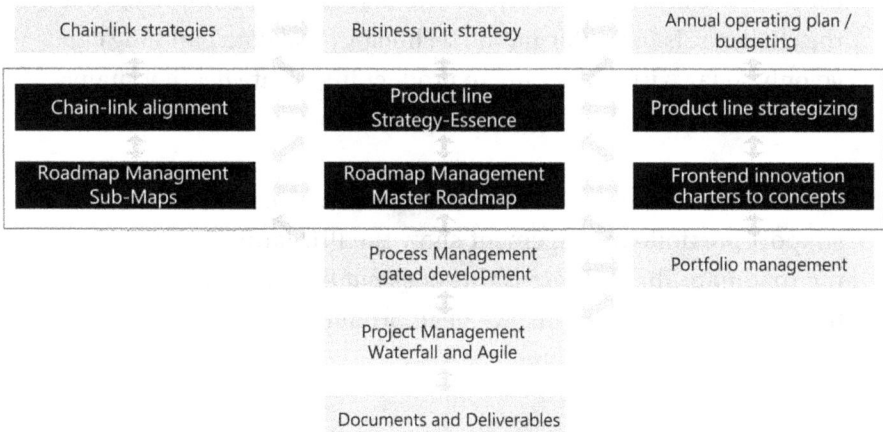

Chain-link strategies
Business unit strategy
Annual operating plan / budgeting
Chain-link alignment
Product line Strategy-Essence
Product line strategizing
Roadmap Managment Sub-Maps
Roadmap Management Master Roadmap
Frontend innovation charters to concepts
Process Management gated development
Portfolio management
Project Management Waterfall and Agile
Documents and Deliverables

The dark-box product line strategy connects project management with business strategy. The result is that project impact on business strategy grows notably. In business strategy, it's important. In product line strategy, it's important. In portfolio management, it's important. And in project management, it's important.

Connecting the approaches helps answer a central question for product line strategies and portfolio management. *Why are certain projects more important at different points in time?* How do business and product line strategy translate to project priorities?

To answer this question, the *PLuS Framework* guides teams in analyzing and setting priorities. The work links directly to the Strategy-Essence and Roadmap Management. It points to what's critical to carrying out the product line strategy and what's not. This then feeds into portfolio-resource management.

Portfolio-Resource Management to Business Strategy

Most large organizations place much attention on keeping day-to-day work and practices lean. The rapidly evolving power of project-portfolio management software focuses direct on this need. But the challenge is that information technology and data handling can go only so far without linking to product line strategies. For many, good product line strategy practices are missing.

Previously, I pointed out how many software companies[27] that support portfolio management show the PID launch schedule as the roadmap. The problem is this does not link to product lines or business strategy. For this, we need product line roadmaps with

27 This includes companies like Planisware, Planview, and Sopheon.

their milestones and deliverables. The is more than just a graphic of launch schedules for products in development (PIDs).

Roadmap management works to solve the issue. It ties project management and portfolio management to product line strategies and the governing business strategy. It is fundamental to good product line strategy execution and forms the second pillar of the *PLuS Framework.*

Carrying out the Strategy

Strategy Execution and Roadmap Management

PRODUCT LINE STRATEGY: GETTING TO GOOD

Seek to:

Gain good strategy execution. It is fundamental to good product line strategy. And it requires the union of Roadmap Management with project, process, and portfolio management.

Use a master roadmap to show how and when technology building blocks should add value to platform-levers to form products that match customer-desired outcomes in verb-oriented market segments.

Use subordinate roadmaps (sub-maps) to help communicate timing of non-product development work. Include all chain-link changes in sub-maps.

Use roadmaps to share a full understanding of the strategy execution plan.

- Create and update the master roadmap and sub-maps as a means to fine-tune the product line strategy.
- Show each platform-lever as a timeline in the master roadmap.
- On the master roadmap, show future/possible products (PICs), products-in-development (PIDs), and key products already in the market (PIMs).
- Visually highlight those projects considered "critical-to-success" (CTS). Such projects, if hindered, will cause unravelling of the Strategy-Essence.

- Include on the master roadmap all changes to your product line strategy and all corrections to execution plans.

Tailor each sub-map's graphics to its intended audience. But always synchronize sub-maps with the master roadmap.

Chapter 9

Measuring and Guiding Strategy Performance *PLuS Framework* Pillar 3

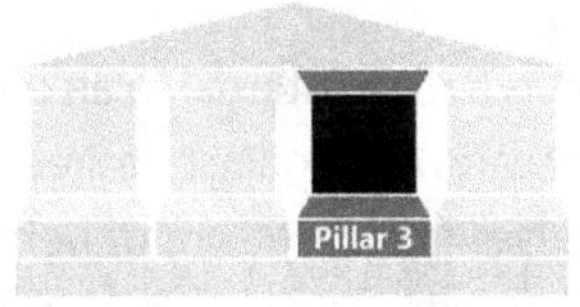

Roadmaps with well-defined milestones are important tools in carrying out good product line strategies. But roadmaps are not enough. Teams also need more tangible guidance for making trade-offs and responding to seemingly random events. This comes from objectives and metrics, the focus of the third pillar of the *PLuS Framework*.

This third pillar of the *PLuS Framework* supports teams in using objectives and metrics to guide and improve the strategy. But much like the work toward setting and updating roadmaps, setting up objectives and metrics is enormously valuable in sharpening the strategy. Teams doing this work develop a deeper understanding of their strategies and gain insights toward improvements.

Like the first two pillars, the third pillar remains focused on one product line. It does not seek to cut across product lines or across functions.

Setting objectives and metrics helps build responsiveness toward influences on the strategy and its execution. It is to guide judgment and behaviors for the better.[28] This is critical in managing good product line strategies.

Most managers quickly see how objectives and metrics help product line strategy effectiveness. Yet recognize a key principle about using objectives and metrics: It goes deeper than just relating objectives and metrics to a strategy. It also relates to behaviors, which combine to form an organization's culture. While it's important to guide and improve product line strategies, it's best to do so by reinforcing positive behaviors to get the job done. This tie between guiding strategy and influencing behaviors is important.

DEFINITION ALERT:
Cultural Inertia

This is a force internal to an organization that can work against desired outcomes. It arises from the sum of behaviors and judgments across an organization. It is an artifact of an organization's culture.

Behaviors Matter

The *PLuS Framework* guides product line teams to first spot behaviors working against their strategy. Next, the approach helps lay out measures and objectives that change those behaviors for the better. The framework does not tackle or push on culture. Experience

28 Hauser, John R. and Gerry Katz, "Metrics: You Are What You Measure!" *European Management Journal*(October 1998)

suggests that pushing culture not behaviors often ends in a naive, Quixote-like fight against an army of windmills.

In the *PLuS Framework*, objectives and metrics become tools for gaining support and directing behaviors. This helps fight **cultural inertia** (*Definition Alert*), the organizational force that pushes in a different direction. When objectives and metrics don't influence behaviors, their relevance may be questionable. In such cases, a team's choice is to either recraft them for greater value or toss them aside.

Strategy Guidance

Product line strategy objectives state the results product line teams seek to achieve. They give guidance and purpose to work and decisions. But objectives, even with good roadmaps, fall short in keeping strategies at their best. For this, teams need metrics to show how both influences, whether internal or external, may affect strategy results.

But what's most critical for good product line strategies? Simple. It is measures of the strategy essence and roadmap milestones. If product line teams keep their Strategy-Essence parts strong and their critical-to-success (CTS) deliverables on time, results should be good. If these slip, changes may be in order. Metrics that track these strategy parts are key to good strategy.

In the next three segments, I discuss how product line teams can best use objectives and metrics to steer their product strategies for greater performance. The first segment shares insights about creating and using objectives. The next segment details how best to use metrics to keep strategy on course while offsetting normal cultural inertia. The two following segments then explore developing insights about the future and using a dashboard to display objectives, metrics, and insights about the future.

9.1: Objectives and Purpose—Where We're Going and Why

Most managers recognize that strategies should have objectives. Product line strategies are no different. Teams need objectives to give focus and direction to their efforts. Good objectives will show where things should be headed. This is especially helpful to teams in guiding the judgments and decisions they'll make along the way.

When thinking about objectives, it's a good idea to go back to basics and consider the purpose for product line strategy. The definition I gave in Chapter 1 is:

"A product line strategy lays out a coherent approach to improve competitiveness, increase customer satisfaction, and maximize income. It does this by astute management of interrelated issues toward creating, selecting, designing, developing, producing, supporting, and retiring related products and services."

Put into action, a product line strategy will capture the deliberate choices and decisions made by management that drive work to achieve certain objectives. That's all good, but the simple statement leaves us hanging on the objectives. What are they? And how do product line objectives differ from overall business strategy objectives?

Objectives for product line strategies usually address three distinct areas or categories. And, as I'll explain, these are not one-dimensional:

1. Cash flow and investments (both time- and growth-sensitive)
2. Customer satisfaction (market segment "stickiness")
3. Competitive/cooperative positions

Recognize these categories are not reflected in a product line roadmap. Instead, roadmaps tie directly to project or event milestones. That's why the *PLuS Framework* encourages teams to highlight objectives separately from roadmap milestones.

Multi-Dimensional

In simple product line strategies, the aim may be to gain more profit. This is one-dimensional. But most product line strategies seldom have just this single objective. In dynamic environments, companies cannot focus on only one objective. They can't just seek improvement in a single direction like more profit, or greater customer satisfaction, or added market share. Instead, their objectives are more complex.

Consider, for example, how Amazon showed us that cash flow objectives could go beyond "seeking more" in near-term profit. Some analysts say that Amazon's near-term earnings are painfully minimal. Yet Amazon has driven up customer satisfaction while *minimizing* competition. Presumably, long-term profits is an added dimension to Amazon's objectives.

The other objective categories also have dimensions other than just "more." Consider customer satisfaction, for instance. In this category, all financial institutions reap the benefits of the "stickiness" of their service. They gain the stickiness from how costly and painful it is for customers to change banks. Stickiness relates to customer satisfaction. It allows banks to create a buffer from less-than-optimal customer satisfaction. Greater stickiness, therefore, is another dimension of customer-satisfaction objectives.

After profit and stickiness comes competition. Today, even objectives related to competition are not always one-dimensional. If they were, all competitors in all industries would be engaged in an all-out war to defeat each other. While customers may appreciate the competition, they may also react negatively toward the resultant monopolies and limited sourcing of goods. Cooperation, not unfair trade practices, may complement work toward competitive objectives. This includes such actions as combining technologies into new offerings, lobbying regulators, and supporting open systems or standards.

Product line strategy objectives most often include all three areas: cash flow, customer satisfaction, and competition. Sometimes, though, a strategy may focus on only one of the three. That's okay, but it's less common. Within good product line strategies, actions and decisions will drive toward *targets related to at least one of the three areas.*

Proximate Targets

As a practical matter, objectives should be achievable without being too specific. Strategy experts will say that "proximate" objectives are more helpful than far-reaching "stretch" objectives.[29] This is because stretch objectives can make contributors question the strategy's validity. You'll seldom see a need for hitting a specific target number. What's important, though, is that the objectives give guidance in the right direction—at targets possible to hit, not pie in the sky.

Product line teams can also set secondary objectives and goals to help shape their strategies. These will address such influences as sustainability, regulations, and market or technology entry. Secondary objectives help clarify what teams want to do and how they can do it. They help explain how a product line strategy might support a business unit or corporate strategy. For example, Nestle's corporate sustainability objective became a secondary objective for the Nescafe coffee product line strategy.

---

29 Professor Richard Rumelt discusses "proximate" objectives in his book *Good Strategy Bad Strategy: The Difference and Why It Matters*, published in 2011 by Crown Publishing Group, a division of Random House.

When setting product line objectives, teams should gain agreement among product line contributors. These are those functions *not* directly involved in product development, especially other key chain-links. As you'll see in Chapter 10, this agreement is an important part of the fourth pillar: the rationale and roll-up.

Setting aggressive objectives is one thing, but delivering on them is another. This becomes crystal clear in top management reviews of product line progress. For that reason, I'd advise having your growth objectives align with revenue and profit forecasts. If you feel those forecasts don't point to enough growth, then consider revamping your strategy to make the strategy create the growth. Don't fudge the forecast. If a strategy can't produce the desired growth, negotiate the growth objective downward.

Articulating Objectives

Clearly stating an objective is important. In practice and specific to product line strategies, it's a statement that includes at least two elements. The first is a stated achievement related to at least one of the three categories discussed above. The second is a date or period of time. A generic format then reads: *To achieve X by Y.* Here "X" is an achievement, and "Y" is a date. Examples of good and bad objectives can be seen in Table 9.1.1.

Table 9.1.1: Good Versus Bad Objectives

Good Objectives	Bad Objectives
To increase customer satisfaction scores by 15 points in our three, core verb-based market segments by year-end 2021.	Increase customer satisfaction
To grow top-line revenue by 15% across all offerings while increasing contribution margins from 35% to 40%. Achieve this by year-end 2021.	To grow by 10%.

Good Objectives	Bad Objectives
To design, develop, and launch at least two specific platform-levers that will generate at least 66% of the product lines offerings by June 2023.	Renew our technologies

Greater clarity also comes from an augmenting statement of purpose—why the objective is needed. The statement of purpose helps create an understanding that becomes useful through the dynamics of managing the product line. A statement of purpose also sets up the importance of one objective relative to another and to the milestones called out on a roadmap.

Recognize, though, that too many objectives can be a problem. More objectives make it harder to balance judgment across them. My rule of thumb is to have more than one and fewer than five for each product line. The logic is simple. Clearly stating the aim of a product line strategy with one objective is seldom possible. Too many objectives dilute the orientation toward each too much. Five are too many. It can be like trying to solve five complex equations simultaneously.

Calling Out Obstacles

Every strategy objective will involve one or more obstacles. If there is no obstacle, I'd argue the product line team didn't set good objectives.

You invariably hear people bringing up obstacles when discussing objectives. These obstacles may be internal or external to the company. They may be hindrances, voids, drawbacks, roadblocks, or hurdles.

Spotting and calling out major obstacles to each strategy objective is very important and should be standard practice. In the *PLuS Framework*, calling out obstacles also sets up the actions, tasks, and changes required to overcome the obstacles. Also, it's helpful in judging where to anchor key actions and milestones in the master and sub-roadmaps. Plus, the actions should be communicated to all influencers and contributors. Figure 9.1.1 shows this relationship.

Figure 9.1.1: Objectives, Obstacles, and Actions

The thought-flow about objectives is as much about feedback and correction as progression. For all objectives, obstacles to meeting an objective may demand adjustment to the objective. Actions that overcome obstacles may also lead to important insights that help redefine the obstacles, the objectives, or even the product line strategy.

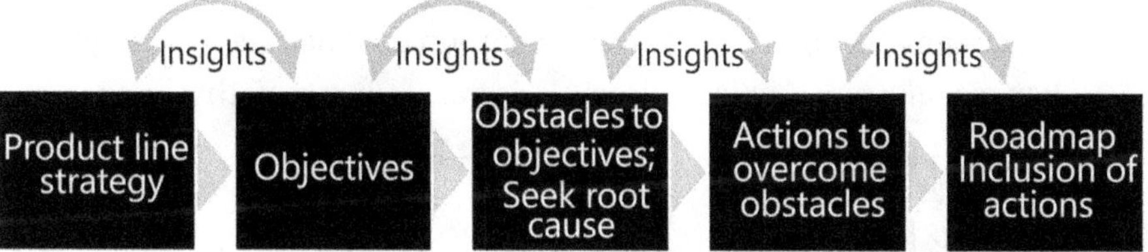

Many managers view the relationship between objectives and obstacles as obvious or trite. I'd agree, except when managers lose sight of the forest for the trees. Each product line can have many projects and actions underway. By themselves, each can demand much attention. The question for product line teams then loops back to whether their actions help to overcome the obstacles and achieve the objectives.

Changing Objectives

As I've discussed, connecting objectives to obstacles to actions is important. Yet another tenet of the *PLuS Framework* is for product line teams to back off from the old-school, unbending approach toward objectives. Yes, teams need them to have a deliberate focus.

Sometimes—and in my experience, more often than not—product line teams find they must *change* objectives.

The dynamic nature of strategy moves and pivots can make rigid objectives more of a burden than a benefit. It's foolhardy to treat product line strategy objectives as being sacrosanct. When organizations insist on that approach, they are usually saying that the strategy should not change.

This could be a mistake. To be effective over time, a product line strategy will be fluid and responsive to opportunities and threats. These challenges may occur in any market segment because of changes in technologies, competition, customers, regulations, and the business environment. Some challenges will inevitably make change necessary. Such changes in product line strategy might include a "pivot," when the change deliberately alters the Strategy-Essence and the interplay between chain-links. When such strategy changes take place, objectives will—or may—change with it.

Adding Purpose

Objectives, by themselves, create focus and intent. When many tasks and projects are in play, as with carrying out product line strategies, this is very helpful. But objectives by themselves may not motivate new desired behaviors. They set the focus, not the motive.

Most managers are reluctant to accept objectives blindly. Instead, they want the "why" behind each objective.[30] The purpose and reasoning behind objectives motivates a higher level of engagement toward the objective than the objective's mere statement. This is an important principle in the *PLuS Framework*. Clearly communicating

30 Phillip Clampitt and M. Lee Williams, *Decision Downloading*, *MIT Sloan Management Review*, Winter 2007

the purpose and rationale of strategy objectives and roadmap milestones is as important as stating the end goal.

Adding purpose to objectives goes far in overcoming cultural inertia. In meetings, you might hear statements like "we don't do it that way," "we don't have enough experience," or "we're not mature enough to do that." These are the pulls and pushes from cultural inertia. Simply offering up an objective to counter the force seldom works. The more powerful recourse comes from the purpose and rationale behind objectives. The same is true for achieving roadmap milestones.

Most rationale statements motivate more by communicating "pain avoidance" rather than "nirvana gaining." This is simple human behavior. But, as I point out in Chapter 13, pain avoidance and gain achievement, together, make the best motivator. It is best then for the rationale and purpose behind an objective to explain the pain being avoided and the gain achieved. This must be fact-based to motivate contributors, especially those not directly involved in the product line.[31]

When a product line team finds it difficult to lay out an objective's purpose with fact-based pain avoidance and gain achievement, it should reconsider the objective. Experience suggests that assessing objectives and their purpose in isolation from the organization often creates issues. Rather, it's best to share "potential" objectives and their purpose before committing to them. When doing so, teams may get their first glance at specific issues arising from cultural inertia. Most often, these issues may be known, but how they manifest may not be.

---

31 You'll see fact-based information critical to creating and improving product line strategies. I address this in Chapter 11. There, I explore the strategizing process as the foundation of the *PLuS Framework*.

As a reminder, the *PLuS Framework* encourages changing individual behaviors, not fighting the entire culture at once. When socializing objectives and their purpose, it's also important to understand what behaviors you are seeking to squash and what behaviors you wish to encourage. Do this, specific to each objective. Even if you find it difficult to call out specific negative behaviors, it's still helpful to call out those behaviors you hope to encourage.

9.2: Measures and Metrics—Current, Future, and Transitions

Measures, or as many say "metrics," complement product line strategy objectives. They show, numerically, whether work is on track or not. While objectives help focus teams on where the strategy is going, metrics reveal forces and influences affecting the direction and the speed of getting there.

The role of metrics evolved with the quality movement of the '70s and '80s and with the lean movement that followed. As Peter Drucker has said and many others have paraphrased: "*If you can't measure it, you can't improve it.*" This maxim also holds true for product line strategies.

Today metrics are commonly used in large organizations to evaluate product development performance. Often, though, such measures address all products being developed, not just those for one product line. This traditional approach also tends not to highlight platform-levers or the Strategy-Essence. Nor does it call out front-end activities and innovation charters. Yet these contributors make or break whole product lines over time.

An absence of product line strategy metrics suggests organizations may realize notable gains from their use. The direct or explicit value of strategy metrics is clear. When values start descending, it's time to take actions to turn them around.

Product line teams may also drive behaviors and influence actions and judgments through astute use of metrics. Researchers call this the "implicit" value of metrics. It comes about because no one wants to be associated with bad numbers. Most normal managers would prefer not to be associated with any metrics that are poor. The connection between behaviors and metrics implies that, if managers don't change behaviors or decisions when a metric's value is poor, they probably don't care about the metric. And if they don't care about a metric, that measure is meaningless. What's surprising for me is to see how many meaningless metrics some managers keep citing.

Our challenge in product line strategy is to use metrics for two closely aligned purposes. First, we need them to give a heads-up to needed changes before things turn south or opportunities are lost. And second, we need them to influence behaviors that drive, not hinder, the strategy.

We do this in the third pillar of the *PLuS Framework* by setting up a dashboard of metrics alongside the strategy's objectives. The dashboard's purpose is to make these values and targets, all related to the product line's advancement, easy to see, analyze, and encourage constructive actions.

Predicting the Future

Metrics fall into four different buckets, based on time horizons. You'll find reactions to metrics differ over different time horizons. A common grouping would look at four buckets, depending on the life cycle duration of underlying platform-levers and products.

1. The current state compared to the past three years
2. The near-term covering the next 18 months
3. The mid-term covering up to five years
4. The long-term (beyond five years)

For product and platform-lever life cycles that nominally reach maturity within a few years, these buckets may have shorter time periods. Table 9.2.1 displays possible metrics that teams might use for each bucket. Many companies have used measures to help carry out traditional product development, even well-formed product line strategies.

You'll find that most teams find figuring out their future-oriented views challenging. These "predictive metrics" include such measures as project-risk assessments, revenue and contribution forecasts, and the portfolio's expected value (as discussed in Chapter 4).

Table 9.2.1: Potential Metrics

Most companies do not use all of the listed metrics. Those metrics following an asterisk are common to product development, but not specific to product line strategy.

Future Buckets	Example Measures or Metrics Specific to One Product line
Current (Compared to past 3 years)	* Vitality index (percent of revenue from products 3 years old or less) * Expected portfolio launch value (risk-adjusted NPV) Complexity of line Product line width and length * Platform-Lever impact 3-year change, and life cycle stage 3-year change * Market-segment count, size, growth, market share, and market-share trend * New products' commercial risk * New technology risk * Milestone slippage, bottleneck assessment * Completeness in Jobs-to-be-Done segmentation, customer desired outcome knowledge Key issue heat maps for technologies; competitor moves/entries; economic changes; customer changes; regulatory changes. * Chain-link specific alignment rating (current and 3-year change)
Near-term Over next 18 months	* All "current bucket" metrics forecast out 18 months Skill-specific bottleneck forecasts * PIM revenue and contribution forecast Impending regulatory changes Possible economic and industry changes Technology "explorations"

Future Buckets	Example Measures or Metrics Specific to One Product line
Mid-term Between 18 months and 5 years	All above metrics forecast to five years Skill-specific resource supply/demand forecast per year Regulatory possibilities
Beyond 5 years	Key trends, changes, and discontinuities Heat map of event likelihoods Technology change forecasts

Key Strategy Metrics

Nearly every company uses metrics to guide their product development efforts. For example, you'll often find companies using time-to-market and new product vitality as their primary metrics. But for good product line strategies, these are not enough.

The *PLuS Framework* encourages companies to add a new set of measures specific to the Strategy-Essence and critical-to-success roadmap milestones. These contribute to good product line strategy. If values for these measures fall short, your product line may be headed for some tough times. If the values stay strong, be happy, but not complacent.

You'll see that eventually all metrics head south, just like their product lines. Good practices, though, place teams in position to respond to such shifts earlier and more quickly, ahead of major problems. Good product line strategy does not wait for "after-the-fact" responses to problems. Instead, teams use metrics to spot and respond to problems before their product line incurs damage. That's what makes this third pillar of the framework so valuable.

Table 9.2.2 lists the key metrics related to product line strategy. Notice measures associated with each of the three Strategy-Essence elements. These are augmented by measures specific to strategy execution (roadmap management), objectives and overall gain.

Table 9.2.2: Product Line Strategy Metrics

Group	Strategy Element	Measure	Note
Strategy-Essence	Leverage rating per platform-lever	Development cost Development time	■ Leverage combines lowering development cost and increasing development speed. ■ How good the leverage is relative to competition and market behavior. ■ Measurement will be specific to platform-lever and its type.
	Attribute Positioning per verb- and noun-based segments	Completeness in JTBD, customer-desired-outcome attribute positioning	Teams should capture and use several dimensions. Consider: segmentation thoroughness; desired-outcome certainty; development specifications to desired outcome completeness; attribute deliverable match.
	Chain-link Alignment across all business-unit links	360-degree feedback across chain-links on alignment to product line strategy.	Assessment of product line's clarity of and alignment with business strategy purpose.
Roadmap Management	**Master Roadmap Milestones**	Attainment Slippage	Knowing slippage after the fact is not as helpful as forecasting slippage. To forecast slippage, use basic critical chain buffer management
	Non-product Sub-roadmap Milestones	Attainment Slippage	Make sure chain-links involved with the milestone know they are being measured. May be a qualitative assessment with empirical back up information.

Group	Strategy Element	Measure	Note
Objectives	**Objective 1 (financials)**	Attainment Probability, Hindrance Removal	First estimate the likelihood of removing hindrances promptly. Next estimate the likelihood of attaining objective on time.
	Objective 2 (customer satisfaction)	Attainment Probability, Hindrance Removal	Periodic, annual or biennial. Grouping on verb- and noun-based segmentation, platform-lever.
	Objective 3 (development efficiency)	Attainment Probability, Hindrance Removal	This is the economic value of new product output divided by the economic value of development resources (output over input).
Gain	**Product Line Vitality Index**	Trend, changes	Percent of revenue derived from products less than 1 year, 3 years, 5 years old… for past, current, and future time period.
	Product Line Project Portfolio Expected Value	Trend, changes	This is the risk adjusted forecast of the product line's forecasted go-forward value (NPV removing sunk costs).

Don't assume that the strategy metrics only give a heads-up when dreadful things are lurking. They also show probable improvements to the product line. Both can be insightful, and both can point to both good and bad events. The main challenge for product line teams is to make sure the measures reflect both external and internal influences on the Strategy-Essence and roadmap execution. Such influence will come from technologies, competition, customers, and industry factors such as regulations and supply chains. And most notably, they come from the organization itself—its work practices, decisions, and its behaviors.

The response to metrics is what makes for good product strategies. Simply acknowledging values isn't enough. A product line team also must adjust strategy or roadmap milestones to counteract poor values and possibly exploit good values. Sometimes this calls for small changes. Other times it may call for grand changes. In either case, allowing poor values or good values to mount without carefully thinking through what to do about them or because of them undermines the strategy. The response is what's important. It's what drives strategies to be good and remain good.

The *PLuS Framework* does not mandate specific metrics. Rather, the approach is to encourage consideration of all those in table 9.2.2 and implement them in the way that best suits the organization and the product line team. But remember, guiding a product line without metrics can be like sailing a ship without a compass or controls. No doubt you'll get someplace, but there's a much greater chance it'll end in disaster.

9.3: Casting to the Future: Strategy Foresight

Looking to the future is an important aspect in determining how well a product line is doing. It's not just about metrics related to the product line strategy and its execution. In reality, no one is perfect at forecasting the future. But a product line team's job is to anticipate it better than the competition can. This is a necessary part of the framework, along with objectives and metrics. Our concern is to trigger smart insights about where the product line is headed considering market and technology dynamics. And it's about getting this in front of all contributors, for all to see. That is the central purpose of the third pillar.

Most companies do little to sharpen their skills and talents toward forecasting the future. But product line strategies can gain an advantage by building these skills and talents. Various tools and techniques also can be very useful.[32] These forecasting tools and "predictive' metrics aid teams with moving down the operational excellence path of product innovation and management. They provide prompts that motivate thoughtful reconsideration of the plans and approaches, helping to counter the inertia that can plague any product line strategy.

This topic is noteworthy. Many experts have written books and given talks on the topic. For instance, Robert B. Tucker's 1991 book, *Managing the Future,* addresses many of these issues, and X Prize Chairman and CEO Peter Dramatis is well known for his talks on the topic.

---

32 For more information on tools, techniques, and approaches for peering into the future, please see our online resources at https://adept-plm.com/plus-resources/

For our purposes, however, the basic challenge is knowing the future when the future doesn't yet exist. Can you know about things that don't exist? Well, no. That's impossible. Somehow our thinking should extend beyond merely extrapolating the past to forecast the future. We need more than just predictions about resource use over the next six months or judgments about project success.

I am reminded of the exercise my friend and leading "Strategy Thinking" expert Greg Githens conducts during his workshops. Greg asks participants to think back over the last decade and jot down those events that affected or changed their life. Everybody seems to come up with quite a few items. Then Greg asks participants to list out those events they expect to impact their lives over the next decade. This list gets interesting. It is events that are extensions of those that happened over the past few years. Revisiting the list of past decade events, it becomes clear how little foresight they have about their futures. It's a powerful exercise that gets you thinking about whether you really can gain insights about a product line's future.

One of the biggest problems faced in dealing with the future is unexpected one-off events. These may include disruptive technology entering a market, a competitor's move, a customer change, an unnoticed opportunity, a new government rule, or a societal event. These—and others—can pop up at a moment's notice.

Consider 9/11 or the market crash of 2008 and 2009. Simple equations and models cannot predict disruptions like these. These "discontinuities," as strategists call them, can either throw product lines into disarray or propel them to new levels. Remember, however, that intelligence agencies, looking back, believe there was enough information to declare *something* would happen in 2001.[33] The

33 A Congressional report released in July 2003 concluded the 9/11 attacks could have been prevented. The terrorist work went undetected because the F.B.I. and C.I.A. worked independently and failed to share information.

failure, analysts suggest, was poor or no transfer of information from one government agency to another (the CIA to the FBI.) It was not for lack of having the information.

And during the real estate market collapse, some market players made extraordinary bets to enrich themselves. *Some people knew something—and made bets in the right direction.* No doubt many metrics from the real estate, and credit markets were crying out for attention. They were signaling a serious reconsideration of future prospects. Those who adjusted their strategies survived. Those who held onto the assumption that real estate values never go down without local markets first seeing other businesses close – failed.

Trying to predict things before others do is important—but also is challenging. Every person tries to do it. It would be stunning to find no one associated with a product line thinking about this. The problem is that teams tend not to do it collectively, purposely, and continually. Nor do they set up a means to enable any insights to flow into their strategy. The creation and continuous flow of insights about possible events should improve the product line strategy. To see this in a real-life setting, I encourage you to check out Case History B about Rockwell Automation in Chapter 15.

Influencing Behaviors

So far, the discussion about metrics has dealt with their explicit value related to strategy. It's about figuring out actions in response to "explicit" numeric values. But metrics can also carry an "implicit" value. Well-embraced metrics can induce behaviors. This is an important concept because it makes metrics a powerful tool in fighting cultural inertia.

Consider organizations that home in on speed-to-market as key to business. Top managers in these companies may review this measure and reward and punish accordingly. Rewards may only be a quick congratulatory smile, and punishments may only be a cold shoulder. In meetings, though, these implicit drivers motivate people. Who wants to attend meetings when their projects, tasks, or whole product lines have poor metric values? When the metrics are deeply entrenched, the only recourse is to get on with improving the metric's value.

Therefore, it can be powerful influence on behaviors when the right metrics become deeply entrenched. Consider the impact when a Board of Directors reviews the vitality index or portfolio launch values for their product line. Top management will not be comfortable reporting these values when they are in decline. This motivates behaviors throughout the organization.

Smart executives understand the recourse to poor numbers is not simply to push harder. Adding greater force to poor product lines strategies and jumbled execution can aggravate problems. No one's career is helped by this. Instead, the recourse is to improve the strategy and embed practices to carry it out effectively. Here is where the implicit value of metrics becomes so important. It's about driving behaviors to support good strategy. And it's about doing this before problems like a poor vitality index and expected portfolio launch values arise.

The challenge is to link the measure to a desired strategy result and to poor behaviors that may impede getting the result. Sometimes, though, the behavior is deeply rooted in the organization and viewed by many as a strength, not a hindrance.

Confirming Strategy

Remember the Keurig case described early in the book? Keurig's culture embraced an entrepreneurial spirit, which supported the flawed "next big thing" approach to new products. Here, the recourse might have been to use measures to assess the validity of customer-desired outcomes in each market segment. Next, product lines teams should want to measure the degree to which product features carry out the Job-to-be-Done, i.e., match a set of customers' desired outcomes. It's about confirming the Strategy-Essence. For Keurig, these values would have been eye-opening. Any measurement on attribute positioning would have shown a mismatch between customer-desired outcomes for making a good cup of coffee and a speculated need for making full pots. And the management team would not have wished to be associated with the values.

The challenge is first to recognize strategy and roadmap execution issues. Only then should teams work to figure out metrics that surround the issues. Once understood and vetted, the metrics may be placed into practice and reviewed continually.

Looking to the Future

The *PLuS Framework* third pillar helps build forward-looking capabilities tied to metrics and objectives. It encourages product line teams to analyze, communicate, and act on their insights. It does this by placing metrics and objectives into the tasks of product line strategizing and management. This makes the third pillar a strong complement to a product line's Strategy-Essence and roadmap (pillars #1 and #2.) Such use addresses dynamically changing situations, often resulting in trade-off decisions. That's the focus of the next segment in this chapter.

9.4: Dynamic Trade-offs and the Strategy Dashboard

When carrying out any product line strategy, lower-level *roadmap recast* changes can mount. Remember, these are roadmap changes that don't change the Strategy-Essence. A collection of recast changes will invariably lead to trade-off decisions like those called for in traditional portfolio management. Unfortunately for product line strategies, things don't always work out as planned. Projects fall off track, technologies fall short, or supply quality decreases.

Trade-off decisions will often be needed. Should one project slow down, and its resources shift to another? Should several small projects be postponed to enable more focus on a new platform-lever? Can the company add new technologies into the mix without stalling projects or changing the Strategy-Essence?

Trade-offs like these are central to the third pillar. Building a means to deal with them is important. It involves creating a decision flow that expects roadmap recasts and seeks to manage them with an eye toward keeping a strategy on track.

Don't confuse trade-offs in product line strategy with the balanced scorecard used in the business strategy. The latter "balances" financial and non-financial objectives for the full business strategy. In this pillar, we're concerned with achieving the product line strategy objectives. Product line strategy trade-offs here in the third pillar need not capture other areas of business not related to the product line. You will see later that such broader trade-offs will become front and center in the fourth pillar. But importantly, the third pillar lays out the need to keep objectives *fluid and responsive* to changes in project status, technologies, regulations, markets, customers, and with competitors.

Product line trade-offs can easily be captured in a spreadsheet. Using the spreadsheet then helps teams oversee and govern the product line's current state and movement toward its future state. Plus, analyzing it helps create insights into how roadmaps may play out into the future. It will reflect the interplay of objectives, actions, and measures. (See Figure 9.4.1)

The Right Objectives

Many key objectives for a product line should come from the Strategy-Essence. Actions to achieve these results are then placed on the master roadmap. This sets up two big questions for the product line team. The first is deciding which metrics to use. The second is how to use them to make trade-off decisions. This job is as much left-brain analytical as right-brain creative. Don't expect to be handed these measures. Each product team must create them on its own.

Figure 9.4.1: Dynamic Trade-offs

The analysis should show trade-offs across changing objectives and metrics (KPIs) while focusing on achieving roadmap milestones. As a product line advances, the spreadsheet should show changes in the trade-offs. This often calls for using graphics to communicate trade-offs visually.

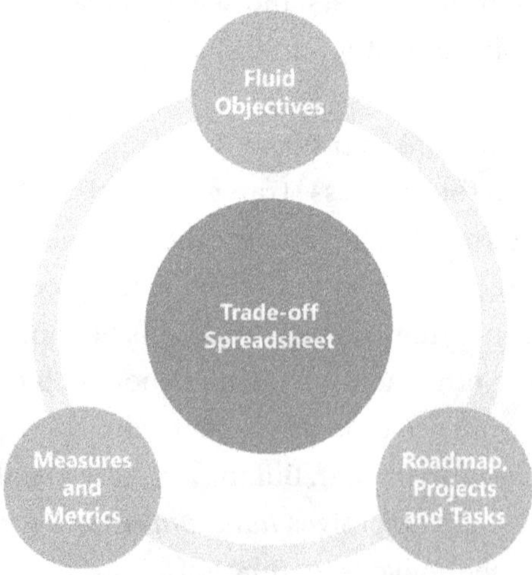

Figuring this out can be helpful. It's as much about examining strategy as measuring its progress. The approach I recommend in the *PLuS Framework* is simple. First, try a set of measures by speculating what might drive their values higher or lower. Second, consider the speculation related to the strategy and to both the internal and external environment. Third, adjust, change, and edit these measures based on the team's collective logic and intuition, but don't worry too much about completeness or accuracy.

More Dashboard than Crystal Ball

The primary goal of product line strategizing is to spot or predict market and technology changes and then work to drive corrective steps quickly. Teams need to see changes and influences faster than others can, and respond more quickly than others do. Speed of observation and reaction is the goal. This is not the old, traditional focus on just speed of development. Instead, it's more entrepreneurial and visionary—based on sales forecasting and diffusion modeling. For many, this is foreign. But in today's world, it's an essential part of real-life business dynamics.

This third pillar seeks to identify discontinuities with indicators or measures of their likely impact. (See Figure 9.3.2 for an example.) The key is for all managers to see all potential discontinuities, not just those easily visible. Carefully facilitating this is crucial to product line strategizing. (Note I stress the "ing" in strategizing. This is the act of creating or improving product line strategies on which I share much more in Chapter 13.) The third pillar helps managers to quickly spot and gain insights from trends, changes, and discontinuities. The intent is to drive responses faster than competitors can.

Figure 9.4.2: Strategy Change Overview

Teams may represent product line strategy changes in different visual formats. Typically, a dashboard displays values related to objectives, trends, changes, discontinuity, key metrics, and roadmap milestones.

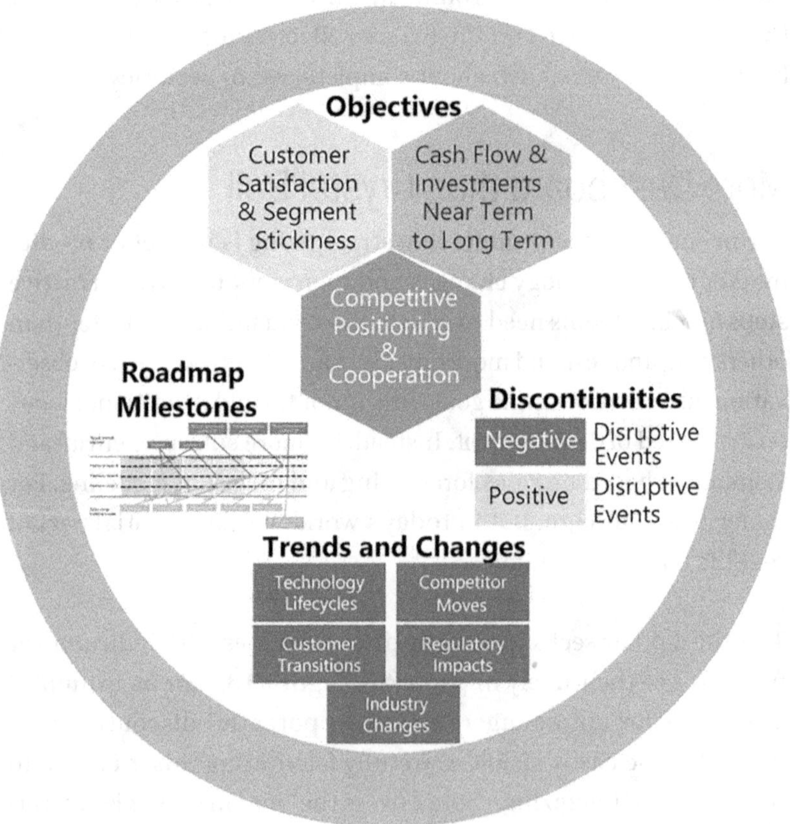

Figure 9.4.2 displays what typically goes into a product line strategy dashboard. The dashboard is a display of gauges, bar charts, and dials. This is more art than science. And interpreting the information it reveals takes a deep understanding of the product line. But this visualization is most helpful for managers in large organizations. After all, most of us are mere mortals. We have yet to achieve the intuitive and visionary skills of an Elon Musk and Jeff Bezos. At least not so far.

Organizing and Relating the Elements of Good Product Line Strategy

Measuring and Guiding Strategy Performance

PRODUCT LINE STRATEGY: GETTING TO GOOD

Seek to:

Use specific objectives to complement project-management milestones and guide work and decision-making:

- Ensure progress toward improved cash flow, customer satisfaction, and competitive positions.
- Have "proximate" objectives that guide work and decisions, and change each when needed.
- Spell out hindrances and hurdles to achieving each objective; match work to overcome them.
- Unite and focus cross-organizational work to achieve the objectives.

Use specific measures and metrics to track a product line's past performance, assess the current situation, and forecast a future state:

- Recognize key metrics as measures of product strategy and cultural influences (inertia). Each reflects how well the strategy is being carried out.
- Build organizational skill to report key metrics through a real-time dashboard.
- Draw up corrective steps that offset poor metrics values.

CHAPTER 10

The Union with Business Strategy: *PLuS Framework* Pillar 4

GROWTH FROM EXISTING product lines is perhaps the most important contributor to both a business's well-being and ultimate survival. This is especially true during economic rough patches. In tough times, it's common for management teams to tighten up core businesses and seek growth only through ventures and partnerships focused on new-to-the-world innovation, vanguard opportunities. But reliance on external, non-core contributions, although helpful, is seldom enough.

Over the period of just one decade, half of existing profitable businesses will experience notable threats to their survival or independence. That's according to results of research conducted by Bain and Company on more than two thousand businesses.[34] They conclude

34 Bain and Company: "Sustained Value Creator Study" http://www.rich-kohler.com/wp-content/uploads/2010/09/growth-strategy-bain.pdf

that a lack of ability to address hindrances will lead to half of the threatened companies not surviving as independent growth entities.

McKinsey and Company adds to the growth discussion through its strong research. It points out that organizations benefit greatly from building skills to address "granular" opportunities within specific growing market segments.[35] The McKinsey work suggests that it is far more important to select and focus on growing market segments than it is to take part in growing industries.

Finding market segments that are growing and then shifting focus to these segments are key for continuous growth. The study states: "Seeking growth is rarely about changing industries—a risky proposition at best for most companies. It is more about focusing time and effort on faster-growing segments where companies have the skills, assets, and market insights needed for profitable growth." According to the McKinsey study, a company's choice of new market segments is four times more important in growth than growing market share in current segments.

In other research, The Boston Consulting Group (BCG) reports that organizations may realize significant benefits to total shareholder return (TSR) by smartly focusing on growth opportunities.[36] BCG highlights managing a growth portfolio. This includes increasing core business, expanding into adjacent opportunity areas, and exploring new frontiers. Internal organic innovation, according to BCG, plays a crucial role in the growth portfolio. Without growth emanating from existing product lines, there is a great likelihood that TSR will decline.

---

35 "The granularity of growth," McKinsey Quarterly, May 2007, by Mehrdad Baghai, Sven Smit, and S. Patrick Viguerie.

36 BCG eBook When the Growing Gets Tough-Charting Your Path to Value-Creating Growth by Kermit King, Gerry Hansell, and Adam Ikdal.

A common theme appears in these studies. It boils down to the notion that business strategies should focus on growth with an emphasis on core, existing product lines. A poorly-thought-out approach toward growing existing product lines will weaken the strategic position of most businesses. The result is a serious threat to organizations and to shareholder value. Therefore, growing existing product lines matters a great deal.

Product Line Strategies and Business Growth

With global dynamics at play, there is a high likelihood that, over a single decade, threats to business growth will happen. Every business will likely have to address economic recessions, significant new technologies disrupting their competitive landscape, or see major shifts in customer behaviors. Through such challenges, those companies with product lines lagging behind market leaders are much more likely to see greater declines in earnings than will the leaders.

This suggests a critical concern for shareholder value—how top management responds to outside threats. An easy action for a business unit's leadership is to cut near-term R&D and product development. The problem is this will, with high certainty according to one econometric research study,[37] also cause a notable hit to shareholder value. Case history C in Chapter 15 on US Gypsum tells this story. You'll see what amounts to sheer courage by leadership to keep a major project on- track (plus encouragement from Warren Buffett).

Keeping a product line's strategy strong is key both to current performance and to long-term growth and survival of a business. But an important warning is in order: Shoring up weaknesses in one

37 *How Innovation Really Works: Using the Trillion Dollar R&D Fix to Drive Growth*, By Anne Marie Knott, McGraw Hill 2017

product line while resting on another line's laurels may be a mistake. "Don't over-invest in the weakest businesses to make them stronger while neglecting the stronger businesses and assuming continued profits. More often, it's the stronger business that has the greatest opportunity for growth," says Chris Zook of Bain and Company. Zook's research delved deep into this topic. He's published extensively about business growth.

Good business-unit strategy demands more than figuring out the growth prospects of product lines. Ideally, it combines the growth prospects of existing lines with the other growth prospects. The challenge is about managing the full portfolio of opportunities, not just each product line.

The focus should be on year-over-year growth, not just on what's happening in the current year. The *PLuS Framework's* fourth pillar does this by helping business units assess growth-related facts and data for product line strategies. But it does this alongside non-product-line opportunities. I refer to this as the Business Growth Portfolio (*Definition Alert.*)

Rationale and the Growth Portfolio

The next two segments of this chapter address the two key orientations of the fourth pillar. The first is about trade-offs within and across product lines. The second is about product lines and their strategies within the business growth portfolio.

DEFINITION ALERT:
Business Growth Portfolio

The Business Growth Portfolio is a compilation of all investments, projects, and ventures contributing to or taking away from the business unit's top-line revenue growth. All of a business unit's product lines are included.

It is important for managers to remain aware of potential trade-offs while they develop the product line strategy and work through the four pillars. Adjustments will be needed—especially when facing changing markets and technologies. The framework's fourth pillar purposely eases such trade-off decisions, driving analysis toward answering key questions such as:

- "Should one development project slow down to speed up another in a different product line?"
- "Should any projects be canceled to enable greater focus on development of ideas for a new platform-lever?"
- "Can the organization add new technologies into the mix without stalling projects or changing the Strategy-Essence?"
- "Would changes to the organization better enable a product line strategy?"

Yet all growth decisions are not just internal to product lines. Consideration of other, non-product-line opportunities also comes into play. This sets the need for managing a growth portfolio at the business unit level.

Changing Our Ways

The full *PLuS Framework's* fourth pillar looks at all product lines within the business strategy. It collects and analyzes all parts of product line strategies with all other contributors to business unit strategy. For businesses with multiple product lines, this pillar is critical. It aids evaluating the why, how, and when of product line strategies. And it does this in relation to the full business unit strategy, alongside all growth opportunities whether product line-related or not.

This pillar also enables teams to figure out how well product lines and their strategies align with other chain-links, and with one another. By doing this, managers can identify any potential conflicts. This is necessary thinking when seeking to maximize a business unit strategy.

This fourth pillar places product line strategies within the core of a business unit strategy. Most important to the product line team is that it confirms their role within their business strategy. Don't underestimate the importance of this contribution. It is the most powerful force a team has for improving its strategy and its execution. It works toward aligning chain-links, gaining recourses for good attribute positioning, and keeping strong platform-levers. And it is a force to offset the cultural inertia working against product line advancements.

10.1: The Rationale and Roll-up

Over the last few decades, I've witnessed several changes in the way large companies conduct business. A notable change happened when the strategic planning groups of the 1970s disbanded in the 1980s and 1990s.

Along the way, the quality and lean movements led to a major push on operational excellence. This gave a serious boost to business performance. However, operational excellence without clear strategies can worsen product line challenges over the long run. The reason is that it tends to maximize the current situation without fostering change. It's about extending life cycles through efficiencies, not building new approaches. The relationship between operational excellence and strategy sets a true need for planning on several levels.

The fourth pillar of the *PLuS Framework* puts overall business strategy thinking back into play. It does so while also evaluating how operational excellence supports or undermines product lines and their strategies.

Business Strategy and Budget Reviews

Today, top managers in most large companies place great emphasis on budgeting for operating and capital expenses. This approach has become an umbrella over strategy. This is good. Who would argue with it?

Budgeting or "annual operation planning," as some companies refer to it, is a means of governance over strategy and all activities across an organization. The budgeting process doesn't care if activities and expenses are for product lines or not. Everything comes into view.

Therefore, product line teams should consider budgetary reviews as part of their strategy work. But many business units don't embrace budgeting within product lines on platform-lever, segmentation, and attribute positioning moves. Instead, the task is more about summing up and "balancing" next year's expenses than it is about trade-offs and decisions affecting growth over longer time periods.

The fourth pillar—the rationale and roll-up—shifts emphasis to pursuing growth. It does this by pulling together the first three pillars and their parts. Most important, it does so with the business strategy—not isolated from it. For businesses with multiple product lines, this pillar helps teams explore each contributing product line, including the role each plays in the business strategy. It also explores relationships between product lines, with other chain-links, and with budgetary oversight. This approach is notably more helpful than the traditional roll-up of only financial objectives and budget needs.

This final pillar helps strengthen the full business strategy, not just each product line. It highlights how each product line strategy works toward its objectives, and so improves its line. However, the key here is to spot conflicts, trade-offs, and opportunities across product lines and other growth opportunities. The fourth pillar seeks to ensure that product line strategies match the business strategy. Together, the strategies should work in tandem. Together, they should address the trends and forces in their industry[38] In

---

38 Some strategists argue that every business works within industries and that each industry places unique forces on the business. These forces then dictate the best position for the company to orient itself within the industry. Harvard Professor Michael Porter writes at great length about this in his books, *Competitive Strategy* (1980) *and Competitive Advantage* (1985). UCLA Professor Richard Rumelt, however, argues that resource management and operational effectiveness affect business performance more than industry forces and positioning. The orientation laid out in the *PLuS Framework* addresses both industry forces and operational excellence—across all chain-links.

some manner, product lines need to address the same market and technology changes the entire business faces.

Without a means to connect product lines to business strategy, companies create environments that result in limp products that don't contribute as effectively as they could or should. Sure, there can be successes, but the challenge is to have a continuous string of successes that yields increased cash flow, greater customer satisfaction, and better competitive positions. This is the thrust of a whole product line over time, not just a "one-off, next best thing" approach.

Product Line Versus Product Line

As product lines within a business unit push to achieve their best, conflicts will arise. This is because resources are limited. Anywhere product lines share assets or people, there will be bottlenecks. This is the same for traditional project resource and portfolio management.

Chain-link changes intended to support one product line may be damaging to another. Product lines might make conflicting demands on chain-links or conflicting positioning moves within market segments. Organizations need a clearinghouse for this. And that's the purpose of this fourth pillar.

Product line teams should include several items in this roll-up to make it work. These are:

- The objectives of each product line, reflecting cash flow (and growth), customer satisfaction, and competitive positions.
- The budgetary needs for all critical-to-success (CTS) projects (PIDs, PICs, and PIMs).
- The Strategy-Essence parts (chain-link changes, platform-lever advancements, and market positioning).

- New-product investments and forecasts (for both current and future developments).
- A clearly articulated business strategy that states each product line's roles, goals, and contributions.

As long as the information and data are available, rolling them up is easy. Unfortunately, that's not the case for most companies. Often, bits and pieces need to be cajoled from key players. Only then can teams rearrange the data to gain greater insights. Unfortunately, in my experience, cajoling is neither easy nor pleasant.

Analysis of the information teams gather takes much time. It requires multiple skills: insight, knowledge, intelligence, and patience. It can also be tough work. It's one thing to review the data and conclude, "Yes there is a conflict between two lines related to some topic." However, the more difficult part is to decide the best resolution. Most of the time, this requires managers to make difficult trade-off decisions.

A major challenge in strategy is that a conflict may be forecasted or predicted to occur in the future, whereas its resolution needs to start in the present. This time separation makes avoiding immediate action seem okay. However, as pointed out in Chapters 1 and 2, companies as large and successful as Kodak once was can fall into this trap.

Please remember this when someone suggests skipping Pillar Four. Doing things that cut across the organization today will affect how things turn out. While this seems obvious, the challenge is that today's actions may need notable coordination across chain-links. But each chain-link's leadership might not have a common view of how near-term actions tie to long-term issues.

Consider, for example, how a focus on growth may play out across different chain-links. Sales may shift things today to sell more later, whether the same products or new products. Operations may make investments today for efficiency gains from predicted greater volume and scale. The supply chain may be contracting suppliers today for their perception of certainty tomorrow. Unfortunately, these orientations may not align with a product change in strategy when seeking greater growth.

The time separation of actions and results makes alignment all the more difficult. But that's the purpose of the fourth pillar: to provide oversight and a control center for the whole approach, regardless of time separation. And it's here where top management can step in to influence chain-link alignment and amplification.

More Lines, More Challenges

The more individual product lines push their limits, the more likely trade-off decisions will be needed. And these trade-off decisions will undoubtedly cause changes in roadmaps and strategies. There can have a cascading effect. And figuring this out before it is too late means taking the product line strategies roll-up and review seriously—this fourth pillar of the *PLuS Framework*.

Because of its importance to the health and well-being of a business, it is critical for all companies. Clearly, top management should be involved in the fourth pillar roll-up and rationalization. This involvement should be at both the business unit and the corporate level. If top management isn't involved, it can be a difficult exercise. Having everyone on the same page, especially with those at the top, helps drive success.

Perhaps the biggest benefit organizations gain from this fourth pillar is commitment and engagement across and up and down its hierarchy. People can see why certain product line strategy moves and roadmap milestones are critical to success. They can then understand the need for specific changes related to functional chain-links that are being managed separately from product lines.

Creating, accepting, and implementing well-thought-out product line strategies can be vital to long-term business success. This fourth pillar helps make this happen by addressing challenges, whether these arise from normal day-to-day occurrences or result from major changes across industries. The fourth pillar does this early and proactively, not reactively and after the fact.

Carrying out this work is the product line team's or function's responsibility. But to make it work, management and administration at the business unit level also need to participate. As a practicality, no matter how much a team may wish for its product line to be reviewed in the context of the business strategy and all chain-links, it will go for naught without top business management involvement.

I first saw this play out just after the takeover of AlliedSignal by Honeywell in 2001. Here, the issue was to focus on growth by highlighting major growth contributors to the new, larger firm. Using research by AD Little and Company, Honeywell's top management sought to collect all of their growth opportunities into one single portfolio. Each product line with growth potential was called out and given "Corporate Growth" status. This title was a clear signal of purpose in business strategy, inducing notable focus from each business unit's top management.

By anchoring a place in the business unit strategy, product lines teams gain assurance their line will be resourced adequately. And when strategy or execution changes are needed, top management will give them full consideration. This is fundamental to good product line strategy.

Evaluation Within Business Strategy

To use this pillar effectively, I recommend rolling up product lines and rationalizing their fit within the overall business strategy. The *PLuS Framework*'s fourth pillar encourages rationalization using multiple approaches. The approaches below reflect those that yield the greatest value. Yet, while doing them all may be helpful, it is also unnecessary. However, I do advise that you consider each approach as you set up your own rationalization and roll-up pillar.

1. **Aggregate Project Portfolio Analysis** (time-sensitive, skill-specific resource demands)
    a. Portfolio reviews should expand to include all projects (PIDs, PICs, and PIMs) within all product lines. This is broader than just traditional portfolio management that only reviews new products under development (PIDs).
    b. Past, present, and future "cumulative expected value" of project portfolios for all product lines should be reviewed. The cumulative expected value is the total risk-adjusted present value for all projects. If this value is trending downward, product line challenges are present or are just around the corner.
    c. Systemic, cross-portfolio risks assessment can be more insightful than just the risks within individual projects. Risks common across projects within each product line need to be understood. Consider how these risks cut across the product line's portfolio of PIDs, PICs, and PIMs. They constitute systemic risks to the line and can be internal and/or external. Internal systemic risks come from resourcing issues or chain-link misalignments. External systemic risks, on the other hand, come from the actions of competitors or customers, from market changes, or from regulatory/environmental influences.

2. **Aggregate Roadmap and Synchronization of Critical-to-Success (CTS)** projects across all product lines (also needed/desired chain-link changes versus planned changes by chain-links).

    a. Management at the business unit level should, at a minimum, govern critical-to-roadmap projects (those needed to carry out strategy designates as "CTS"). Given the importance of CTS projects, their timing, and their inherent risks, the concern is whether teams should reasonably expect to complete them successfully. Otherwise, other approaches should be considered to bring success to each line.

    b. Changes to benefit a product line strategy are not the only reason chain-link strategies might experience change. In each chain-link's pursuit of excellence, they'll seek new methods, approaches, and systems to support their work and decisions. Business units need to compile and analyze chain-link changes, whether for product line purposes or not. This analysis focuses on the change: its practicality and time-sensitivity. Plus, it points to how easy or hard it'll be to carry out the strategy.

3. **Platform-Lever Analyses** (These analyses compare all platform-levers for growth in absolute and percentage terms, and for life cycle stage changes and trends.)

    a. All platform-levers have life cycles. This impacts the growth and profitability of their product line. The analysis calls for plotting growth rates and profitability versus life-cycle stages for each platform-lever across all product lines. The focus should be on comparing the past, present, and future to create a trend line for each platform-lever. Growth rates and profitability can be derived from historical data, good cost accounting, and forecasting. This graphical plot should capture the relative leverage from (and scale of) each platform.

4. **The BCG Growth-Share Matrix**[39] and its cousin, the **Directional Policy**[40] **Matrix**

   a. It's always easier to succeed in growing market segments than in shrinking segments. The Boston Consulting Group's matrix recognizes this at the business unit, product family, and product line levels. It does so by considering competitors in its market share analysis. The directional policy analysis adds to the BCG matrix by adding an assessment of "strategic fit." It shows how product lines have a "right to win" in certain market segments.

   Each approach recognizes two fundamental principles in product line strategy:

   i. It is easier to succeed in growing markets with limited competition.

   ii. It is easier to change the inner-workings of an organization than it is to cause existing markets to grow or convince competitors to exit.

   b. A word of caution is in order. Good product line strategies define market segments by Jobs-to-be-Done segmentation. Remember this from Chapter 7.2. These are verb-oriented, not noun-oriented, market segments. Segments should be defined by how customers gain benefit or satisfaction. This is different from noun-oriented segments like product type, geographies, or customer classification. However, the traditional

39 Boston Consultancy Group Matrix helps evaluate growth possibilities in market segments and industries. The BCG Matrix best applies to noun-based, not verb-based, market segment analysis.

40 Directional Policy Matrix evaluates the attractiveness and fit of market segments compared to one another. This is helpful in verb-based segment assessment and much needed for good product line strategies.

approach to market segmentation is noun-oriented. Sometimes it's necessary to use noun-oriented segments to satisfy others in your company, like the sales force or operations. They may divide themselves by noun-oriented segments. Nonetheless, *do not* abandon using verb-oriented market segments in your product line strategy.

3. **Porter's Five Forces[41] and Diamonds[42]**—This thinking produces a deeper industry analysis, one that focuses on playing fields both for driving profit (five forces industries) and driving shareholder value (diamonds for countries and geographies).
   - **a.** This Five Forces analysis focuses on forces that drive your position in an industry. These include the threat of new entrants, the threat of substitutes, the bargaining power of customers, the bargaining power of suppliers, and industry rivalry. Academics and consultants have written copious amounts on each force. Please take time to read what you find.
   - **b.** The Diamond analysis looks at geographies or countries in which industry players interact. Note that in the diamond analysis, competition can mean growth to the entire market, plus the sharpening of skills to survive. This contrasts with the Five Force model suggesting the opposite.
   - **c.** The Porter analyses seek to give managers high-level insights to better position their business and product lines. Depending upon how you define industries, a product line may cut across several industries. This may lead to discussions on whether the business—and its

41 Michael Porter, "The Five Competitive Forces That Shape Strategy," *Harvard Business Review* (January 2008)

42 Michael Porter, "The Competitive Advantage of Nations," *Harvard Business Review* (March–April 1990)

product lines—should move into different industries, and with which competencies.

d. Industries and market segments have close ties. The Porter analyses may shift the discussion from verb-oriented to noun-oriented segments. That's because most industries are classified by noun-oriented segments. Once again, *do not* abandon verb-oriented segmentation because of industry analyses. Use industry analyses to feed understanding of all verb-oriented segments.

6. **Learning, Visionary, and Entrepreneurial Explorations**

   a. If an organization sticks only with its industries, market segments, technologies, and platform-levers, it faces the risk of being left behind. Clearly, many businesses have benefited significantly from visionary and entrepreneurial approaches that enabled them to get out in front of markets. And others have suffered from a lack of vision. Entrepreneurial explorations should add to business strategy what product lines and their markets and technologies cannot. In this context, intrapreneurship and new ventures, both internal and external, find a home in strategy.

Compiling, comparing, and joining insights from several of the different analyses given above will help boil things down. The goal is to advance business strategy while spotting necessary changes across chain-links and within product line strategies. You'll find discussions about these insights quickly shift from misalignment to future alignment and the actions to get there. That's the aim of this fourth pillar.

Table 10.1 below lays out potential questions to guide full strategy reviews within and across a business unit. The intent is to get both facts and helpful insights out on the table for all to see.

Table 10.1: Pillar 4 Analysis Across Product Lines, Within a Business Unit

Questions to Address in Pillar 4
1. Do the product line strategies complement or conflict with each other? In market positioning? Chain-link demands? Technology developments?
2. Are all chain-links aligning and building synergy with each of the product line strategies? Should the product line strategies change to help the chain-link functions?
3. Are skill-specific resources (quantity and quality) available for all product lines to succeed over the next year? The next three years? What skills will cause bottlenecks?
4. What product line strategy pivots are being called for—or seem likely—over the next year? The next three years? What demands will these pivots place on the organization?
5. Should any product lines be seeking new platform-levers? Why? When are they needed?
6. Should the organization start initiatives to create new product lines? Or should they pursue major opportunities outside existing product lines?
7. What technology scouting activities should the company emphasize over the next six months? 12 months? 36 months? Why? What's hoped for?
8. What market or customer-research activities should the company emphasize over the next six months? 12 months? 36 months? Why?

Making It Happen

How companies carry out the fourth pillar should be specific to each organization. The first rule of order is to make the approach common to all product lines. Next, it's best to complement or add to the processes and approaches that already exist. Let me give an example.

Consider a business unit that has its project management office (PMO) along with the head of technology review a portfolio of projects currently underway. This may take place on a monthly or quarterly basis. As the core construct of product line strategies and roadmaps get formed, it would be a mistake to skip over strategy priorities and critical-to-roadmap information before setting project priorities across the development portfolio. This is especially true because the top person in the business would be deeply involved in product line strategy reviews.

This fourth pillar helps product line teams gain insights into changes that drive stronger business strategy. It is helpful to bake these changes into each product line's strategy before budget/strategy reviews. If the budget review occurs in October of each year, then the Pillar Four analysis should be conducted in July or August, allowing time for the product line team to incorporate changes and revisions.

For most businesses, the role of aggregating and analyzing product line information can be a new undertaking. I recommend adding this work to the group responsible for product development portfolio management. If no portfolio manager exists, management should create the role.

Recognize that adding the fourth pillar creates responsibilities (and potential results) that are much needed. This is a step up for portfolio managers. Yes, the pillar adds much strategy thinking to a job that has, up to now, been project management-oriented. However, without this fourth pillar, company portfolio managers will eventually become frustrated. They simply won't have enough insights about product lines and business strategy to guide them in project prioritization.

Part of Culture

Adding this fourth pillar goes far toward embedding the continuous improvement of product lines and their strategies into a culture. This is fundamental to the *PLuS Framework*. This, then, brings us back to adding product lines into the business unit's growth portfolio, the topic of the next segment in this chapter.

10.2: Rationalizing and the Business Growth Portfolio

The fourth pillar of the *PLuS Framework* also ties product lines to a business unit's growth initiatives. Business units do this by managing what many call the Business Growth Portfolio. It is specific to a business unit.

The Business Growth Portfolio

The business growth portfolio differs from the product development portfolio. Business growth portfolios are collections of initiatives, projects, and investments that contribute to or take away from a business unit's year-over-year growth. Product portfolio management is only about PIMs, PIDs, and PICs as I described in Chapter 8.2. The business growth portfolio stresses investments of money and people's time to all initiatives affecting growth. (See Table 10.2.1.)

The product development portfolio should include projects across all product lines and is a subset of the business growth portfolio. Nearly every successful business sees its product development portfolio as a key contributor to their business growth portfolio.

Table 10.2.1

The business growth portfolio is more inclusive of growth opportunities than just overseeing products under development. Looking over different time periods (e.g., one, three, and seven years), the business growth portfolio includes:

- NPD Portfolio (PIDs, PICs, PIM Improvements) – Product line-specific.
- Technology Building Block Moves (licensing and development).

- Market and Marketing Moves such as major promotional campaigns. Need separation line
- Sales Expansions -- geographic, regional, and market segment-specific.
- Platform-Lever Moves.
- Intrapreneurial Activities.
- Business Acquisitions, Ventures, Lean Startups, and other Business Investments.
- Core Business (current PIMs) Growth or Decline from baseline revenue and earnings.
- New Product Lines.

The focus of the business growth portfolio management is to induce a positive change in top-line revenue. This means top management needs to view facts and analyses about both positive or negative contributors. For product lines, a good analysis also breaks down contributions to specific platform-levers and market segments.

Near-term Versus Long-term

Product lines are unquestionably important to growth. However, those companies that stress earnings growth over top-line revenue miss the strategic importance of the growth portfolio. There is a strong argument that overemphasis of near-term earnings is harmful to product line strategy success. It leads to trade-offs of strategy moves for short-term financial rewards. Consider failed corporations like Kodak, PanAm, Polaroid, and Borders. All failed following years of profitability. That's what makes this so interesting. It turns out a strong near-term profit orientation is a defining characteristic of the dreaded "Success Trap"[43,44] conundrum.

---

43 Levinthal, D.A. and March, J.G., "The myopia of learning." *Strategic Management Journal*, vol. 14, 95–112 (1993)

44 Adams, M. and Boike, D. (2004), "The PDMA foundation 2004 comparative performance assessment study." Visions, 28, 26–9.

Stressing revenue growth can create a positive influence on product line strategies. Consider, for example, how Amazon optimized growth while managing earnings to barely tolerable levels. (See Figure 10.2.1.) Stock market analysts continually criticized Amazon's skinny earnings. One analyst said, "Amazon is a charitable organization being run by elements of the investment community for the benefit of consumers."[45] Jeff Bezos, CEO of Amazon, responded to the "charitable" statement through a letter to shareholders. Bezos stated, "Take a long-term view, and the interests of customers and shareholders align." Jeff Bezos has purposely stressed customer satisfaction and competitive positions over earnings. Much to the chagrin of analysts, shareholder value has soared. (See Figure 10.2.2.)

EXPLANATION:
Success Trap

The term "Success Trap" refers to a conundrum in which companies can find themselves. Companies get "trapped" by overemphasizing the very practices, behaviors, and strategy that made them successful. Caterpillar, Kodak, Polaroid, and Rubbermaid are companies commonly cited for having been victims of the Success Trap phenomenon.

For a product line strategist, the question is whether the Strategy-Essence and its three parts (chain-link alignment, platform-lever effectiveness, and attribute positioning) causes or contributes to the Success Trap.

---

45 Matthew Yglesias, Moneybox blog; *Slate*, 29 Jan 2013

Figure 10.2.1 Amazon's Revenue Versus Earnings, 2010 Through 2014

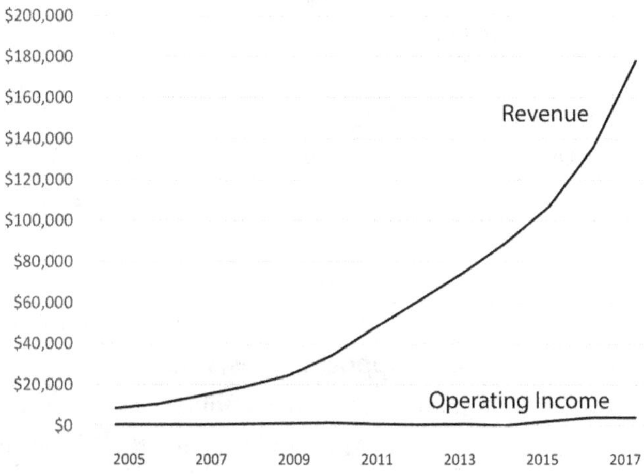

Source: Google Finance

Figure 10.2.2 Amazon's Market Cap 2008 Through 2015

Source: Google Finance powered by YCharts

There is a common belief that growth portfolios are like financial portfolios, those containing assets such as stocks, bonds, and real estate. This is true, to a degree. There are likenesses toward diversification and risk mitigation. The difference, however, is the business growth portfolio is far more affected by time, uncertainties, and competitors. It's also affected by synergies among its contributors and projects. And it changes constantly. This makes its management much more demanding.

Keeping a certain mix of projects within a growth portfolio helps address trade-offs between risk and rewards. The idea is to desensitize the complete set of contributors from the negative possibilities of just a few. It's about seeking an optimal mix. But figuring out what is "optimal" is difficult, and, at times, seemingly impossible. It depends on likelihoods, opportunities, and many unknowns. Moving toward a best business growth portfolio needs more analysis than just counting each contributor and totaling the investments.

Extraordinary Benefits of a Business Growth Portfolio

By specifically focusing on growth, organizations gain both in strategic planning and the well-being of the firm. Consider these key benefits:

1. Gathering, analyzing, and creating a visual representation of data helps engage top management. Such engagement sends the organization a clear message. Growth is crucial to the organization's well-being. It is critical to shareholder value. And, growth is equal to or more important than earnings.[46] Smart use of business growth portfolio management develops a full view of how those responsible for producing growth expect it to occur. It also communicates the key influences, both positive and negative, to achieve the growth. This common understanding helps promote collaboration across

46 The exception to this rule is only when a business faces impending failure.

an organization, create new synergies, and build greater insights.

2. The business growth portfolio spells out how each growth opportunity contributes to the business unit strategy. This includes new ventures, forward-looking investments, intrapreneurial work, and other non-product development activities. This relevance helps. It matters in understanding different perspectives. Plus, it aids in communicating the importance of activities to those working through critical day-to-day practices.

Business units realize the benefits of a growth portfolio through its consistent use. To do so, managers, shareholders, and key stakeholders need, at a minimum, an annual readout of the growth contributors, individually and as a set. Leadership should also build the skills to understand how best to exploit growth portfolios in business strategy.

Upholding and growing contribution margins and net earnings are focal points for the growth portfolio, although secondary. Most organizations find such accounting measures important to track and analyze, but not an endpoint. Consider how the contribution margin of a product line may change in a different direction than top-line revenue. This may happen, for example, during the mature stage of a product line life cycle. This is when product line teams may see revenue growing and contribution margins declining.

Business Growth Mix and Balance

A common approach in managing the growth portfolio is to seek "balance." This is depicted in a four-quadrant-type graphic such as a Boston Consulting Group Grid or McKinsey and Company's Nine

Box Model.[47] These can be very helpful. However, mix management of a growth portfolio is more like seeking balance in a three-dimensional Alexander Calder mobile than plotting bubbles on a static four-quadrant chart. And the balance becomes more difficult because, over time, the objects (contributors) change in size and weight, plus the external forces on each shift continually.

Balance can also find its way into the product portfolio conversation. I find, for example, that many managers believe balance in the product portfolio to be smart. Unfortunately, this is not the case. There is no strong empirical evidence that points to gaining benefits from an optimal mix of product development projects. The few completed longitudinal studies on the topic do not support the notion there is a best or ideal mix of projects.[48]

This then leads to a principle of the *PLuS Framework.* It's this. *Business units should seek balance in the growth portfolio, not the product development portfolio.* The focus for product and project-portfolio management should be on ensuring product line success, regardless of balance. Do <u>not</u> confuse the business growth portfolio with the product portfolio.

The longtime duration over which portfolios play out makes them difficult to analyze quantitatively. Many years may have passed when portfolio results become available, enough time for an entire industry to change. The best mix a decade ago may not be the best going forward. So, the growth portfolio should orient toward

---

47 BCG will quickly declare what percent of a business's investment should be in each quadrant. The approach leaves the impression that to create new opportunities top executives need only pick up a phone and place an order to their staffs, much like buying stocks and bonds. Obviously, this is not the case.

48 "Predicting Project Portfolio Success by Measuring Management Quality—A Longitudinal Study," Jonas, Daniel; Kock, Alexander; Gemunden, Hans Georg; Engineering Management, IEEE Transactions on 60 2 215-226, 2013

avoiding lopsidedness. And, it should stress helping each product line strategy and each venture. The mission of business growth portfolio management is to achieve overall growth objectives, not to gain a specific mix or balance.

Analyzing the growth portfolio can be tricky. The variety of growth contributors requires teams to pay careful attention to normalizing data. The challenge is that each contributor may have different and unique characteristics. Timeframes may be different. Risks may be different. Even the units to capture revenue and earnings may look different. This may make comparisons difficult. It often takes ingenuity to create a level playing field among the opportunities.

Picturing the Business Growth Portfolio

The graphics that I share go a long way in explaining a business unit's growth portfolio. They also help to think through how it might play out at your company. (See Figures 10.2.3, 10.2.4, and 10.2.4.)

The bar chart depicts the expected growth for each of three product lines within a business unit. The next figure, the first bubble chart, depicts the growth trajectory over ten years for the three product lines. In this chart, the Y-axis is the cumulative revenue growth for each product line. The X-axis shows the year for the revenue gains. The size of the bubble represents the investment being made back into each line. For the three product lines, we see Product Line # 3 moving past maturity and into decline. Product Line #2 is moving to maturity, while Product Line #1 is undergoing growth.

Figure 10.2.3: Expected Three-Year Growth for Product Lines Within a Business Unit

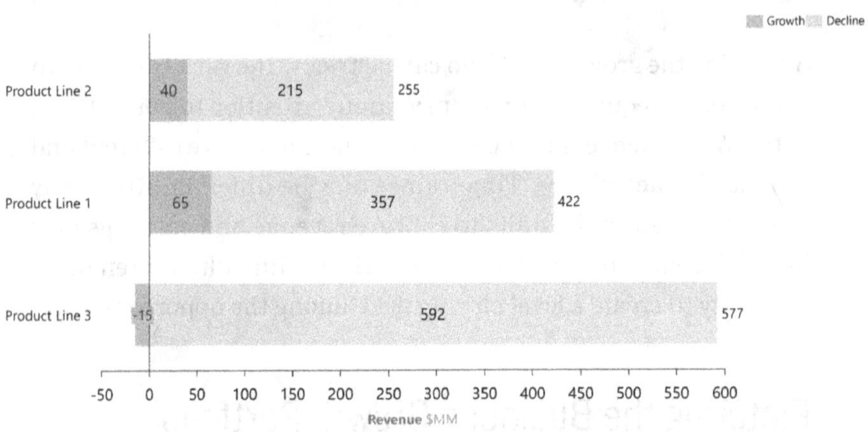

Figure 10.2.4: Growth Trajectory for the Product Lines Within a Business Unit

The second bubble chart in Figure 10.2.4 below shows all of the business units' growth opportunities, not just the existing product lines. This is the overall forecast for three years.

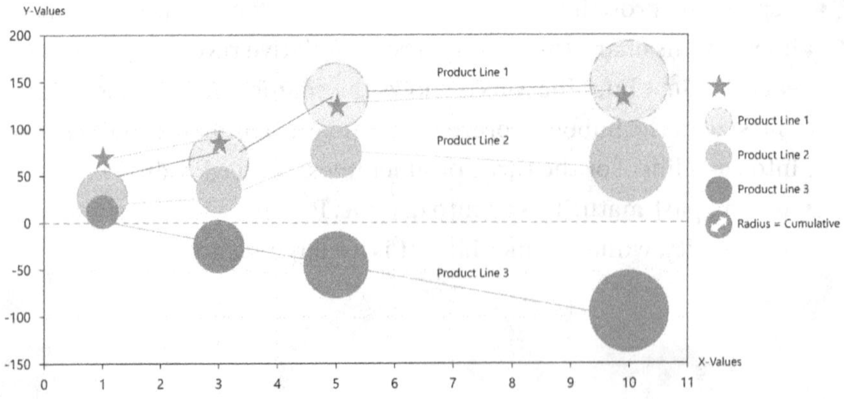

Figure 10.2.5: First-Year Growth versus Third-Year Growth for All Growth Entities

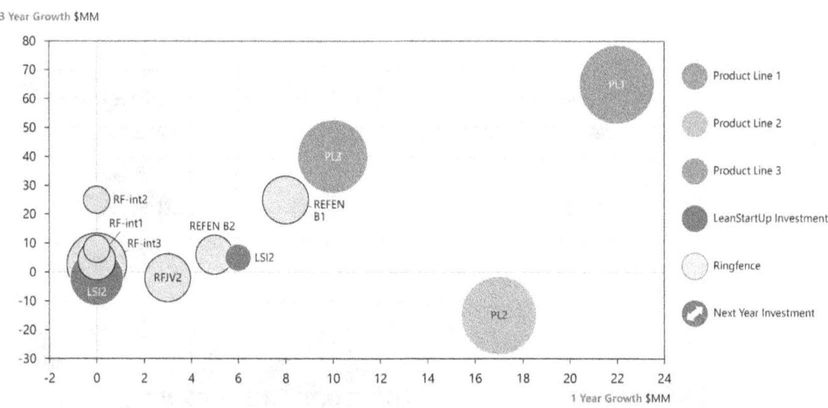

Notice how the three product lines (PL1, PL2, and PL3 in Figure 10.2.4) dominate both growth (positive) and decline (negative). This is common in large businesses. Non-product line activities like investments in emerging businesses, ring-fenced ventures, and standalone intrapreneurial work tend not to contribute markedly. The problem is the base revenue in year zero is so large. Their top-line revenue contribution to growth tends not to be as large as most top managers would hope. Instead, the fate of large businesses tends to ride on existing product lines. Hopefully, these are lines with good strategies and smart execution and roadmap management.

Every business unit approaches its growth portfolio differently. Don't expect a one-size-fits-all approach here. The example graphs above simply give a starting point. You'll find analyzing and presenting a business-growth initiative has many challenges, and it's surrounded by many uncertainties.

EXPLANATION:
Operationalizing the Growth Portfolio

One form of analysis I encourage as part of the PLuS Framework is to cluster projects and initiatives by their growth types. You'll see that a product line strategy may contribute to any of the five growth clusters. These clusters are:

1. **Core Growth Cluster**: The roll-up growth contributions, both positive and negative, from existing product lines. These are the PIMs coming from established platform-levers, using technology building blocks and going to core market segments.

2. **Redefined Core Cluster**: These opportunities are strategy moves (projects and initiatives) related to core product offerings. Their purpose is to create new business models and/or reform chain-link strategy alignments and synergies. They may also seek to alter market segment positioning. This cluster includes projects and initiatives like:

    - Radical innovation (new platform-levers, new Strategy-Essence) in product lines.
    - Reconfigure chain-link strategies and business models.
    - Reorientation of the organization culture or behavior.

3. **Adjacency Growth Cluster:** These are strategy moves to extend product lines into new market segments. The new segments are near or similar to existing segments.

    - Product line adjacency is a higher-payoff, higher-risk growth opportunity than the core product line offering. Such adjacencies may also be subdivided as "far off," "moderately far," or "close-in" adjacencies.

4. **Whitespace Growth Cluster**: This is the set of opportunities needing new product lines to be created. A whitespace opportunity implies that organizations use internal resources to carry out most of the work to create it.

5. **Vanguard-Pioneering Growth Cluster**: These growth opportunities help to take a business in a new direction. They include:

    - Exploring growth in new areas, independent of organizational boundaries.

    - Ventures held purposefully separate from the core organization. These may include ring-fenced, lean startups, or investments in independent startups or joint ventures.

At the business unit level, it is helpful to assess the mix of financial contribution and uncertainty. First, do this within each cluster, and then across clusters. The message the consulting firms communicate in their research findings boils down to a few key points:

- Adjacency clusters (#3), whitespace clusters (#4), and redefined core clusters (#2) are critically important. This is because they are the easiest to focus on and need the least product change. The consulting firm's research suggests they offer the best return for the amount invested. Each should be present in the growth portfolio mix.

- It is a mistake to complement a core growth cluster (#1) only with a vanguard-pioneering growth cluster (#5). Yet some executives do this when seeking growth while cutting out waste by using lean practices without a strong product line strategy. This approach, the consulting firms' research suggest, offers the least return for investment and the risk incurred.

It's Growth that Matters

Stressing growth related to core product lines is important. The evidence from the cited research suggests that much of business growth comes from core product lines and their strategy moves. This makes it critical for organizations to gain a clear focus on their product line strategies. This is a key purpose of this fourth pillar of the *PLuS Framework*.

The central focus of managing the business growth portfolio should be on improving revenue and earnings contributions. It is not on specific new products or resource consumption.

Consider, for example, adjacent market opportunities that may extend the life of existing PIMs. Keen analysis should call out revenue from PIMs extending to new markets.

This needs to be separated from the same PIMs' changes in revenue in core market segments. The idea is to give credit for growth to the strategy move seeking adjacent opportunities. It should not bundle growth into data reflecting the core offering. Such "growth strategy accounting" is notably different from typical cost accounting.

Direct Value and Real Options Value

One tendency in managing the business growth portfolio is to include only new products or new businesses. This limited approach, however, misses the extraordinary real options value.[49] This can be from entering new growth markets with existing products, developing new technology building blocks, or setting up new platform-levers and product lines.

---

49 Real Options Value is often designated as the ROV or ROA (real options analysis) of an investment.

In time, such opportunities should transition into new cash flows. Yet it's often difficult to predict a product's resulting cash flow or when it will launch. But good growth-portfolio management works to capture, analyze, and report the real options value for each project and each group of projects within the growth portfolio.

Nurturing the Goose that Lays the Golden Eggs

In the next chapter, I address workflows, decision flows, and information flows. These are the foundational parts of a product line strategy process. You'll see that oversight of the Business Growth Portfolio, often referred to as "Governance," plays an important role. Together, good product line strategies and smart Business Growth Portfolio Governance form a healthy, thriving enterprise. When combined, they can create a productive goose that lays many golden eggs. And it turns out the goose is far more valuable than any single egg.

Organizing and Relating the Elements of Good Product Line Strategy

The Union with Business Strategy

PRODUCT LINE STRATEGY: GETTING TO GOOD

Seek to:

Gain and keep a purposeful role for your product line strategy within your overall business strategy:

- ▶ When lines are too small or offer little impact on a business unit's growth, their role in business strategy decreases ... size and growth matter.

Aim for growth in fast-growing noun-based market segments. Position product attributes against verb-based segments:

- ▶ Build the skill to assess both noun-based market segments and verb-based segments ... and the talent to communicate about both.

Work in unison with your business unit's other product lines to maximize shared support from other chain-links:

- ▶ When product lines work separately, the chance of harming one another increases.

Recognize the line as a contributing part of a business growth portfolio, not separate from the business unit's other opportunities, whether the product lines exist or not:

- ▶ Compete for resources within, not isolated from, the growth portfolio.

SECTION 4

WORKING THE FRAMEWORK

Strategizing and Execution – Orchestrating the Flow

Gaining the Profound Value of Good Product Line Strategies

- Structure, Teaming, and Process–The Framework Foundation
- Strategizing as a Fluid Process
- Workflow and Information Flow
- Deliberate Decisions–The Framework Roof
- Governance and Decision-Making
- The *PLuS Framework's* Principles

CHAPTER 11

Structure, Teaming, and Process: The *PLuS Framework* Foundation

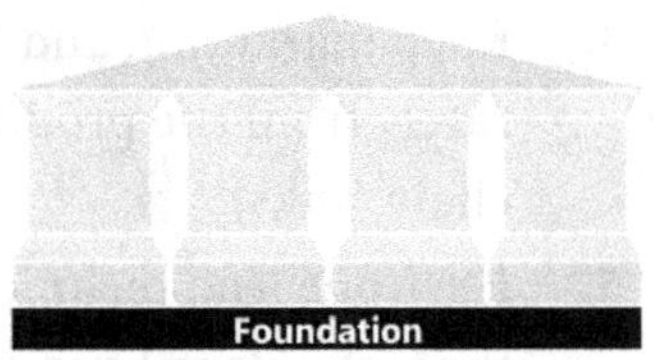

BEFORE DIVING INTO process flow and decision-making that support good product line strategies, we need to look at who will be doing the work. What roles with what responsibilities are best? As I stated earlier in Chapter 6, this is situational. But the *PLuS Framework* gives guidelines for good structure and teaming.

Organizational Structure

The best way to discuss organizational structure is with a diagram. You'll find an example structure, although fictitious, in Figure 11.1 below. It shows several key principles that are earmarks of good structure. Not all business units need the same functions nor will they have multiple lines. And not all are large enough to support the roles.

Study the organizational chart for a moment. The chart is not intended to be specific to your organization, or any other organization for that matter. Rather, it's laid out to share how best to set up an organization for good product line strategy. Here are the six guidelines for adapting an organization's structure for good product line strategies.

1. Make sure product line strategy is a separate chain-link.
2. Make sure one person with suitable staff has responsibility for each product line.
3. Try to have one full-time manager with suitable staff responsible for achieving and maximizing leverage from each platform-lever.
4. Keep marketing and technology managers reporting separately from the product line chain-link (these are different chain-links).
5. Have one lead technical person per each product line under the technology head or engineering head.
6. Have Project Management (PMO), Portfolio Management (PPM), and Roadmap Management (RM) report through product line management. Do not have them report through another chain-link. Remember, though, the decision-flow and its governance should cut across the President/GM and heads of each chain-link.

By setting up roles specific to each product line and their platform-levers, the organization enables intense focus where needed. Following these guidelines helps achieve the needed focus. These dedicated managers must then cut across the organization to do work. This is classic matrix management. Remember the product line team's two key responsibilities laid out in Chapter 6 are.

1. To draw up strategy and strategy improvements.
2. To carry out the strategy and manage the product line.

Perhaps most important for good product line strategies is making product development and management a separate chain-link. If not, the product line's role in overall business strategy will be suboptimal. All product line strategy issues and opportunities would be addressed only by part-time teams.

Perhaps more problematic, smart product line moves would fall secondary to other chain-link needs. Such moves might include building new platform-levers and targeting new market segments.

This is important because failing to make notable product line moves and pivots early enough is a major cause of a business collapse.

When there is just one product line in a business unit, assigning roles and responsibilities may seem easier. But it's not. Here, it would seem the product line leader takes on a senior role as head of product development and management. But the conjunction "and" between "development" and "management" makes matters more complex.

You'll often find that senior executives need to share the responsibility. This usually falls to the head of technology and the head of marketing and product management. In effect, you're asking these two people to share a single role. Conflicts are bound to arise. The alternative is to push responsibility to the business unit head, or the general manager. In either of the approaches, the product line strategy and execution task is a part-time job.

Unfortunately, this is not best for good product line strategies.

When it's not possible to dedicate managers to each product line, the recourse is to set up part-time managers in a cross-functional team. Their job is just the same, but their focus on it is not. This is suboptimal but could be necessary.

Figure 11.1: Example Organizational Structure for Good Product Line Strategies

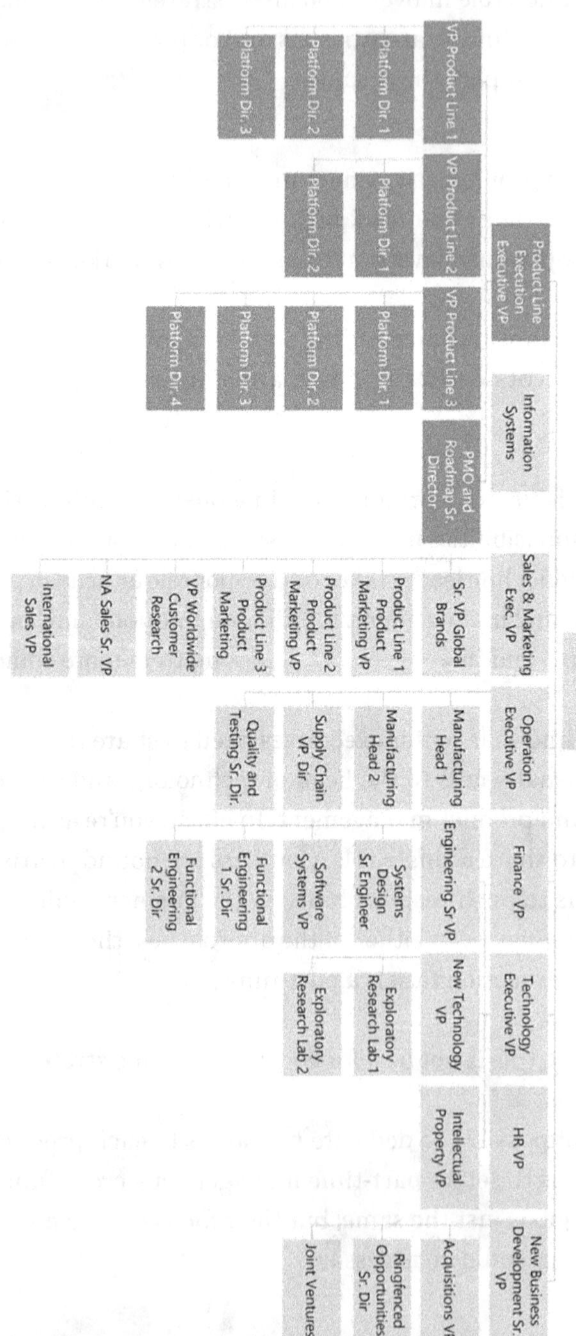

Teaming Across Chain-Links

Good product line strategy always needs input from across chain-links. It comes from managers deeply knowledgeable and insightful about the product line. And they know how it fits into the overall business unit strategy. Consider the knowledge that's needed. It can involve many functions and disciplines. And while having knowledge is important, it is not the most important factor to consider when forming strategizing teams. Rather, the most important factor is the participants' intelligence.

I am trying to make a few points by stating that intelligence is most important. Taking part in a product line strategy team is a unique responsibility in any large business. It demands breadth and depth of knowledge, an ability to merge seemingly disparate thoughts, and a passion for strategic thinking. Don't expect anyone from a function to fill the role. And don't expect senior managers to be better than junior managers.

Those joining a product line strategizing team can't be shy about stating their thoughts. Much like in scrum meetings for agile work, topics need to be fleshed out. And those who can't add to the discussion don't belong on the team. The only way the strategizing process works is for people to speak up.

Processes and Practices

The next few chapter segments describe a process flow that teams may follow to create good product line strategy. It is the product line strategizing process, and it incorporates work, information-gathering, and creation, and decision-making.

11.1: Strategy Moves: Aiming at Moving Targets

Today, most product managers recognize that product lines and their platform-levers have life cycles. Trying to change —or "pivot"—quickly out of a decline stage may be the last solution a team tries. Quite a few notable companies have found their way to bankruptcy because of the failure to refresh or replace mature product lines. Consider the challenges faced by Kodak, Polaroid, Hostess, Saab, Chrysler, and The Tribune Group. Sticking to strategies and doubling down on their existing platform-levers for too long led these once-stellar companies to bankruptcy.

Spotting the need for change and then doing it early works much better. I call this keeping the strategy on target—or, in simple language, "smart." The bankruptcy cases mentioned above show why flexibility and rapid response works so much better than doubling down on old strategies and leaning out (removing waste or slack from) existing plans. Companies need new dynamics addressing the whole approach. Indeed, roadmap recasts and pivots must be considered before it's too late. This means a process must continuously address change and its dynamics.

All product lines will die eventually. Working only to cut costs and extend life cycles can become a race to the bottom. Equally important, without change to strategy, major opportunities will be lost. The problem is in figuring out what changes to make—and when and how to make them.

Some teams always include a multi-generational dimension to their product line. Failing to do so can quickly result in evaporation of a product line's impact. Such failing will also expose weaknesses and forfeit opportunities to increase customer satisfaction.

Some companies have, however, addressed multi-generational dynamics successfully. Amazon's E-reader product line under the Kindle brand name is one of those. Each generation's goal has been to deliver greater customer satisfaction and so improve the line's competitive position. It would be impossible to do this with just one generation of an E-reader.

This responsiveness is a common thread in every high-tech company. It's especially true for those that have been successful over a decade. I point to high-tech companies and a decade because it implies they have progressed through several life cycles of their products. You simply can't survive in fast-paced industries without regenerating your product line strategies.

Keeping product lines strategies current and at their best is a constant job. You'll find that many activities can help. Almost every business writer today shares at least one technique or another for analyzing product line strategy topics. For example, many authors focus on life cycle analyses, technology-readiness charting, market segmentation techniques, or the voice of the customer explorations. All these approaches, and others, matter. I refer to each as a "*PLuS Lens*." Teams use *PLuS Lenses* to build insights and understanding about both the product line's present and future.

Teams select *PLuS Lenses* they believe are most helpful, adapt the steps to fit their situation, and then get on with the analysis. The idea is to produce more information and new insights that help advance the product line. Lenses provide the input for crafting the strategy. They aid teams in forming the Strategy-Essence, plus aid in setting up objectives and metrics, the Roadmap, and the Rationale and Roll-up. These are the four pillars of the *PLuS Framework*.

Diving into all potential *PLuS Lenses* goes beyond the scope of this book. If you're interested though, check out The Adept Group's resource page (www.adept-plm.com/PLuS-resources.htm). You'll find discussions on over thirty lenses specific to product line strategies, each with step-by-step instructions, templates, and examples. The site also shares whitepapers and articles discussing how to customize and set up a flow of *PLuS Lenses*.

But what's not available in templates or methods is "smarts." That ingredient comes from within the organization. By "smarts," I don't mean those with the knowledge to carry out one function. I am referring to the people who have cross-functional insights and understanding across chain-links. These rare "T-shaped" people[50] are those with *deep* knowledge covering several topics, coupled with *strong* knowledge of all the topics. These topics can include technologies, markets, competition, regulations, finances, sales, or operations. You name it; they have some knowledge of it. Working with those "T-shaped" experts, you and your team can create a flexible, realistic a product line strategy and roadmap that helps you succeed, both today and over the long run.

Putting "smarts" into a process flow can be enormously helpful. Doing this purposely to support the four pillars is like nurturing the goose that lays multiple golden eggs, not just a single golden egg—"the next big thing"—by chance.

50 "T-shaped" people is a term coined by David Guest in "The hunt is on for the Renaissance Man of computing," published in *The Independent* (September 17, 1991).

11.2: Product Line Strategizing as a Fluid, Agile Process

Perhaps the most difficult challenge in product line strategizing is to spot and understand how the many influences interrelate. These influences include everything from market and technology changes to skills, competition, and even the unknown. Teams will spot these influences not just within the product line strategy itself, but also within seemingly unrelated discussions across the organization. In this segment, I detail how the process[51] works to corral such influences and relate them to strategy.

Process-oriented people might have preferred a discussion of this in earlier chapters. However, to understand the approach, it's helpful first to understand a good product line strategy's core parts. These are the Strategy-Essence (Pillar 1) and Execution and Roadmap Management (Pillar 2). The understanding sets the stage and lays out a language for how the process works to improve product line strategy and keep it good.

Carrying out practices that cut across an organization has been a cornerstone of good product development and management. To some extent, most large organizations do this through gated or agile practices. Or it may be through hybrid processes that combine both staged and agile practices. They also may carry out portfolio management and idea generation with cross-functional contributions. The full process then links these practices to business strategy.

---

51 The PLuS Framework strategizing process uses a workflow, a decision flow, and an information flow. Together, these flows seek to achieve goals, milestones, and objectives specific to a product line strategy.

From Beginning to End

Getting the most from product development is difficult without good product ideas. The challenge is coming up with product ideas and then deciding if they are good. Traditionally, companies tackle this challenge in that exact order: ideation first and screening second. Find the concept, and then decide if it's good. If you hear people calling for better screening, you'll know your organization is in that mode.

Unfortunately, this is backward. Instead, the approach should be to figure out what characteristics lead to "good" products. It should then seek to scout, work, think, and create a product having those characteristics. Building skill in product line strategizing brings with it a better understanding of what "good" means. Let's look further at this idea.

Consider how business strategy connects to creating, producing, and managing products. Figure 11.21.1 shows how they relate. You'll see the output from one process is the input to the next. In the full flow, product line strategy sets the characteristics of what's good and what's not. That is the role of a strategy's core—its Strategy-Essence.

Figure 11.2.1: Product Development Process Flow

Product development flows from targeting innovations to forming ideas. It then leads to product realization in staged and/or agile development. Throughout the flow, the quality from one subprocess notably affects work in the next.

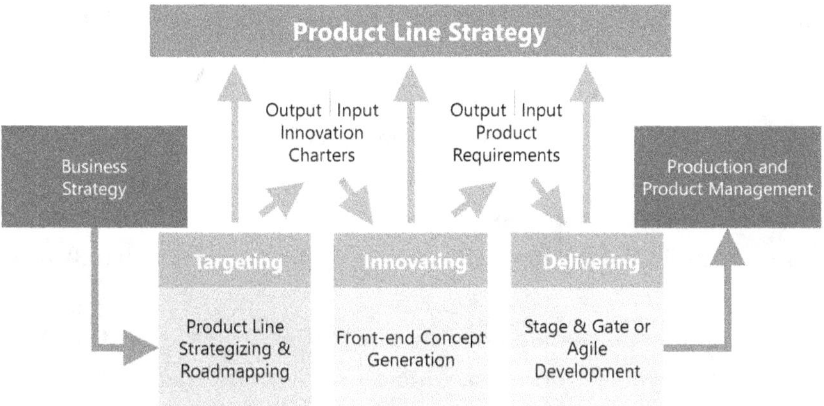

This simple output-to-input connection leads to an obvious fact. To have good products in the market, you first need good products to come out of the development process. Stepping further back, getting good products out of development practices demands having good projects. This starts with how to set up product idea generation.

The output-to-input connection is important. It means that good output from one subprocess will improve all remaining work. Note the opposite is also true. The poor-quality output from one subprocess will undercut the remaining work efforts.

Adding strategizing to traditional product development demands a broader view of the development cycle. Figure 11.2.2 depicts this by what I call the "full architecture" of new product development.[52]

A traditional view of the "front-end" includes work performed after the business strategy but before staged or agile development. Managers often call this the "fuzzy front-end." This means that what goes on there can be uncertain.

In the full architecture, the front-end divides this, with creating the roadmap and forming PICs (Pillar 2) coming next. Then come concept generation and feasibility assessments. In the full architecture, portfolio management then wraps up all practices (Pillar 3).

Overall portfolio management in the full architecture extends beyond the typical approach, which includes only staged and/or agile development projects. Instead, PICs and PIMs also become included. Together, these changes to the process are a major difference from typical staged, agile, and portfolio management approaches.

52 I first introduced the full architecture into five distinct chevrons or flows. Early work focuses on rationalizing product line strategies with business strategy (Pillar 4). Creating or improving the Strategy-Essence (Pillar 1) follows on product development in 2005 and advanced it in the years following. It was published as Chapter 4 in The PDMA Handbook 2 for New Product Development (Hoboken, NJ: John Wiley & Sons, Inc., 2005), pp. 59-72. Credit for the original architecture should also be given to Beebe Nelson and Robert Gill. Beebe has co-authored two books: New Product Development for Dummies and Innovation Governance: How Top Management Organizes and Mobilizes for Innovation. Beebe is more than willing to take on complex organizational topics. She is a one-of-a-kind expert with a Doctorate in Philosophy from Harvard working deep in the throes of innovation and product development. Bob became president of PDMA years after I held the position.

Figure 11.2.2: Full Architecture of Product Development

The full architecture integrates all processes from business strategy through managing products in the market. The architecture connects subprocess workflows and information flows. Notice the placement of *PLuS Framework* pillars within different subprocesses.

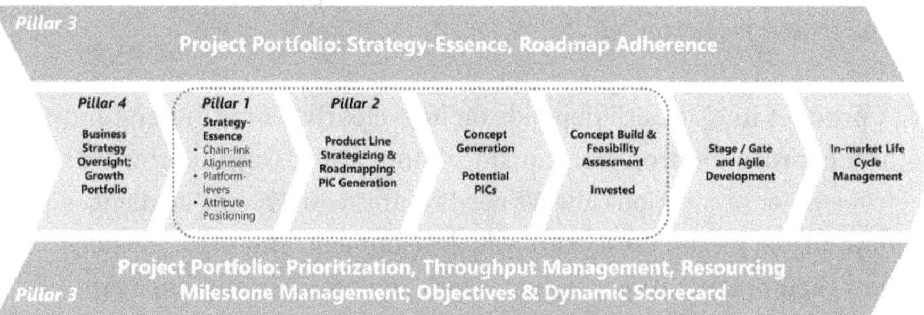

This fuller view also suggests a proactive and purposeful approach toward advancing product line strategies. It pushes strategy work and planning to the front-end, before development.

This proactive front-end loading has a major influence on product management practices and investment decisions. It also helps drive product lines forward, which helps deliver greater customer satisfaction, competitive advantage, and cash flow.

Smart strategies deliver greater value from product lines and their product development investments. As I discussed in Chapter 4, they yield bigger, better bubbles and often also create synergistic gains across products.

In the previous segment, I shared how setting up a process is like creating the goose that lays the golden eggs. A well-thought-out process can keep product line strategies at their best and, when needed, can help create new lines.

Information and Insight Flow

The nature of product lines and innovation makes for demanding dynamics within any organization. All innovations influence strategy, and strategies influence innovations. The challenge is understanding and communicating the work and projects that improve a product line and those that do not. Clarifying this makes product line strategies better.

A product line's health depends on how clearly teams understand and coordinate projects. Consider innovation. Gaining rewards from major innovations always needs teams to overcome challenges beyond just product discovery and development. This often includes how their organization conducts work, makes decisions, and transfers information. Rockwell Automation, one of The Adept Group's clients, offered a case in point described in Chapter 14.

Previously I mentioned Greg Githens, a leading expert in strategic thinking. Greg calls insights the "magic sauce" of strategy.[53] Good strategies need smart insights, and bad strategies stem from poor insights. Creating good strategies, I would argue, demands having smart approaches toward forming great insights. *(Definition Alert.)*

The work is to form insights from data and information and then move those insights toward realizing improvements to the product line. Good product line strategies need high-quality information transformed into high-quality insights (see Figure 11.1.3). Getting high-quality insights calls for analytical analyses, creative thinking, and systems thinking. It also needs subjectively judging how random influences might affect one another and the product line. Most important, it needs contributors to gain an ability to speculate how the future might unfold.

---

53 Greg Githens, The Strategic Thinking Coach, points out how "Strategic Thinking" is a competency. You can learn more about strategic thinking at his website https://strategicthinkingcoach.com/

Figure 11.2.3 Insight Flow: From Information to Value Realization

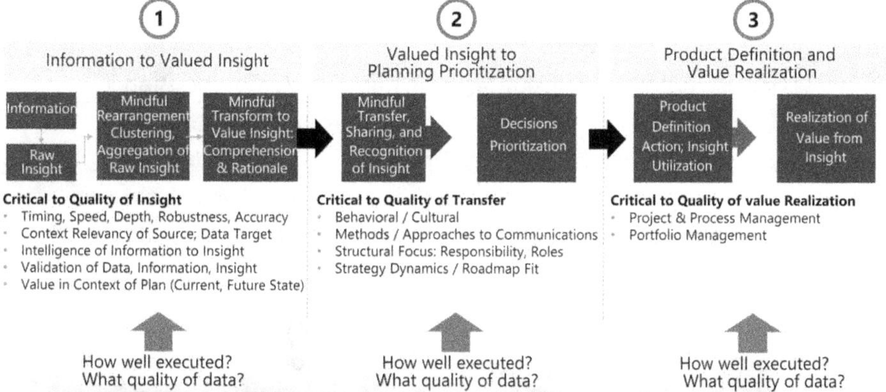

The *PLuS Framework* calls for teams to craft strategy by exploring topics both certain and uncertain. Without a deliberate approach that cuts across all four pillars, many managers will find this difficult to tackle. The challenge comes from deeply seated assumptions—those woven throughout product line discussions. Assumptions are helpful. But they can also bind the organization and product line teams in approaches and tactics.

EXPLANATION:
Insight

For our purposes, an insight is an instance of comprehension about influences on and hindrances to a product line strategy. An insight comes from combining fact-based information, creative thought, and intuition. New insights also arise from exploring or testing prevailing assumptions, and from merging and testing insights.

Good insights about product line strategy are those that yield impact. This sets guidelines for driving good insights into product line strategy. And the guidelines help shape practices within the *PLuS Framework*. They also help form *PLuS Lenses* useful throughout strategizing work.

Analytics and analysis within each *PLuS Framework* pillar should contribute fact-based information. Creative and intuitive explorations should cut across pillars. Teams should stress gathering information related to the Strategy-Essence pillar. This includes chain-link alignment, platform-levers, and attribute positioning.

To form good insights, I recommend:

1. Employ continual efforts to develop fact-based information about the product line. This includes information about technologies, markets and customers, competitors, and the line's measures and metrics.

   Consider, for example, how product line teams may conduct market research. An effort may seek to evaluate desired outcomes in verb-based market segments. This may take several months to complete. The resulting data and following cluster analysis are fact-based information. By itself, however, the information may be interesting but of little value.

2. Share all fact-based information in venues designed purposely to help creative and intuitive thinking across information sets. The goal is to produce relevant, good insights.

   Going one step further with the verb-based market research example described above, teams can share the research with technology-aware contributors. Insights will accrue from intuitively matching specific technologies to defined desired-outcome clusters.

3. Explore possible impacts of insights (individually and in combination) on strategy. Enable individuals and groups to explore all insights. Some groups should be functionally oriented. Other groups should cut across functions. Capture and make available all new insights that arise.

   In another step, insights about technologies that match desired outcome clusters might suggest a need for a new platform-lever. By definition, creating a new platform-lever would be a "Strategy Pivot." It may set up organizational and chain-link business strategy challenges and issues.

Assumption Dynamics

Most managers recognize that assumptions help cut through complexity. It is impossible to confirm every view about markets, technologies, customers, and the world. Instead, it is much easier to use assumptions that help cut through the morass of details and uncertainties. Often, most of us aren't aware we use assumptions. They are shortcuts to help us avoid having to rethink everything.

Yet no assumption will prevail forever. Assumptions that held true early in a product line's life will not necessarily hold up later. Too often, bad product line strategies exist because an assumption is held to be true for far too long.

Consider that almost everyone at Kodak understood the likely impact of the digital world on traditional photography. Yet Kodak held onto the assumption that film use and photography would remain set in consumer behaviors. Eventually, they changed their assumption. But "eventually" was too late.

Product line failures tend not to be about the lack of awareness. Instead, contributors to the product line errantly hold onto certain assumptions longer than they should. The difference between poor and good strategies is knowing when to abandon these assumptions. Being aware of this is the first step toward improving a product line strategy.

Many assumptions are woven throughout behaviors and an organization's culture. This may prove problematic, because it sets boundaries within which managers feel comfortable thinking and working. Assumptions, or presumed constraints, then define the proverbial "box" outside which we are told to think.

Teams should deconstruct their assumptions periodically. This is why the *PLuS Framework* process foundation encourages teams to set up lenses that help identify and explore assumptions. Each strategy lens helps teams mindfully explore assumptions alongside new information and insights.

Lenses help spot and test assumptions. And purposely, lenses should help develop new insights to improve the strategy.

Notice the three keys directives at play:

1. Mindful attention to specific influences on the product line
2. Identifying and continuously testing assumptions
3. Developing new and relevant insights

Mindful Analysis

Mindfulness in business is about nurturing an openness to new thoughts not burdened by assumptions. It also seeks a freshness toward mundane circumstances and drives a deep awareness of details. In complex assumption-ridden topics like product lines, there are many contexts in which to be mindful. Consider, for example, segmenting markets, analyzing technologies, and assessing the competition. Each presents a different context or set of circumstances and situations that surround the analysis.

Creating smart strategies calls for mindful analyses from many contexts, not just one. It is the product line team's job to be mindful in the analysis of all topics. It is also their job to combine these analyses into a single diagnostic. This then leads to forming the Strategy-Essence and Roadmap.

Gaining mindfulness across topics comes from using a flow of methods and approaches. Product line teams set this up to drive awareness of details and deep analysis. It should also inspire smart and creative thinking, plus focused and informed judgments. And as with all processes, it combines the flow of work, information, and judgments.

Ultimately, brilliant strategies stem from good insights. Therefore, the approach used to gain these insights matters a great deal. Ideally, the approach is mindful and aids contributors not familiar with the discipline.

Connecting Lenses into Process

The strategizing process uses lenses to address all *PLuS Framework* pillars and their parts. Correctly, it uses lenses to inject a full body of facts, insights, and creative thoughts into deliberate decision-making, the framework's roof. I call these *PLuS Lenses*™[54] *(Definition Alert.)*

The big task for product line teams is then to tie together the different insights. The process also helps here. It purposely moves teams beyond a mindless acceptance that "the product line is what it is." Product line teams use the process to foster a deep perspective on the product line. The intent is to form smart insights and make those insights understood by team members and key players.

DEFINITION ALERT:
PLuS Lens

"PLuS Lens" is The Adept Group name for methods and approaches that aid gathering and using facts to generate insights. PLuS Lenses are specific to forming and carrying out a product line strategy. Teams may use different PLuS Lenses in series or in parallel throughout the product line strategizing process.

Some *PLuS Lenses* are specific to the framework, others not. But each lens helps teams explore information, data, and assumptions while discovering insights. The *PLuS Lenses* help teams be mindful across several topics. For example, they delve into customer needs, technology advancements, and platform-levers. Each lens uses exploratory questions, specific techniques, and team exercises. By forming and rearranging insights, a team sets the stage for forming a superior product line strategy. This takes a certain discipline. And a key purpose of the process flow is to enable such discipline.

Design Thinking and Agile Sprints

The lens flow and strategizing work uses Design Thinking and Agile Sprints. **Design Thinking** *(Definition Alert)* orients toward understanding, framing, and creatively solving the strategy challenge ... improving product line results.

---

54 PLuS Lenses and PLuS Lens are a trademark of The Adept Group Limited, Inc.

Conducting most *PLuS Lenses* as **Agile Sprints** *(Definition Alert)* works to ramp up insights quickly. Sprints also aid teams in responding to their situation and to the insights they gather or create.

DEFINITION ALERT:
Design Thinking

Design Thinking is an approach or method for understanding, framing, and creatively solving problems. It began to aid industrial design. Today, businesses use it to address a wide variety of problems. Our focus is on creating the best possible product line strategy. The PLuS Framework encourages Design Thinking to create or improve the Strategy-Essence, the Roadmap, and Innovation Charters.

Not all lenses, however, can be conducted in individual sprints. Some, like conducting Job-to-be-Done segmentation coupled with determining customer-desired outcome clusters, may be too large to think of as a single sprint. These are more like projects within which a few sprints may take place.

Teams need two levels of learning and understanding throughout product line strategizing. The first is about insights gained from an individual *PLuS Lens*. Each lens brings unique insights to the forefront. One by one, they should be examined and assessed. The second level is the big-picture integration of insights. It is about the collection of insights garnered from the lenses and other sources. How do they relate? Are there root issues? Are there insights about the insights? This is the big picture of the strategy puzzle.

DEFINITION ALERT:
Agile Sprints

An Agile Sprint is a work effort spread over a few days and up to a month. For product line strategizing, each Agile Sprint usually involves three or four team members. Their job is first to shape the strategy lens (PLuS Lens) to fit the situation. Next, Agile Sprint members carry out the work and compile insights relevant to the product line. Using Agile Sprints keeps the work flexible and helps teams respond to unknowns inherent in each situation.

As part of the process, teams then must translate their full bucket of insights into actions and development projects that advance the line. Translating insight is the magic of product line strategizing. It's where creativity, intelligent analysis, and strategic foresight play an important role.

Figure 11.2.4 depicts the product line strategizing process as a flow. It fits into the full development architecture's front-end. The approach to the strategizing process takes advantage of Agile work with a Design Thinking approach. Notice how Agile Sprints are conducted by strategizing team members to carry out lens work. This is part of the Design Thinking approach of empathy (needs analysis), and problem definition and framing. But our use of these methods is not about one product. It's about the whole product line and its strategy. And our job is to improve the whole product line strategy.

Figure 11.2.4 Design Thinking Approach to Product Line Strategizing Process

Product line strategizing happens before concept generation. The flow diagram below depicts the strategizing and roadmap management process. The process delivers a renewed Strategy-Essence and an Execution Roadmap. It also delivers innovation charters to concept generation. The flow takes advantage of Design Thinking to understand, frame, and creatively solve the product line strategy-improvement challenge. Small groups contributing to the strategizing team carry out strategy lens work through quick Agile Sprints.

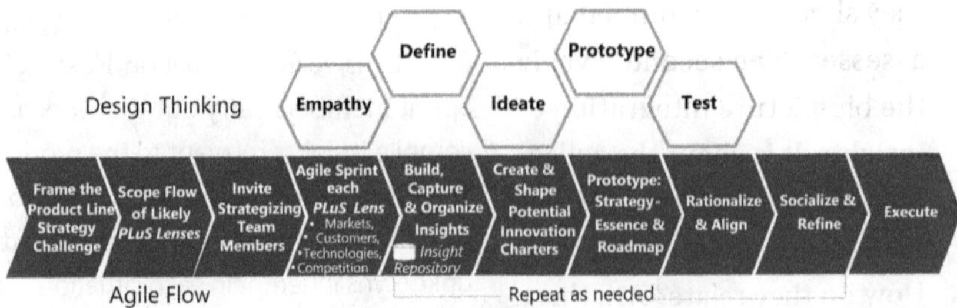

A warning is in order. Often, over-simplifying lenses and their flow is a mistake. It can undermine the quality and thoroughness of insights. The challenge is to keep mindfully aware of challenges and opportunities over a product line's entire life cycle. The problem is that without revisiting insights and their quality, they can evolve into errant assumptions. While keeping discipline about insights over one year may be easy, good product line strategies may depend on keeping insight quality over many years.

Using Agile methods to work through a Design Thinking approach helps maintain freshness toward information while forming insights, regardless of life cycles or a product line's age. But be aware: *Creating insights needs smart people covering relevant topic subjects.* The job is not "strategy by the masses." This usually means involving part-time contributors. These managers should have deep knowledge that may affect the product line and be capable of manipulating and integrating insights from many thought worlds.

These "smart contributors" working with core product line team members must understand, analyze, and create their way through the process. Fortunately, the step-by-step, yet flexible, approach laid out in *PLuS Lenses* helps. Ultimately, though, it's brain power that matters. The lens flow works by keeping the team on track toward the product line strategy challenge – to improve a product line's Strategy-Essence, and its execution, and its objectives and fit within the business unit strategy.

More About Lenses

Lens[55] selection and how they flow are specific to the product line and its circumstances. Good lens flow recognizes the output from one to be input for another. For example, Jobs-to-be-Done market segmentation is a single lens. Teams need its output before defining

55 The Adept Group maintains a library of dozens of *PLuS Lenses*. Each lens lays out step-by-step work and examples of insights to be garnered. Each lens starts by restructuring its generic work steps to fit the product line strategy challenge.

customer-desired-outcome clusters (another lens). And they need customer-desired-outcome clusters before creating potential innovation charters (a third lens). Also, depending on the circumstances, teams may recognize the need for other lenses when creating innovation charters.

A key to crafting and keeping good product line strategies is spotting and quickly recalling insights that arise when working the topic. These become pieces of the strategy puzzle. When mindfully assembled, the pieces should form a picture of a coherent product line strategy.

Depth and diversity of the lenses will benefit teams by helping create many unique and relevant insights. Some insights may add to the team's collective thinking. Other insights may seem disjointed and random. Smart product line strategies come from coupling accepted insights with these new insights. Collecting and examining all insights will then help create higher mindfulness toward the strategy and its execution.

In building out a strategy, teams pull together all insights with all assumptions. The question is whether the insights affect assumptions or the other way around. Speeding up insight formation is also important. Insights flow matters. Doing this faster and better than the competition is key to good product line strategy. This is where whole markets are won or lost.

Figure 11.2.5: Product Line Strategizing Lens Flow

The workflow depicted below goes one level deeper than that shown in Figure 11.1.4. Here, work is specific to *PLuS Lenses* and flows across four phases. The lenses are practices, methods, and techniques designed to gather and analyze information. The intent of each lens is to create good insights. The lenses divide across different contribution areas. The top swim lane of lenses addresses market and customer information. Next down is technology. At the bottom are lenses about the product line Strategy-Essence and the Execution Roadmap. All lenses are conducted using Agile practices.

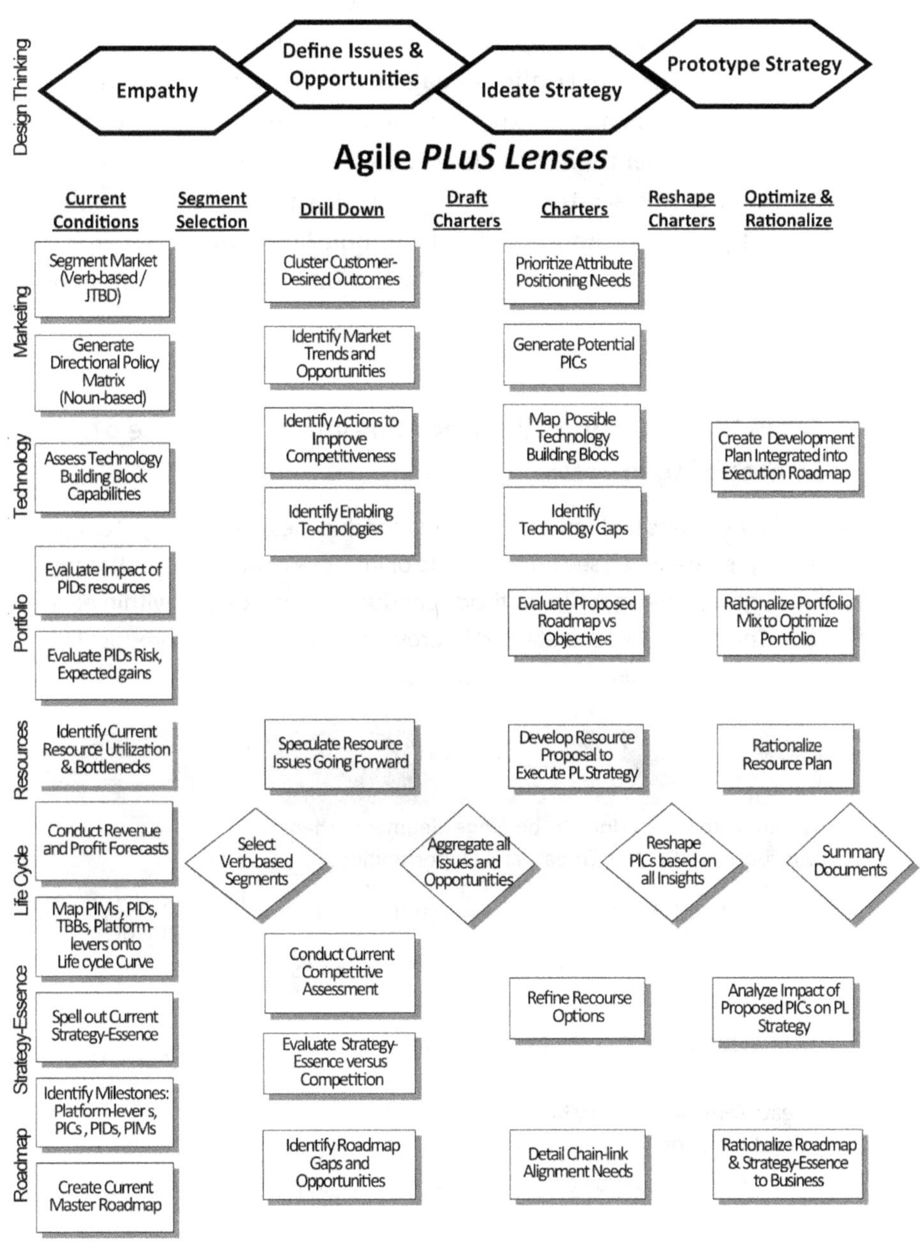
Design Thinking
Empathy
Define Issues & Opportunities
Ideate Strategy
Prototype Strategy
Agile PLuS Lenses
Current Conditions
Segment Selection
Drill Down
Draft Charters
Charters
Reshape Charters
Optimize & Rationalize
Marketing
Segment Market (Verb-based / JTBD)
Generate Directional Policy Matrix (Noun-based)
Cluster Customer-Desired Outcomes
Identify Market Trends and Opportunities
Prioritize Attribute Positioning Needs
Generate Potential PICs
Technology
Assess Technology Building Block Capabilities
Identify Actions to Improve Competitiveness
Identify Enabling Technologies
Map Possible Technology Building Blocks
Identify Technology Gaps
Create Development Plan Integrated into Execution Roadmap
Portfolio
Evaluate Impact of PIDs resources
Evaluate PIDs Risk, Expected gains
Evaluate Proposed Roadmap vs Objectives
Rationalize Portfolio Mix to Optimize Portfolio
Resources
Identify Current Resource Utilization & Bottlenecks
Speculate Resource Issues Going Forward
Develop Resource Proposal to Execute PL Strategy
Rationalize Resource Plan
Life Cycle
Conduct Revenue and Profit Forecasts
Map PIMs, PIDs, TBBs, Platform-levers onto Life cycle Curve
Select Verb-based Segments
Aggregate all Issues and Opportunities
Reshape PICs based on all Insights
Summary Documents
Strategy-Essence
Spell out Current Strategy-Essence
Conduct Current Competitive Assessment
Evaluate Strategy-Essence versus Competition
Refine Recourse Options
Analyze Impact of Proposed PICs on PL Strategy
Roadmap
Identify Milestones: Platform-lever s, PICs, PIDs, PIMs
Create Current Master Roadmap
Identify Roadmap Gaps and Opportunities
Detail Chain-link Alignment Needs
Rationalize Roadmap & Strategy-Essence to Business

PLuS Lenses work to aid thoroughness in insight creation while speeding insight flow.

However, not all insights accrue from lenses. Most organizations have other notable initiatives underway. This includes work like continuing R&D, portfolio management reviews, sales win-loss assessments, and brand-extension inquiries. This work may extend beyond or deeper than individual *PLuS Lenses*. It would be wasteful for product line strategizing to ignore this work. Instead, teams should purposely add insights from non-lens work to a central repository. Then, they should use the insight repository throughout the process.

Table 11.2.1: Design Thinking "Empathizing" Phase of Strategizing Process

Below are lenses that teams may use to conduct design thinking's "empathizing" phase when seeking to create or improve a product line strategy. Small groups using Agile methods conduct the work steps within each lens. The goal is to generate and improve insights about the product line and future possibilities.

PLuS Lens	Orientation
Create Verb-based (Jobs-to-be-Done) Segment Schema; Attribute Positioning, Threats and Opportunities	Market
Assess PID Risk, Portfolio Risk, Systemic Risk	Portfolio-Resource Management
Forecast PIM Revenue and Profit: 1 year, 3 years, and 5 years	Finance
Articulate Current PL Strategy-Essence and Assumptions	Strategy-Essence
Create Directional Policy Map of Verb-based & Noun-based segments	Market Segmentation
Review synchronization of PID Tasks, Gate & Launch Schedules	Roadmap
Assess Life cycle Status of Key PIMs	Life cycle
Define Current Platform-Levers, if any; Create Current State Roadmap	Platform-Lever

PLuS Lens	Orientation
Create Preliminary, Current State Strategy-Essence, and Roadmap	PL Strategy
Assess Skill-based Resource Use and Need: 1 year, 3 years, 5 years	Resources
Prioritize Market Segment	Market
List Available and Potential Technology Building Blocks	Technology
Conduct Preliminary Chain-Link Alignment Assessment	Strategy-Essence
Compile Insights and Assumptions	Insights

Insight and Assumption Repository

Insights often go for naught. Teams may hold meetings with other chain-link contributors and top managers at which one person or another states or explains an insight. Yet, within days after the meeting, the insight floats into the organization's ocean of knowledge and waits for rediscovery. While one such instance may not hurt the product line team's work, many will. This is especially true when rediscovery of insights does not happen quickly.

Managers capture such insights in their brains. In business, we call this "product knowledge." Having deep product knowledge or not, coupled with personalities, dictates how teams interact and build new insights. Problems with this approach arise when the brains are absent, or potential insights go beyond one person's product knowledge. This sets up a need for a repository of product knowledge, easily accessible by all team members. It is a knowledge base of information, data, insights, and assumptions related to the product line.

EXPLANATION:
Multivariate Cluster Analysis

With a good computer program, someone with a table containing the distances between cities could plot their relative locations. You could not tell north form south, but you could see their relative distances from each other.

Multivariate cluster analysis makes a table specific to the insights and information. Then the technique plots the relative positions for each insight and bit of information. Software then calculates mathematical clusters, akin to drawing a circle around those that bunch together. The product line team then tags each cluster with names and descriptions using their own logic.

How do you get the right values into the table? Simple The values come from people knowledgeable about the product line. They respond to survey questions that compare each bit of information or insight with all other bits. This work is more than filling in a form.

The survey may also capture characteristics of each insight or bits of knowledge. For example, the importance and the insight's type (marketing, technology, competitor) may also be captured. In the plot, the characteristics may show as size and color of the insight. This makes the graphic more like a topography than a flat geographical map.

The team then uses the plot to develop new insights. It may also use the plot to figure out a path that navigates the clusters and exploits relationships.

A repository of insights and assumptions gained from *PLuS Lenses* helps speed creating and improving the strategy puzzle. Most companies are already familiar with similar approaches set in place as a "knowledge-base," "content repository," or "wikidata." When made specific to a product line, its content or information may seem unstructured and random. That's OK at the start. However, over time, strategizing teams should both build on the information and insights and develop means to organize and analyze it.

While I wish there were one magical algorithm to pass the information through and organize everything, that is not the case. Instead, what I see is combining hard work and intuitive analysis to yield organization and more insights. An example of the hard work is to use multivariate cluster analysis on all accrued bits of knowledge and insights. (See sidebar explanation.) The technique plots all insights and information in relation to one another. Teams complement this with their intuitive understanding of relationships between information and insights.

11.3: Detailing Future Platform-Levers

I'd like to address a specific lens that is enormously useful in figuring out the best path forward for a product line. It is a method or approach for defining possible platform-levers and new generations of current platform-levers. Because new platform-levers can be key to a product line's vitality, I'd be lax if I did not share a description of the lens.

My goal here is not to make you an expert in the approach. Rather, I wish to convey how the approach works and suggest how to learn more. This understanding gives insight into where and how a product line should advance. Equally important, though, exploring the approach shares what makes for good product line strategies.

This is where understanding product line strategy fundamentals pays off. Knowing some basics helps enormously in figuring out possibilities for new or renewed platform-levers. Let me explain.

First, consider the simple product line roadmap in Figure 11.3.1. See how it details technology building blocks adding value to a platform-lever to create products. Each product is, in effect, a bundle of attributes.

At the top of the roadmap, you also see a line connecting each product (attribute bundle) to a verb-oriented market segment. The connecting line suggests the match between attributes and sets of needs. In Chapter 7.2, I discussed at great length that verb-based needs should be defined as customer-desired outcomes. Then at the top of the roadmap, we see the verb-oriented segments associated with noun-based segments. This is where the approach gets interesting.

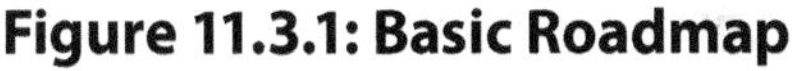

Figure 11.3.1: Basic Roadmap

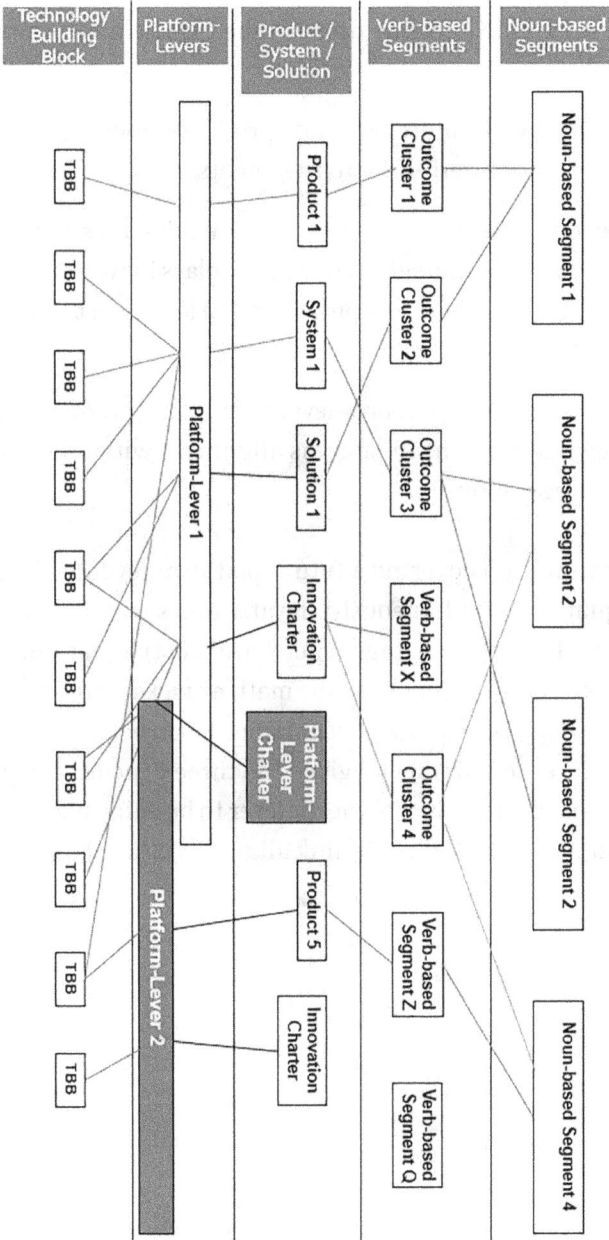

There are three conditions necessary to make a strategy work. This may be better stated as conditions to a good product line strategy. These three conditions line up with the three components of the Strategy-Essence.

- First, the attribute bundles (products) must match sets of needs in the verb-oriented segments.
- Second, the platform-lever must enable leverage. In good product line strategies, leverage displays in two ways: 1) speed or quickness of development and 2) lower cost in delivering the desired attribute set.
- Third, the new platform-lever results in a product line strategy that remains in or gains alignment with other business strategy chain-links.

In other words, discovering a future platform-lever is like solving three equations simultaneously: the attributes matching customer needs equation, the leverage (speed and cost) equation, and the chain-link alignment equation. The math nitpickers among us might say the analogy is more like optimizing the objective variable (the platform-lever requirements) given the three dependent equations (attribute-need matching, platform-lever to building block integrating speed plus cost, and chain-link alignment.) (See Figure 11.3.2.)

Figure 11.3.2: New Platform-lever Equation

1st Matching sets of customer-desired outcomes with possible platform-levers; 2nd assessing the ease (cost and speed) of combining technology building blocks with platform-levers, and 3rd assessing chain-link alignment with the new platform-levers.

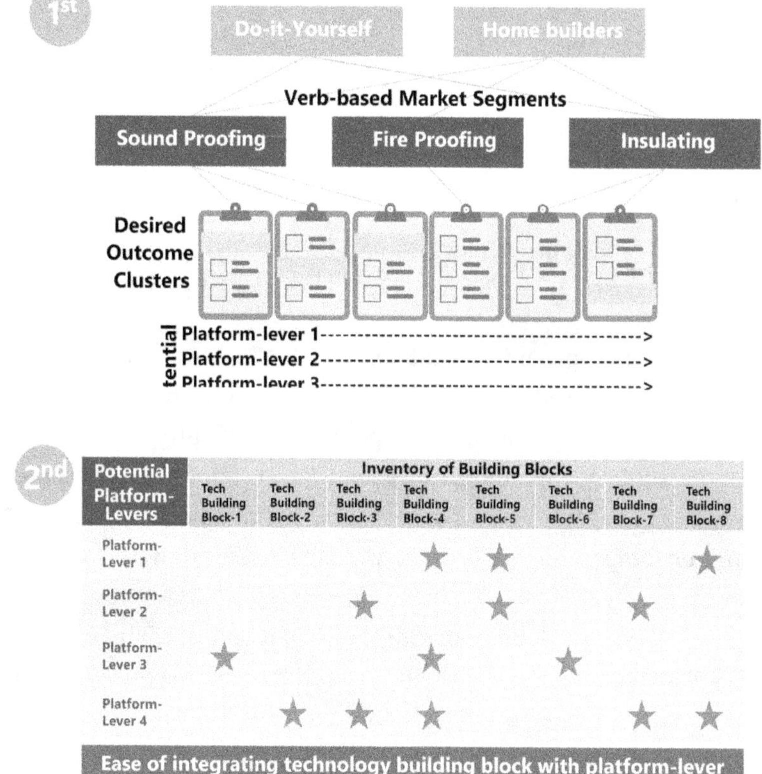

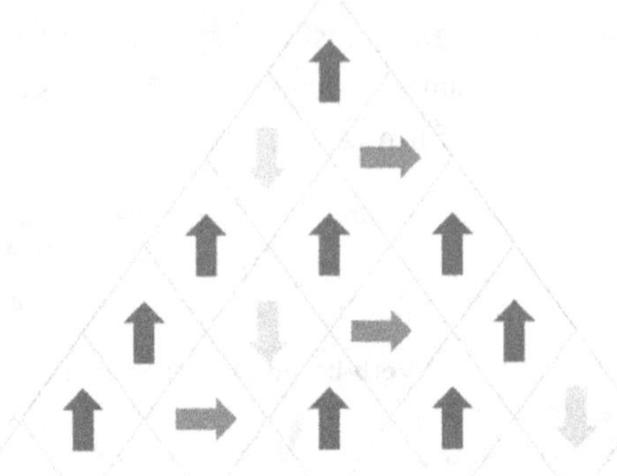

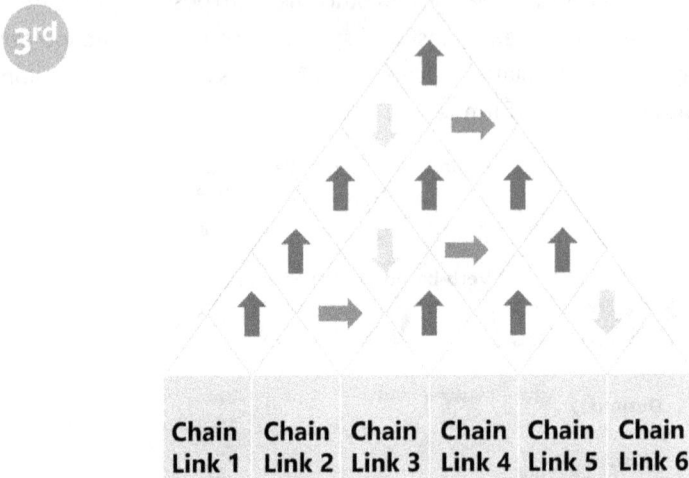

Chain Link 1 Chain Link 2 Chain Link 3 Chain Link 4 Chain Link 5 Chain Link 6

The analytical approach should start with attribute-need matching. Using verb-based, Jobs-to-be-Done segmentation, the analysis requires analytically assessing a large set (think greater than 50 and fewer than 200) of customer-desired outcomes across a large statistically significant sample of customers. The most useful analytic technique for the analysis is multi-variate cluster analysis.[56]

The key to defining good platform-levers is to detail their requirements. It's not to try to form them through creative exercises, brute force declarations, or praying for serendipity. The requirements, then, should guide teams in forming the new platform-lever specifications. The single-product equivalent would be translating user requirements into product specifications. This is akin to using quality-function deployment[57] for platform-levers.

56 Girish & W. Stewart, David. (1983). "Cluster Analysis in Marketing Research: Review and Suggestions for Application." *Journal of Marketing Research*. 20. 10.2307/3151680.

57 Quality Function Deployment (QFD)

While analytical in nature, the platform-lever requirements lens is not purely number-based. It also calls for qualitative assessments and judgments being interpreted as rating values. It also calls for a bit of brute force trial-and-error learning.

Be aware, though, for large product lines, the platform-lever requirement lens is not a simple, quick task. It requires notable input and much knowledge. This is justified because its economic impact can be great. It's about the whole product line, not just a single product. Be aware that this difference can cause organizational antibodies to attack the proposition—a cultural inertia phenomenon.

EXPLANATION:
New Platform-levers

When seeking new platform-levers, teams need not wait for all market research and technology building block assessments to be complete. Knowledge, without such analytics, is also useful. Usually, teams can get two-thirds of the way toward good definitions for new platform-levers definitions without such analytics.

The approach is to use available knowledge while building analytics to detail the specifications for a new platform-lever. Teams do this by creating and reforming "potential" Platform-lever Innovation Charters (PLICs.) The term "potential" means the charter is not fully formed nor included on the roadmap.

11.4: The Workflow and Information Flow

Business processes divide into three parts: a workflow, information or data flow, and a decision flow. The same is true for creating and roadmapping product line strategies. And it is true for waterfall development, portfolio management, and idea generation. (See Table 11.3.1.) Our concern is how well the flows align with and complement one another. This is both within each subprocess and across the full architecture. The product line strategy process is just one of the subprocesses.

Table 11.4.1: Components of Process

Flow	Type
Workflow	Tasks, stages, activities, practices, analyses
Information Flow	Data, knowledge, insights, documents, reports, presentations
Decision Flows & Governance	Judgments, choices, go/no-go, resource investments, prioritizations, rules

The challenge with process alignment for product development became clear in the late 1990s. This is when organizations began using software to support the flow. Many organizations had processes in place. It turned out workflows and information flows were well-formed, but decision flows were not.

Decision flows at the time were amorphous. The method and basis of decisions were, in some ways, being recreated with each decision point for each project. This is top management's prerogative. Unfortunately, it makes it nearly impossible to streamline the flows. How can you align a workflow and information flow when a decision flow changes constantly?

The decision flow is perhaps the most critical of the flows. In fact, it is so critical that I break it out as a major contributor to the *PLuS Framework*. It is a central feature of the framework's "roof"—making deliberate decisions. This includes governance of product lines and development work. All parts of the framework work to support the decision flow and decision-making. Therefore, I choose to discuss deliberate decisions and the decision flow in chapters 12 and 12.1.

In this chapter segment, I address the workflow and information flow. I do this in conjunction with decision-flow. The discussion cuts across the product line strategizing process and all other subprocesses in the full product development and management architecture.

Mapping the Flow

When I ask companies about their product development and management processes, I often hear responses suggesting a flow of work that needs to happen. What comes to mind for many people is a Gantt chart detailing work steps anchored by deliverables and milestones. It's about completing tasks related to a project. This is good. Thankfully, many companies do this well. In product line management, however, the workflow is about multiple products and projects, not just one.

The product line roadmap gives a high-level view of the workflow product line teams should focus on. But roadmaps don't address resourcing issues. Nor do they deal with uncertainties related to tasks and deliverables. For this, teams need to rely on project management practices coupled to process flows.

Many experts have written about, taught, and set up good project management practices related to product development and dealing with unknowns. I do not wish to dive into this. For those who wish more insight on the topic, I suggest checking out the Project

Management Institute (PMI). PMI is a professional association that offers many resources on the topic.

For our purposes, I wish to explore process flows tied to good project management. The contributing flows matter a great deal. These address work, information, and decisions across all subprocesses and the full architecture. When setting up the contributing flows or working to improve them, I recommend teams first deal with the flows separately before merging and streamlining them.

Deconstructing Flows

The preferred order for such process "deconstruction" is first to lay out needed documents and deliverables. Next, add the work, at a high-level, needed to create the documents and deliverables. For example, developing a tangible product will need to deliver a bill of material (BOM.) Much work must go on by different functions to create a BOM. The work is always unique to the business, its business model, and the industry. Nonetheless, this work will flow from certain design documents considered predecessor deliverables.

Smart process flow deconstruction, for individual developments, will extend through an offering's whole life cycle. This begins with crafting targets for innovation (Product Innovation Charters--PICs) as part of product line strategizing. It then extends across development and launch, and through in-market management and retirement. But recognize this is for a single product. To improve product lines, organizations must also address different product types, from incremental to radical. Also, new processes need to address new platform-levers, new generations of platform-levers, and technology building blocks.

The *PLuS Framework* changes traditional process flows. It pushes certain work and decisions to be done earlier. Many experts and academics argue the benefits and avoidance of problems from doing this.[58] [59] The new approach never starts with a concept. Instead, it begins with a charter for a product, platform-lever, or technology building blocks.

Sometimes an executive, customer, or someone else will propose a concept for development. In such cases, the *PLuS Framework* calls for a team to translate the idea into a "potential charter." Work then takes place to shape the potential charter for fit with the product line strategy. A decision follows about whether the charter, not the concept, is worth placing on the product line's roadmap. Doing so is a deliberate and openly communicated decision.

For an individual project, the flow of documents starts with a potential innovation charter. Work continues with building out the charter's core parts: an objective, a purpose in strategy, and development guidelines to fit within the strategy. Document deliverables also need an assessment of the economic value and risk toward realizing that value. A management group then assesses the information and data. They decide whether the innovation charter should become "invested" and placed on the product line roadmap. If not, the management group must decide whether the innovation charter should be revamped, delayed, or shelved. (See Figure 11.4.1.)

---

58 Wheelwright, S. C., and K. B. Clark. Leading Product Development: The Senior Manager's Guide to Creating and Shaping the Enterprise. New York: Free Press, 1995.

59 "Why Firefighting Is Never Enough: Preserving High Quality in Product Development." Black, Laura J., and Nelson P. Repenning. System Dynamics Review Vol. 17, No. 1 (2001): 33-62.

Figure 11.4.1: Document Flow in the Front-end

This diagram displays an example of how documents flow in the front-end, between product line strategizing and staged development. Work and decisions or judgment happen before and after each document. Notice the Product Innovation Charter evolution from potential to invested to developed.

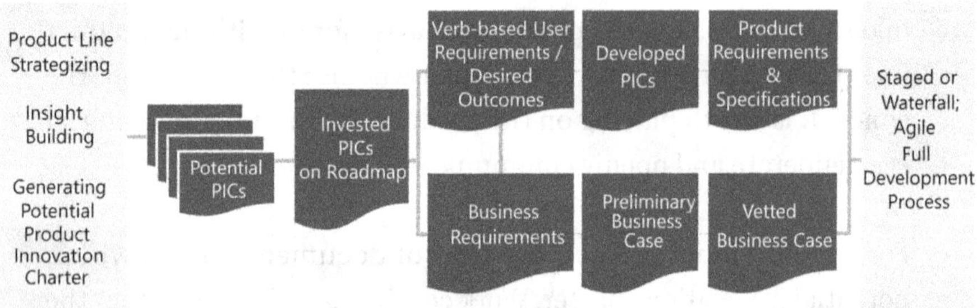

Once on a roadmap, a product innovation charter (PIC) will need resources to move forward, hopefully to become a development project. This is a unique principle of the *PLuS Framework*. When potential PICs advance, they also enter the project-portfolio management process. It is here that resources get assigned. It is also here that managers review details about status and deliverables. Note how in the *PLuS Framework* portfolio, management includes what, in traditional practice, were front-end projects separated from portfolio management oversight. This is a notable advancement.

Often, managers who work with traditional approaches like open innovation and intrapreneurship argue against this approach. They believe including front-end projects in portfolio and resource management decisions stifles creativity. Doing so, they say, hurts value creation. In the *PLuS Framework*, however, concept generation is driven by, not independent from, the product line strategy. The question is whether the activity will advance a product line's Strategy-Essence. And the answer to this question needs to be deliberate and purposeful.

Creative projects, those known to diverge from existing product lines, need their own path. They should not be tethered to a product line. Nor should the product line be burdened by them. Here is where the business growth portfolio and end-run approaches like intrapreneurship become so important. If warranted, business unit management needs to support these efforts separate from the product lines. More to the point, such support should not be with the same resources needed for successful product line strategy execution. And in keeping with business strategy, such projects should be focused on building completely new product lines, not just adding separate products into existing lines.

Matching Subprocess Flows

Deconstructing process flows reveals another interesting principle regarding the *PLuS Framework*. It's that teams and their organizations must recognize that all subprocesses in the full architecture relate to one another. Work conducted, information generated, and decisions made in one process can affect what's happening in the other subprocesses.

Consider, for example, that validation work on a new platform-lever suggests flaws that require notable resources and time to correct. The outcome of this work could impact everything the product line team has underway. It might change the Strategy-Essence, the Execution Roadmap, and portfolio resource allocation. It depends on the project. Yet, at times, outcomes from even well-done work can reverberate across a product line.

The same is true about changes to a roadmap. An accumulation of many small changes across projects can greatly impact the strategy. I refer to this as "roadmap entropy." It is a normal occurrence that if left unmanaged leads to product line chaos.

The *PLuS Framework* stresses management and oversight of changes and entropy influences both within and across the subprocesses. By doing this, the framework seeks to unify the full architecture's subprocesses, so they operate as a whole.

This then leads to the final part of the *PLuS Framework*, its roof. As I discuss in the next chapter, the roof is about deliberate decision-making and clear governance of product line strategies and their execution.

Portfolio Management & Roadmap Responsibility

One of the most important changes that the *PLuS Framework* places on the product development process comes with the need to unify project-portfolio management and roadmap management. These seemingly different subprocesses are two sides of the same coin. If a product line's roadmap changes, the implication is that resources must shift to make that change. However, shifting resources from project to project has been in the portfolio management domain. Similarly, if a current project hits a snag, the portfolio management process may seek to shift resources to correct the situation. That's fine, except the resource shift may cause the roadmap to fall off track if it is not taken into account.

The recourse calls for portfolio management and roadmap management to be carried out by the same group within an organization. (I also made this case in Chapter 8.3.) Most large organizations have a group, perhaps a PMO, in charge of portfolio management tasks. With the new product line strategy approach, tracking and assuring updates to roadmaps should be assumed by this group. It is, without question, a major addition to the portfolio management team's role and responsibility.

Similar to portfolio management, the new Roadmap Management team is not responsible for making decisions. Rather, it is responsible for collecting and analyzing data. And it assumes responsibility for analyzing potential scenarios of both portfolios and roadmaps, and making recommendations accordingly. No doubt this is a major job in many organizations.

Implementing for Rapid Gains and Orchestrating the Flow

The Process Foundation

PRODUCT LINE STRATEGY: GETTING TO GOOD

Seek to:

Build a fluid process that continually works to improve the line. Use a Design Thinking approach to understanding and responsiveness. Use Agile methods with *PLuS Lenses* to address uncertainties.

- Enable the transition from facts and data to insights and foresights; focus on purposely forming smart insights quickly.
- Use methods and practices (lenses) to speed fact-gathering and insight-development.
- Deconstruct the process into a workflow, an information flow, and a decision flow. Work to streamline the flows as an interrelated set.

Connect the process to front-end concept generation; staged/waterfall and agile development, and project portfolio management.

Test your organization's assumptions about your product line and its relation to customers, competitors, and technologies.

Chapter 12

Making Deliberate Choices and Strategy Moves: The *PLuS Framework* Roof

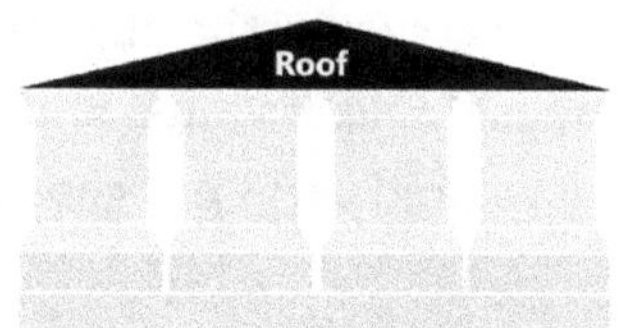

I HAVE ARGUED THROUGHOUT this book that creating and carrying out good product line strategy is vital for most companies' growth. It's clear that top management knows this, and that's why there is an increased focus on product lines and their strategies. To me, good product line strategy is what enables large- and medium-sized companies to compete successfully in multiple markets over the long run.

In the previous chapters, I've laid out four pillars and a foundation to the *PLuS Framework*. Together these work to create strong product line strategies that are also flexible and responsive to change. The goal is to ensure long-term success and growth.

The *PLuS Framework* encourages managers to make "pivots" and major changes when conditions call for them. Although it's possible to use workarounds, as discussed in Chapter 2, these are not as effective as creating a product line strategy that responds to conditions and opportunities. A smart strategy can create a major change in direction for an organization. Going outside the company, however, is often only a stopgap measure.

To pull off any strategy, however, management teams must make deliberate choices. Product line strategy is no different. Each part of the Strategy-Essence is a choice. It doesn't matter if you keep things as they are or if you radically alter them. It's a choice. And this choice always involves a platform-lever, attribute positioning, and chain-link alignment.

What goes on the roadmap and what doesn't is also a choice. The same is true for the objectives you set and the measurements you make. Managers must make these choices deliberately if they wish to form and carry out good product line strategy.

The Decision Flow

The roof of the *PLuS Framework* works to coalesce deliberate decisions and choices. It purposely guides decision-making as a flow from forming product line strategies to carrying them out. And notably, it ties product line decisions to business strategy.

A product line strategy's decision flow is a set of events where managers, whether low-level or senior, make choices, declare decisions, or fund investments. Consider, for example, the gate meetings within a staged development process. Coordinating and aligning these decision points sets them up as a decision flow for development projects.

For product line strategies, the decision flow goes further. It includes portfolio management, roadmap management, and forming the Strategy-Essence. And it extends to front-end idea generation and back-end life cycle management. Most important, it links to business strategy planning and refinement.

Seeing and communicating the decision flow both as a whole and in its parts is important. Teams do this as part the framework, what I refer to as its roof. It involves compiling and analyzing a series of spreadsheets to deconstruct the full set of decisions and choices. Each spreadsheet reflects a decision point. It shows which managers make each decision or choice, and what information they can expect to have.

The framework intentionally calls out all decisions, choices, and investments. It makes each a deliberate statement. Individual managers or an executive can't add projects into development or onto a roadmap without purposely and openly doing so. This can be a valuable step forward for many product lines. It helps minimize project creep and its first cousin, portfolio chaos. It also requires strategy moves to be purposeful. They should not be an unintended collection from appeasing key executives or individual customers.

Deliberate strategy decisions make a Strategy-Essence become crystal clear. This can be powerful. It enables chain-link alignment, attribute positioning, and platform-levers to be understood and ready for action. This is critical to crafting superior strategy with improved execution and more-impactful results.

It's Not Easy

Here is a heads-up to all managers who want to be involved in making deliberate decisions. Choosing one path over another always leaves someone disappointed, disillusioned, or downright mad, and it's hard to be objective about this across the board. People can have their entire professional lives wrapped up in certain projects or activities. Dealing with this is part of the leadership role.

Thinking the leadership role is only consensus management is a mistake. Sure, people might be happy when everyone falls into line and agrees with the choices. Strategy by consensus, however, tends not to be good strategy. Happy people with bad strategy is a great way to shorten careers.

Making good product line strategy demands smart, insightful choices tied to rigorous follow-through. This calls for leadership and collaboration at the product line team level. It's not just about assigning tasks and compiling outputs. It's also about guiding and shaping, molding, and morphing. It's about judgments and decisions on the smallest of things. It's also about governance of the whole. These don't just happen on their own. Leadership is crucial.

Top management's effect on product line strategy choices and follow-through is always significant. Governance with an inadequate understanding of business and product line strategies is a problem. However, I have rarely seen all functional leaders share a collective understanding. Without question, most know their own and other chain-links' contributions to business strategy. But great business strategy governance demands a *full* understanding. To gain advantage from good product line strategy, top managers across all roles must recognize and understand the strategy and the desired actions that make it possible.

What Moves, When?

Most managers have heard consultants, gurus, and academics sound smart by giving names to strategy moves. You'll hear titles like "dominant," "differentiated," "disruptive," and "sustaining." Or you may hear discussions about being a fast mover or fast follower, a price leader or a performance leader. These descriptors give context to communicating about strategy but are seldom the starting point. Plus, they tend not to describe a product line's whole approach over time, but rather a single product's approach or a platform-lever's role at a given point in time.

In product line strategy, conjuring up and creating alternatives is as important as making deliberate choices. Without alternatives, there is no choice. In fact, creating alternatives is itself a choice. This work starts with the exploration and formation of the Strategy-Essence and its three parts. It involves looking at how teams divide their markets and how attributes position products within each resulting segment. The product approach within each segment can and likely will be different. Plus, over time that approach or any single-product strategy can and should change.

The same is true for platform-levers, also part of the Strategy-Essence. Each platform-lever has a life cycle. As it advances toward maturity and decline, certain actions may be more beneficial than others. Choices about those actions must be deliberate and take into account the impact on attribute positioning and chain-link alignment.

Building scenarios about how choices might play out on roadmaps and in the market can help guide choices. This too is part of the strategizing process and links directly with the *PLuS Framework's* roof.

Governance Versus Day-to-Day Choices

All product lines and their strategies need good oversight. Some call this governance. At the same time, those managers working on specific tasks must also make choices like "use this software code or routine rather than some other approach." Without these choices, projects will freeze. What's important to recognize is that governance and day-to-day choices are part of the same decision flow. Without good day-to-day choices and good governance, there won't be good product line strategy.

The issue, though, is that day-to-day choices tend to relate to a single project. Governance, on the other hand, relates to the whole product line. This is like comparing the single project decision flow with the product line plurality decision flow. They're different, yet each affects the other.

When advancing product line strategies, the issue is usually about transferring understanding of governance into day-to-day choices, not the other way around. I do not mean this from a perspective of governance dictating choices. Rather, it is better for smart governance based on good product line strategy to influence day-to-day choices. Such influence should help keep individual projects as strong contributors to good product line strategy. It also helps avoid ending up with great individual products being hampered by the product line strategy.

Using the Framework

I lay out the *PLuS Framework* in a format that aids teaching and communicating product line strategy. It's accessible and understandable from the bottom of the organization to the top and across all functions. It provides a lexicon that's specific to product lines and their tie-ins to business strategy, and to creating and evaluating potential moves. It provides the models to think about its distinct parts. And it's flexible enough to embed into organizational practice. Once the *PLuS Framework* is in place, it will enable teams and executive leaders to make smart and deliberate choices for good product line strategy.

Moving forward with the framework is itself a deliberate choice. But to get to that decision, many people in the organization need to learn about it. This calls for workshops, training, reading, and, most important, following through with action. No organization easily jumps to the end-game of developing great strategies. First, leadership has to recognize a need for improvement. It also must see how its organization needs to learn what improvements are all about. This should happen even before stepping on the ladder to develop more-impactful product line strategies. This is a serious climb, demanding many deliberate choices.

But remember, it's worth it. The *PLuS Framework* will yield powerful results. It will enable product lines to grow market share. It will help increase customer satisfaction and will improve cash flow while using resources more effectively. All of these are important goals for organizations committed to long-term growth.

12.1: Governance and the Decision Flow

Making deliberate decisions and choices is key to good product line strategy. So too are oversight and **governance** *(Definition Alert.)* They're so important that, together, governance and decision-making form the roof of the *PLuS Framework.*

DEFINITION ALERT:
Governance Flow

Governance is the act of setting and managing policies, principles, and rules. Governance is carried out by members of a governing committee or team. Members are usually executives or senior management.

Governance and decision-making are managerial partners of two separate but intertwined topics: policy and strategy. Policy is about rules, principles, and setting roles. Policy sets guidance and orientation. Strategy is about objectives and methods. Strategy drives action. In large organizations, policy and strategy are more powerful together than apart. Let's explore why and how this affects product line performance.

What is Governance?

Try a word game with me. Put the word "governance" behind any of these words or terms: Corporate, IT, Innovation, Health and Safety, Human Resource, ISO, Technology, and Product Line Strategy. You'll see it matches up in a buzzword-like manner. That's fine so long as we can get at its meaning.

Governance is leadership, shepherding, and encouraging. It is about setting the stage and giving players reassurance in their actions. Let's be clear, though. In large organizations, governance is meaningless without decision-making. Somehow decisions must be made.

First, though, governance needs to set clear roles and responsibilities toward decision-making. And most important, good governance sets decision-making authority, or, as some call it, **decision rights** *(Definition Alert.)*

DEFINITION ALERT:
Decision Rights

A decision right is the authority and responsibility to make specific decisions, choices, or judgments. A governance body empowers managers with decision rights.

In their book *Innovation Governance*, Jean Philippe Deschamps and Beebe Nelson lay out the topic in relation to innovation in general, not product lines. In case after case, the book shows how senior executives carry out governance. The cases describe setting up oversight, enabling processes, providing guidance, and settling roles and responsibilities. And it's about removing obstacles and installing rewards.

Governance allows the doers in an organization to create workflows, decision-flows, and whole frameworks. And it's governance that sets up boards, committees, and councils to create linkages across practices and functions.

Smart governance is key to good product line strategy. That's because it allows setting up approaches like the *PLuS Framework*. This includes the strategizing process. As part of this, governance also sets roles and responsibilities associated with product line decisions. Here, we see decision rights—declaring who has responsibility and authority to make certain decisions—as critical to a product line. Good product line strategies come from doing this smartly.

To underscore this point, consider the opposite. Lack of good governance leaves decision-making unclear. In such cases, organizations struggle to gain intense focus on a platform-lever. Or they dance around the need for deliberate attribute positioning. And, when overbearing governance demands decision-making only at the top of an organization, product line strategies also suffer. Actions bog down while awaiting decisions, after which those doing work may need to deal with inconsistencies and incoherencies.

Who Governs and Who Decides

Governance for product lines always comes from the top of a business unit. The common governing body is the business unit head, plus her direct reports. Typically, these are functional heads, those that comprise the business unit's chain-link strategy.

It may be heresy to say this in many organizations, but often the governing body is incapable of making good product line decisions. This isn't because they're not smart enough. It's because they don't have, nor should they be expected to have, the knowledge, information, or relevant skills for any single decision. This is perhaps the most significant factor making the practices within large companies different than practices in small companies. It's also the biggest problem small companies must overcome to become big companies.

Over my career working for big companies, I have heard more than one top executive state "I do not believe in processes" or "I've had my fill with frameworks. Just do your work." These comments do not reflect realities or the need for good governance. Often such comments come from a strong, positive "can-do" entrepreneurial mindset. But unfortunately, this mindset can seep into an organization's culture. It can drive behaviors that act counterproductively to good product line strategy.

Governance should recognize the need for others, lower in the organization, to make decisions. At the same time, governance should channel entrepreneurial and intrapreneurial support into ring-fenced work. This work should not sidetrack existing product line strategies.

Let's be clear. Entrepreneurial work should not be slowed down by a single product line's strategy. Nor should a product line's strategy lose its focus on platform-levers and market segments to help entrepreneurial freedom. This is why governance becomes so important. Governance needs to make both approaches work, and it should do so concurrently. Many experts refer to this as enabling an ambidextrous organization.[60] In fact, keeping a focus on product lines is why the *PLuS Framework's* fourth pillar ties product line strategy to the business growth portfolio. It's within the business unit strategy and its growth portfolio that both product lines and entrepreneurial work gain purpose.

Before going too much further, I'd be lax to not address one key question. Does the governing body ever make product line decisions? Yes, it does. These individuals, because they sit at the top of a business unit, must remove their governance hat and put on their decision-making hat when needed. In good product line strategies, this can be for key project selections, approvals, and investments. It is also key for Strategy-Essence changes.

Why Decision Flow?

Setting up decision-making seldom is about making one decision isolated from other decisions. Rather it is series of decisions, choices, and judgments that connect. Every **decision flow** *(Definition Alert)* produces a series of results or choices, even if it is to do nothing.

Let's look at product line decision-making in a simple way. In good product line strategies, governance sets up a clearly defined decision flow. Those given responsibility to make decisions should do so using fact-based information. And when such information runs dry, they should use their best judgment before reverting to intuition. Teams

60 Tushman, Michael L., Wendy K. Smith, and Andrew Binns. "The Ambidextrous CEO." Harvard Business Review, 89 no. 6 (June 2011)

then record all decisions and communicate them to all managers who might be impacted.

The Full Architecture

Allow me to reference the Full Architecture of Product Development again. I presented this in Chapter 11.1. This is a set of subprocesses that make for good product line strategy and good roadmap execution. Each subprocess and the connection between them have points at which decisions must be made. Please consider its decision flow a series of choices or judgments that advance individual projects and the strategy as a whole. (A principle I've learned in consulting is that if you wish to improve a company's product development productivity, first improve the decision flow.)

DEFINITION ALERT:
Decision Flow

A decision flow is a series of decisions that result in multiple related actions. The decisions made across multiple gates in a state-and-gate development process is an example of a decision flow.

Figure 12.1.1: Decision Flow in Full Product Development Architecture

This is the same as diagram as 11.1 but with decisions points added and the workflows faded. Focus on the diamond shapes. Together, they create the full architecture's decision flow. Governance sets the decision flow, assigns responsibilities, and grants authority (decision rights) to make it work.

Getting it Right

Pointing to governance mistakes in some organizations can be like saying "the emperor has no clothes." But I don't mean this to point at one top manager. Rather, it's the collective responsibility of the whole executive suite—the top person and her direct reports. Yet governance shortcomings do happen. And, they can be costly. Let me give an example.

When governance pushes certain decisions too low in the organization, problems arise. Consider the governance mistake many companies have made toward a product development phase or gate reviews. This process is geared to manage project risk. At each gate, managers decide whether projects should move forward to the next work "stage." Let's say a following stage of work costs $10,000 to complete. This means the decision makers are choosing to invest $10,000 in more work.

The error is made when selecting gatekeepers—the decision makers. The thinking is "this is $10,000; just put a decision team together where each person has authority to spend $10,000." There are two problems with this, though. First, by governance enabling this approach, the following gates will have managers more senior in authority. The next decision gates might need $50,000, $300,0000, and $1MM authority levels. The issue is that managers with more seniority tend to second-guess less-senior managers. This is natural, and, from my experience, to be expected. The result is that those projects going through this decision approach have a great likelihood of cycling back at each stage. Each successive set of decision makers is likely to second-guess previous decision makers. This does not help any product line or its strategy.

The second issue starts right at the beginning of staged development processes. Here, many companies begin the process with the selection of what to work on. If those making the selection are low in the organization, it's unlikely they will select large projects. When governance enables this, don't expect new platform-levers or major market segment moves to happen. In fact, it's much more likely many more small projects will be allowed to enter development. This can be a surefire approach to clogging development pipelines. It can cause very difficult portfolio management problems.

But when governance keeps all decision at the top of a business unit, product lines can stall. This approach causes decision-making to become a bottleneck in getting work done. You'll know this to be the case when you hear statements like "let's wait to see what '_____' says." (Fill in the blank with the name of a senior executive.) Or, someone will say "we'll know which way we're going after the governance council meets two months from now." And while this can be good for some circumstances, always pushing decisions to the top will surely stall product line actions.

These are not decision-making mistakes. They're governance mistakes. They reflect faults in setting decision authority and responsibility. Without doing so clearly, decision-making becomes a burden on product line strategies.

Table 12.1.1 below lists good governance actions and deliberate decisions that, together, make for good product line strategy.

Coupled with anchoring decision rights and decision flows, good governance also makes sure the resulting decisions are smart. And governance should make sure decision-making, like other parts of the business, continuously improves. Here's what's needed for good product line strategy decision-making.

- Map the decision flow graphically. Show decision or judgment points, and who has a role in and who carries responsibility for the decisions. This should visually communicate decision points and involvement of boards, councils, approval committees, and review teams.
- Each player in the decision flow should have deep understanding and knowledge of the whole product line, its Strategy-Essence, and Execution Roadmap. Plus, each player must recognize and embrace the product line purpose and contribution to overall business strategy.
- Roles on the decision-making body must be clear, spelling out responsibilities for each member. Each decision-making body should have one final decider—a person assigned responsibility for the decision.
- All decision flows need rules of exception. These are unique or exceptional situations that demand sidestepping the normal flow to get to the top of the business unit as soon as possible. Clarifying the exception path is a hallmark of a good decision flow.

Table 12.1.1

Some Key Governance Actions	Some Deliberate Decisions
Embracing the PLuS Framework, being engaged throughout implementation	What is and is not a platform-lever, and the best form for each fulcrum
Approving and declaring roles and responsibilities related to the Framework and the product lines	Which market segments (noun- and verb-oriented) on which to position attributes
Structuring (or restructuring) the organization	The Strategy-Essence, what it is
Defining decision rights (decision authority)	Pivots and roadmap recasts
Funding and resourcing	Who works on which project, at what time
Rewarding individual managers	The roadmap and project scheduling
Oversight of chain-link alignment	Innovation charter progression
Orchestrating business strategy and the business growth portfolio	Starting and terminating projects

Governing bodies do not actually set up decision flows. Rather, they empower others, lower in the organization, to figure out what works best. This empowerment is critical to effective design and implementation, as you'll see in the next several chapters. During design and rollout, those creating the decision flow need to ensure that process workflows and information flows feed into and match the decision flow. Nonetheless, the governing body is responsible for making sure the decision flow is streamlined and clearly understood.

Each decision point within a flow has several common parts. Yet for each decision point, there may be different people involved. Figure 12.1.2 lays out the common parts.

Figure 12.1.2: Decision-Making Roles and Responsibilities

There is a common set of roles and responsibilities for every decision. First, scenario creators and choice recommenders provide input to a decision-making body. Within the decision-making body, a single person holds the "rights" and responsibility for the decision. Analyzers and approvers work within the body to influence and guide the decision maker. The decisions then move to performers who carry out actions associated with the decision.

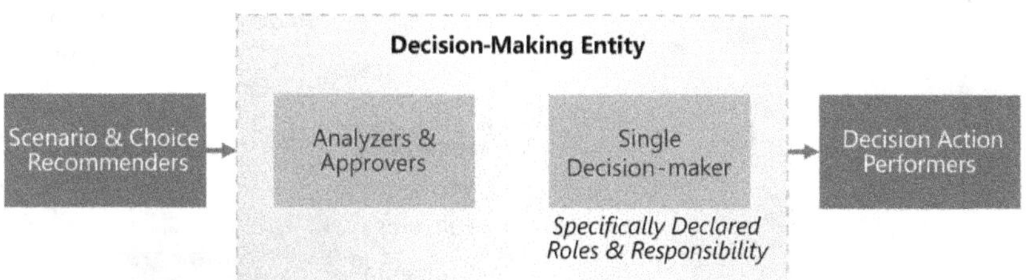

Table 12.1.2: Example: Decision Rights Within Product Line Strategy

Contributors		Product Line		Top Management	
Individual Contributors	Development Project Teams	Product Line Strategizing Team	Product Line Team (Function)	BU Management	BU Governance Body
Problem-Solving Approaches	Design choices	Growth Segments	Roadmaps	Strategy- Essence parts & union of parts	Framework Implementation
Creativity Approaches	Knowledge Interpretations	Platform-lever Generations	Roadmap Recasts	Strategy Essence Pivots	Decision Rights
Problem Definitions	Scrum Judgments	Roadmap Milestones	Gate Review Meetings	Chain-link alignment	Ringfencing work

Contributors	Product Line		Top Management	
Quality Reviews	Potential PICs	Project Prioritization	Project Portfolio Management	Roles & Responsibility Assignment
Milestone Determination	Technology Readiness Ranking	Technology Building Block Selection	Business Growth Portfolio	Organization Structure
Readiness	Issue and Insight Ranking	Objectives	Business Unit Strategy	Approval or Disapproval of Process Metrics
		Platform-Levers & Fulcrums		
		Segmentation (Noun & Verb)		
		Life cycle PIM Termination		
		PIC Selection		

Recognize the four contributors to each decision point.

1. Scenario and Choice Recommenders. These are managers who do work to create or identify the decision to be made, lay out possible decision alternatives, and recommend possible decision(s). The quality of this group's work and input to decision-making affect how smart each resulting decision may be.
2. Analyzers and Approvers: These managers aid and influence decision-making. They use knowledge, understanding, and experience to debate possible decisions.
3. Single Decision Maker: The governance body assigns this person the responsibility for making certain decisions. This

person holds the decision rights for that decision. Good decision flows do not cause the manager to share the role.

4. Performers: These managers carry out the work that results from the decision.

Good decision-making spells out who's responsible for the four roles for each decision point. Individual performance appraisal would then review the thoroughness and quality by which those assigned the roles perform.

For high-level or top management decisions, there is a fifth role that is often overlooked. This is a person to administer the decision point. That person's responsibility is to set up the decision meeting, encourage the quality of the input, and record conclusions.

Throughout the decision flow, participants may overlap as members of different decision-making bodies. This is helpful because it aids fluidity of the flow. Members know why, or at least should know why, other decisions were made. They also should understand information and insights that contributed to those decisions. This helps make sure decisions align, and the flow does not become disjointed.

Inputs, Outputs, and Decision Types

It's important to recognize different decision types for creating and keeping good product line strategies. You'll see decisions handled much differently lower in the organization than at the top. But decisions also have common parts needing to be tracked.

Consider decisions and choices in a staged development process. Some may be formal gate decisions. Others are less formal reviews and project choices. They happen within stages, not at gates. The same is true in the strategizing process, roadmap management, and portfolio management. Some are formal. Some are less formal. But all decisions always have inputs and outputs.

Organizations often overlook an important part of decisions: recording both the decision and the decision rationale. In good decision flows, the decision record is a key output of each decision. It should capture six facts.

1. What decision was made?
2. What actions are expected from the decision?
3. Who made the decision? (the decision maker with decision rights)
4. Who were the scenario and choice recommenders?
5. Who were the analyzers and approvers? Who influenced the decision?
6. Why was the decision preferred? What is the rationale for the decision?

The decision record helps communicate outcomes and track the decision flows. But most important, an analysis of a full set of records helps to improve the whole process.

Deliberate Decision-making

Smart, deliberate decisions are critical to good product line strategy. That's why the *PLuS Framework's* roof works to ensure involvement with decision-makers and the business unit's governing body. It does this by setting up decision rights and responsibilities, while streamlining decision flows coupled to work and information flows.

Implementing for Rapid Gains and Orchestrating the Flow

Making Deliberate Decisions

PRODUCT LINE STRATEGY: GETTING TO GOOD

Seek to:

Make deliberate choices, decisions, and investments regarding the product line. Do not enable happenstance decisions to mount.

- Communicate the deliberate decisions when they happen to all involved with the product line.

All decisions must tie to the product line strategy and its execution and to the business unit strategy.

Understand your decision flow and its match to a work flow and information flow. This flow will include portfolio management, roadmap management, and forming the Strategy-Essence.

A governing body of top executives needs to oversee and set "decision rights" for each product line. This gives key managers specific authority to make certain decisions within the decision flow.

SECTION 5

IMPLEMENTING THE *PLuS FRAMEWORK*™

Realizing Profound Gains

How to Set Up and Gain Benefit from Good Product Line Strategy

- Organizational Change and Change Management
- Integrating Into, not Against, Current Practices
- The Big Reason Behind Great Roll-outs
- SpiralUp™ Capability Maturity Levels
- The Value Proposition
- Guidelines for Successful Implementations

CHAPTER 13

Implementing The *PLuS Framework*™

IN LARGE ORGANIZATIONS, it's humorously common to hear people use the idiom "you can't teach an old dog new tricks." Even today's old dogs used that phrase when they were young. The problem here, though, is not about the dog. And it's not about the trick. It's about the teaching.

Building the new trick, in our case the *PLuS Framework*, is only partially about teaching. Rather, you'll see it's mostly about designing, doing, and improving. Implementing this new trick for good product line strategies is not a "one and done" job. Don't expect to go to workshops, read a few books, or scan online templates and consider the implementation complete.

As we watch the generational mix within large companies shift from Baby Boomers to Baby Busters to Millennials, and to Gen Z, we see many values have changed. But there are two values I believe are still common. The first is that each generation always wants the previous generation to change. Consider, for example, how organizational change as a topic began with research and efforts in the years before and after World War II. Change was the call-to-order for the Baby Boomers who brought us Positioning Strategy, Staged Development, and Intrapreneurship. Even new-age-like Agile practices were brought to us by a mainly Baby Boomer cast, sprinkled with a few Busters.

The second common value is almost the opposite. Once in positions of authority, people tend to seek a steady state. They do this by pushing harder on the same practices and behaviors that got them in their position. This is to be expected: If you got promoted by doing a job well, it makes sense to do more of what you've been doing. Now, simply do it better. In some ways, this is like saying the change agents evolve to be old dogs.

Herein lies the challenge. Getting the new *PLuS Framework* installed and functional calls for a notable organizational effort. It starts with top management, those who govern the business unit and head up each function. Let's face it: If you consider yourself a top manager in a large organization, the onus for change is on your shoulders.

My call-to-action for top managers is to understand the framework and its parts and put it to work in your organization and business. Without a solid understanding, the framework offers little value. Most important, however, is recognizing how a less-than-stellar product line strategy sells your organization short. You forgo creating an economic moat, building stronger business strategy, and delivering greater shareholder value.

Adapt not Adopt

I am not suggesting your organization adopt the framework. I am rather suggesting you adapt the framework. Adapting is much more helpful than adopting. The idea is to make the framework work for your organization, not the other way around.

To start the implementation discussion, let me share few important principles right away. I call these "Implementation Facts." You may consider reinventing the wheel about these, but before doing so, consider my experience. These are truths or facts about implementation, not just suggestions. In the next chapters I delve into the facts. I explain them and give actions to deal with them.

Consider, please:

- **Fact 1**: Implementation is about change. Changing how a company works and makes decisions is taxing because it bumps up against an organization's culture—its behaviors and norms. Deploying new practices using sound principles toward organizational change is important.
- **Fact 2**: The *PLuS Framework* must interact with other subprocesses. The full benefit of the *PLuS Framework* accrues only by setting up the full architecture. Your organization is likely to have many pieces of this in place, just not aligned and streamlined in a manner helpful to creating and keeping good product line strategies. And a full architecture's details—its flows and decision points—are always unique to each organization.
- **Fact 3**: Creating and improving product line strategy is itself an Agile process. It has a workflow, information flow, and decision flow. But these flows need to be flexible and adaptable to insights and needs, plus the need to cut across the four-pillar *PLuS Framework*. Then, as an organization's capability maturity increases, they too must advance. Gaining benefit tracks with building strategizing capability.
- **Fact 4**: Top managers' involvement is more important than commitment. The measured time top managers take part

in the framework implementation will make or break the initiative. Top management is the set of senior managers who head each chain-link function and those who govern the business unit.

- **Fact 5**: Implementations should advance one skill level at a time. This helps keep framework components working in unison. Jumping ahead on one skill can be counterproductive. Adept's maturity model helps keep implementation on track.

Let me knock out a common misconception about implementation. You can't train or teach your way through implementations. However, building a shared understanding of the *PLuS Framework*—what it is, how it works, and what to expect—is critical. Training contributes to this, especially among top managers. But training by itself cannot realize the desired benefits of good product line strategy. For this, we need more.

All implementations start with the same first task—to figure out what to change, how big a job it is, and whether it's worth it. As simple and straightforward as this seems, the results greatly influence the change effort. The four areas to look at are:

- Structural changes to the organization.
- Process changes or additions to the full architecture of product development and management.
- Information and data systems to support and enable new practices.
- Knowledge, understanding, and awareness.

Although there are many details in each grouping, the biggest issue is communicating the need for and potential value of the change. Let's look at what makes for a good implementation.

13.1: Organizational Change and Change Management

Putting the *PLuS Framework* into practice demands, to one degree or another, an organization to change. Work, decisions, and information use will be different. Yet a collective norm for organizations is to avoid change. For change to succeed, people must support the approach and be motivated to overcome their natural resistance to change.

Fact 1: To Gain Benefit, Companies Must Change

Behaviors that inhibit change are normal. They can be found in every meeting, email, or decision. Our challenge is to redirect or overcome that force. Let's take a look at what the research and experts tell us about this challenge.

Concern about organizational change goes back as far as World War II. Kurt Lewin's research, conducted at MIT in the 1940s, is foundational to understanding how to change an organization.[61] Lewin focused on forces that drive or hinder change. He points out how organizations must "unfreeze" from a current state before the change occurs. This unfreezing, he points out, eases the move toward a new steady state.

Lewin's work explains how unfreezing an organization demands purposeful actions. People, he says, should sense the future state gain plus the current state pain as greater than the cost of change. If they

61 Lewin, Kurt (June 1947). "Frontiers in Group Dynamics: Concept, Method and Reality in Social Science; Social Equilibria and Social Change."

don't, change is unlikely. The pain, gain, and cost of change are inputs to Lewin's change equation. (See Figure 13.1.)

Figure 13.1: The Organizational Change Equation

Implementation teams "unfreeze" their organizations and induce change by influencing views that the left-hand side of the equation is greater than the right-hand side.

of current practice | of desired practice | both economic and psychological

PAIN of inadequate Product Line Strategy (Seek to increase perceptions)

Derived from: Project and Productivity Analyses Internal Interviews External Benchmarking

GAIN from executing good Product Line Strategy (Seek to increase perceptions)

Derived from: Conducting In-Use Case Analyses Summary Literature Reviews External Presentations

COST OF CHANGE (Seek to lower perceptions)

Derived from: Using Expert Facilitation Involvement / Participative Design Following SpiralUp Capability Maturity Model

The equation's right-hand side shows the cost of change. It reflects both economic costs and psychological costs people associate with the change. On the left-hand side, the pain and gain reflect opinions toward the current state and a future state. Unfreezing the organization, according to Lewin, is about making the equation's left-hand side greater than the right-hand side.

Working the Change Equation

As you step up to rolling out the framework, first consider who's on the implementation team and the work they must take on. A key part of their job is to take actions and share insights that minimize the perceived cost of change. Are they up to the task? They must be able to influence perceptions toward each side of the equation.

Therefore, those taking on the job should be skilled communicators who understand how to influence others.

Now, consider how many top managers might sense the cost of change. Some might believe a new approach only adds work and slows down important projects. And others might believe the cost of setting up the new approach is too great. An implementation team's job is to "unfreeze" the organization by offsetting these opinions.

When someone suggests the rollout is wasted expense, it implies there is no financial return on the new approach. The implementation team should not let that perception prevail. Here, the recourse is to position the rollout as an investment, not an expense. In good implementations, this happens at the start and through concerted efforts.

Dealing with the psychological cost of change is much different. For example, using the *PLuS Framework* often calls for change to an organization's decision flow. Some decision makers may feel the change is taking away their authority. Undermining authority, if so perceived, will undoubtedly increase the cost of change for certain managers. If some managers sense the cost of change is high, the implementation team should work to make perceptions about pain and gain also be high. They need to "unfreeze" the situation by factually arguing down the cost of change. This can be done by conducting a thorough diagnostic and creating a well-thought-out value proposition.

The Diagnostic

Good diagnostics *(Definition alert)* should reveal the pain an organization endures from not having a good product line strategy. This, as I've explained earlier, shows itself as poor growth and declining impact in the market. It's interesting to note, though, how receiving permission to conduct a diagnostic suggests someone already feels the pain.

Be aware, however, problems can arise when internal managers carry out diagnostics, and other managers don't accept the conclusion. To avoid this, it's best to use an outside expert to conduct diagnostics. Experts will analyze all practices regardless of maturity level and can sidestep internal politics. They'll keep an eye toward identifying key hindrances in finding and developing bigger, better product offerings.

Assessing alignment between product line strategies and other chain-links is also important. It adds to the diagnostic. It gives a broader view that ties product line strategy to business strategy. It makes the diagnostic more relevant to the whole organization.

Going forward and throughout the rollout, implementation teams must figure out actions that influence views about pain, gain, and the cost of change. The idea is to preserve the equation tilt throughout implementation. Because setting up a new approach through all maturity levels may take a few years, the challenge is notable. It's easy to see how problems can occur when key managers leave. And the longer the rollout, the greater the likelihood of top management turnover. But the equilibrium must remain tilted in favor of change no matter the duration.

Implementations = Organizational Change

Implementations are always about organizational change. You shouldn't sidestep this. Instead, it's more helpful to use organizational change principles to boost the implementation.

DEFINITION ALERT:
Diagnostics

Diagnosing a product line's situation is the first step toward its improvement. Experts do this through interviews, data and report analyses, surveys, and comparative benchmarks.

A diagnostic should include:

4. Review and assessment of financials, new-product vitality and other measures and metrics.
5. Assessment of method and approaches for identifying opportunities, developing new offerings, and managing products and services in the market.
6. Review of the product development portfolio including changes in expected value and project slippage.
7. Assessment of coherence of the line on platform-levers, technology building blocks, and market segments.
8. Review and assessment of governance and decision-making.
9. Chain-link alignment assessment.

Results of diagnostics should be candid and presented formally to the organization's top management.

13.2: Integrating Into, not Against, Current Practices: The Full Architecture Is More Than the Sum of Its Parts

The *PLuS Framework* needs good inputs to yield good deliverables. The inputs come from knowledge and insights. The deliverables are innovation targets, the Strategy-Essence, and the Roadmap. As part of the full front-end to back-end architecture, the *PLuS Framework* feeds other practices such as concept generation and business unit planning.

Enjoying good product line strategies and having them add value to your business unit's strategy is a "no-brainer." Who wouldn't want this? But to do so, you also need to consider your existing product development and management processes. For this, the product line strategizing needs to tie into front-end concept building. It also needs to tie into development and portfolio management practices. Together they create the full architecture of product development discussed in chapter 11.

Fact 2: The *Plus Framework* Must Interact With Other Subprocesses

Each subprocess in the full architecture adds to creating and improving product line strategies. And the *PLuS Framework* becomes part of the full architecture. In other words, the subprocesses work together and complement one another. Therefore, to get the most out of the *PLuS Framework*, organizations must work toward setting up the full architecture and integrating its subprocesses.

While the architecture's subprocesses may seem simple to design, gaining consistent use in each is a formidable challenge. Luckily, there is much experience installing a full architecture and its subprocesses. Most companies have a running start on this with existing Staged, Agile, or combined Staged and Agile development processes. Many companies also have established portfolio-management and front-end practices. The challenge is these practices may not be mature or integrated and streamlined. Building maturity while integrating and streamlining practices is a common need in large organizations.

There is a logical order to setting up subprocesses. (See Figure 13.2.1.) It begins with stage- and-gate, or Agile development. Next, companies add portfolio management for those projects in the stage-and-gate, Agile, or hybrid of both development process. Concurrent to portfolio management, yet somewhat delayed, companies also build out front-end practices. This usually starts with flows related to concept-generation methods and approaches.

Streamlining Work, not Burdening Managers

Many top managers express concern about how the full architecture with the *PLuS Framework* adds more work to what they are already doing. But that's not the case. Rather, the full architecture shifts the work. It moves from development to the front-end and into improving product line strategies. It also helps organizations avoid investments in poor projects. The greatest contribution from well-thought-out product line strategies is a shift in focus to the best projects and away from poor projects.

Much work also gets streamlined and "tilted" to the front-end of the full architecture. Consider, for example, creating a business case. Typically, this is stage-two work in the development process. Creating a business case is a major job without sound product line strategy. It's much easier, however, with the *PLuS Framework* in place, because a business case arising from a strong strategy foundation is more about assembling insights than about creating new insights.

Figure 13.2.1: Implementation Progression of Full Architecture Subprocesses

To gain the most from the *PLuS Framework*, an organization should set it up with the other subprocesses within the full architecture discussed in Chapter 11. This diagram portrays the implementation progression.

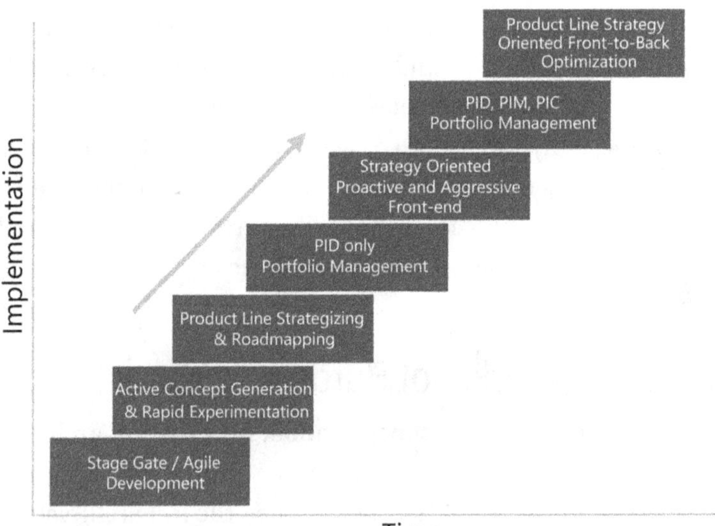

Robust product line strategies also push gains from platform-levers matched to verb-oriented segments and aligned across chain-link strategies. This leverage, as I've laid out in previous chapters, enables faster and more-cost-effective development. It does this by helping avoid product quality and performance issues otherwise addressed in the back-end of development.

All companies have skills to carry out each subprocess. If they did not, they'd likely be out of business. Perhaps product line teams did not coordinate work across functions. Or perhaps they did not streamline decision-making, or focus on a Strategy-Essence.

No matter the case, the seeds of many capabilities exist. The challenge is identifying and advancing these skills.

Implementation is about transforming and advancing current-state skills to address the future state. Shifting work toward improving product line strategy creates an emphasis on critical-to-success (CTS) projects. If the strategy is good, resulting investments should yield greater gains. The goal is to improve the portfolio by aiming for major products.

The goal is to find and develop bigger, better product offerings— or, as I shared in Chapter 4, *bigger, better bubbles.*

Organized Implementation

To make the full architecture work, product line strategizing must deliver innovation charters, the targets for innovation, to front-end concept generation. This is important because it ties product line strategies to development work. A more detailed view of this was shared in Chapter 11.2.

In Figure 13.2.1, notice the overlap of subprocesses. The duration of the full architecture implementation may last a few years. Each subprocess cannot work properly until the full architecture is in place.

After the subprocesses are running, the focus should shift to streamlining the flow between them. This includes workflows, decision flows, and information flows. The approach is to progress toward true front-to-back, full architecture optimization.

Fact 3: Creating and Improving Product Line Strategy Is an Agile Process

In chapter 6, I shared how product line teams have two missions. The first is to formulate and improve strategy. Their second mission is to carry out the strategy and manage the product line. A smart approach is to set up strategizing as a process that strives for continuous improvement. And it's also smart to make sure the process integrates into the full architecture.

The strategizing process includes a flow of strategy explorations called lenses. In the *PLuS Framework*, I call these *PLuS Lenses*. Chapter 11.1 discusses lenses and their flow.

The strategizing process needs an Agile approach more than a staged work effort. Here, product line teams may view each lens as an agile scrum. Output from the scrum-like lens then helps select the next lenses and the work within each. Declaring a full strategizing process in terms of waterfall project management, therefore, is impractical and not helpful.

Each lens chosen by a team needs to be flexible in response to existing insights or the lack of insights. Such adjustments are more art than science. They are about smart strategic thinking—understanding the situation and casting a view to the future. For this, it's important to think through team membership carefully.

Choosing an annual cadence to product line strategizing is common, but not a strict rule. Your key concerns should be in matching the timing of other practices in your organization like creating the annual operating plan or rolling up budget needs. Nonetheless, product line strategizing is more about building from or upon previous work than starting with a clean slate. Therefore, having insights available can be helpful to speeding the strategizing flow. It's why, in chapter 11.2, I stress setting up and using an insight repository.

Iterative Approach

Setting up the strategizing process is about simultaneously doing it and improving how it's done. The goal is to improve the Strategy-Essence and roadmap using insights from previous work as the starting point. And it's to create bigger, better opportunities set up as innovation charters. The only way to achieve these goals is to form better insights. Capability toward strategizing therefore reflects in the quality and importance of insights.

13.3: The Big Reasons Behind Great Roll-outs

How implementation teams carry out the implementation affects the benefits gained. Consider research The Adept Group conducted on setting up the stage/phase gate process.[62]

This research looked at implementations for twenty companies. The research goal was to discover the difference between good and poor implementations. What causes some to yield benefits quickly? And what causes others to drag on without delivering any benefit? Results are displayed in Figure 13.3.1; a scatter chart shows how the companies fared. It shows benefits gained versus implementation duration for each company.

So, what separates good from poor implementations? The answer comes down to one dominant reason.

---

62 "Implementing a Product Development Process" by Paul O'Connor. Chapter 7 of The PDMA Handbook of New Product Development, Rosenau, Griffin, Castellion, Anschuetz (Editors) September 1996, Wiley

Figure 13.3.1: Implementation versus Time – The Good Versus the Poor

Research by The Adept Group pointed to senior management involvement as a key determinant that separates good from poor implementations. Top management involvement, measured by time, is more than commitment or support. The data in this chart represent setting up a stage-and-gate process in 19 large organizations.

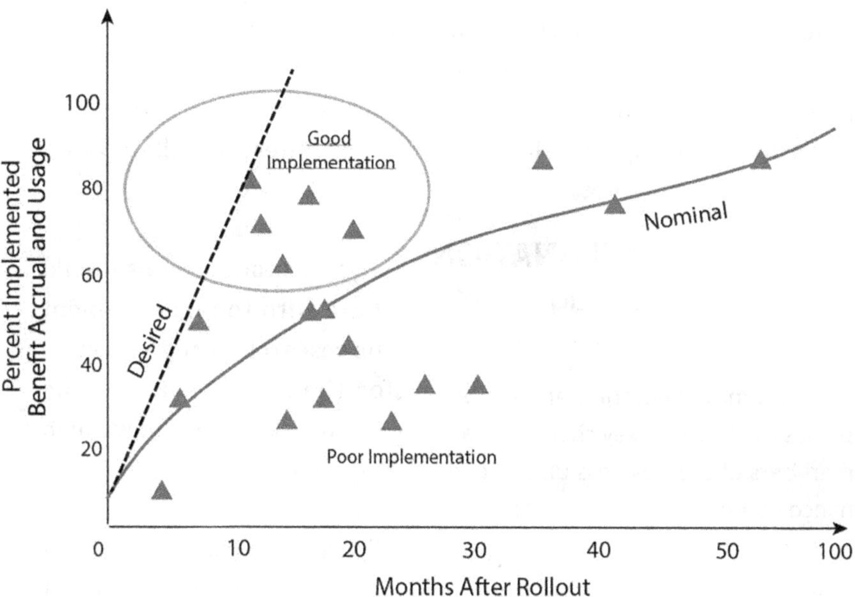

Most managers speculate the answer to be a need for "*senior management commitment.*" Yes, that's helpful, but it's not correct. Research suggests what matters is not merely commitment. Rather, it's the amount of time they take part in the implementation. Involvement is more important than commitment.

Fact #4: Top Manager's Involvement Is More Important Than Commitment

The more time top managers devote to an implementation, the faster benefits accrue. Strong benefit gains come from top management involvement, not commitment. The hours per month top management spends on the implementation matters.

Commitment turns out to be cheap to secure. Involvement by senior management, however, is not cheap. It changes the implementation dynamics. The importance of top management involvement leads to an obvious and important question: How do implementation teams secure top management involvement? The answer is equally obvious. You ask for it.

EXPLANATION:
Top Management & Governance

Top or senior management encompasses the heads of key chain-links and members of the business unit's governance board.

Implementation teams should share with top management the research-based rationale for their involvement. The next questions are "how much time, and do what?"

The Adept Group's research and experience suggest there is a target or goal for management involvement. It even suggests the time top managers — those with authority over the people and resources being employed — should involve themselves during maturity levels one and two. Estimates are between two and four hours each month per top manager. The work should focus on reviewing product line strategies and roadmaps. Plus, top management should also evaluate the practices or lenses that teams use to lay out their strategy.

Early in implementations, these top managers should participate as members of an "Executive Implementation Oversight Team." The normal time commitment is only a few hours each month. The oversight team will focus on how well the process works and what product line teams must do to succeed.

The top managers should also consider how they wish to review alignment among chain-links. Plus, they should examine how managing the portfolio and creating product line strategy can work together. These are the critical decision points in overall product development. Their involvement helps them learn the approach. But it should also help remove hindrances to work and provide support along the way.

The nature of senior manager involvement changes once product line teams complete their first run of the approach. Attention should shift to reviewing each product line strategy and the roll-up of all strategies. The average time top managers contribute will grow to six to eight hours per month, depending on the number of product lines in their business.

A common mistake is to declare top management involvement to be good when it's not. This happens when higher-level managers second-guess decisions by lower-level managers. It disrupts the decision flow. From a process view, this drawback will cause decisions to detach from the workflow and information flow.

Some implementation teams may find they cannot gain direct involvement from top managers. There can be many interests competing for top management mindshare. Because strategies shift focus to the future, some senior managers may think this to be unimportant.

When top management involvement is impossible, implementation teams should secure participation from as high as possible. Typically, this is through implementation team meetings. Connections to the top, then, should happen with reports, presentations, and informal discussions

The idea is to use every opportunity to tell senior managers about the approach and product line strategies. Roll-outs should keep a goal of securing more direct involvement from the top of the business.

Training and Knowledge Transfer

Teaching and training product line teams in the new approach to product line strategy are the first step in implementation. Training is not implementation. It's part of the implementation.

Teams about to work through their product line strategy should learn the topic. But it's best done in ways that match their business and product lines. Implementation teams should consider three types of training:

1. Building a common understanding of product line strategies and their value to the business.
2. Just-in-time training of product line teams doing work within *Strategy Lenses.* Coaching the oversight team about what they are reviewing and what is needed from them.
3. Coaching (teaching) in-meeting discussions that move toward judgments and decisions.

Improving product line strategies is about creating and using insights. Training does not deliver these insights, but it provides participants with basic understandings. When trained, teams should be able to form better insights and create smarter strategy moves.

Gaining involvement across the organization can be helpful in setting up a good product line strategy. It enables analysis that includes information and insights from across chain-links. This is important to drive the creative thinking. Training outside the product lines teams, therefore, also contributes to good implementations.

Non-product-line team training is best done while seeking chain-link alignment. Training should build an understanding of the impact of product line strategies. It should also show strategy influences on chain-links and the other way around. Plus, it must drive home the importance of creative and critical contributions from each chain-link.

Expert Facilitator-consultants

An expert facilitator-consultant can provide important help during implementations. An expert works alongside both the product line teams and the implementation team. They should contribute knowledge, expertise, and work templates.

An expert's role should be to speed up implementations and help teams avoid mistakes and missteps. The expert should also contribute a deep understanding of product line strategy alternatives.

An independent expert should also be neutral politically. Outsiders don't carry the same political baggage as insiders. And they don't have the same superior-to-subordinate rapport as do team members. During change initiatives, it's often helpful to use an expert independent of the organization.

Team composition is also important. Each team should have members who can contribute deep knowledge. Often, the work in this knowledge process is engrossing. At other times, it can be contentious.

Team members must understand what they are talking about. Plus, they must feel comfortable with discussions that are not always black and white. Teams achieve this by combining knowledge and working collaboratively. Taking guidance from a facilitator-consultant is also helpful.

Data and Information Quality

Data handling and insight tracking are important technical issues when creating or improving product line strategies. On startup, it's advisable to consider using the *PLuS Framework* and software tools.

Such tools divide into two categories. One category is the set of tools for designing, setting up, and using a repeatable approach. These are specific to improving product line strategies and roadmaps. They include templates for workflows, information flows, and decision flows.

The other category is about creating strategy presentations and roadmap graphics. These topics are not mutually exclusive. One complements the other. It's important for implementation teams to use both.

Graphic plots won't display all the information about a product line strategy. Teams must also embrace other forms of sharing such reports, textual comments, and presentations. Therefore, it's helpful to include document management alongside any data management supporting the approach.

Often, there are useful data that teams can gather from software in use across their organization. For example, front-end systems keep data for concept generation and idea tracking. And portfolio management software will provide data on PIDs. Such systems can offer rich information.

Analyzing information is always useful in forming strategies. Consider, for example, how a team might explore information about each concept that does not pass screening. This helps teams improve their concepts.

Then too, analyzing why multiple concepts do not pass certain hurdles can help improve the approach. There may be common factors across hurdles with a greater effect on the product line than just a concept. An analysis of systemic risk across PIDs may reveal insights about a platform-lever or chain-link. For example, results may show common competitive threats or common resource shortfalls. These can be important pieces of the product line strategy puzzle.

Many insights from many analyses will help shape a product line strategy. Employing all insights is important.

Software Tools

Software tools not specific to product development or management also play a role in improving product line strategies. Consider online meeting rooms, information rooms, and even peer-to-peer communication tools. Each can help in analyzing data, sharing knowledge, and forming insights. These tools may be useful when dealing with the common challenges of global teaming.

Creating brilliant product line strategies is about the data and information quality. Plus, it's about forming new, smart insights. Information systems, thankfully, can help in this.

Implementation teams often overlook the challenge of systems implementation. Often, it's looked at as an Information Technology challenge, not an implementation concern. This orientation, however, causes problems. Information Technology departments may tackle setting up a system through a simple approach. They ask the implementation team to tell them the details of what data they need. They then promise to deliver a system that resolves those needs.

The problem is that no implementation team understands all the details of what they need when they start. Out-of-the-box systems rarely match process needs.

Any software that supports product line strategies needs also to integrate with other software. To reach high maturity levels, teams must streamline the subprocesses. This demands software that supports each subprocess and integrates across the full architecture.

Implementation teams should consider how software tools may help productivity toward forming and improving strategies. Flexibility from simple applications may provide better support during early maturity levels than larger enterprise systems. Issues will arise, though.

This happens when demand for productivity is greater than the simple app can deliver. Eventually, the organization will need integrated and automated software.

A good approach is to work with your IT department early in the rollout. Start by building a vision of an integrated support. Then, over the first two maturity levels, select separate point solutions to build the envisaged integration. Teams may then alter and customize the software as the implementation gains higher capability maturity levels.

13.4: SpiralUp™ Capability Maturity Levels

Fact # 5: Implementations Should Advance Capability One Level At a Time

Organizational change related to product development can be complex. It's nearly impossible to take an existing, large organization to peak performance quickly. There are just too many changes.

Along the way, there will be notable, yet natural, "push-back" to the changes. You'll hear statements like "this doesn't fit us," or "it's too academic for us." This is natural. The job calls for teams to space out the implementation and address these views over a reasonable time-period—one capability level at a time.

From 2001 through 2003, The Adept Group undertook research on setting up portfolio management practices. Roughly 200 firms joined the research. Our findings were interesting because they showed how complex it is to set up good practices. The research found that organizations are at different levels of ability which matched the benefits realized. The higher the maturity level, the greater the benefits.

Figure 13.4.1: SpiralUp™ Implementation

Implementation divides into maturity levels. Implementation work should focus on one maturity level at a time.

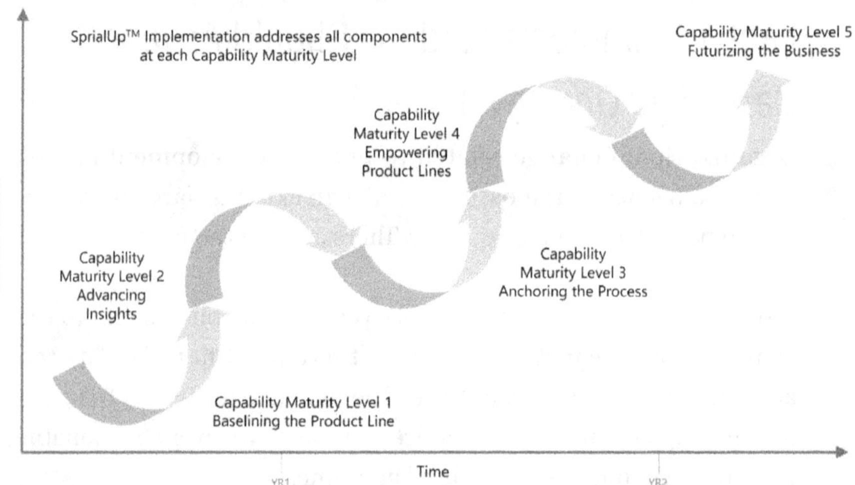

The research suggests that at each skill level, companies must set up different supports and practices. Also, to advance to the final level, organizations must mature through the previous levels. This is not a single jump to an endpoint. This means teams should orchestrate implementation to advance one maturity level at a time. SpiralUp™ is then about achieving goals specific to each maturity level. Using the change equation also makes sense in the maturity model. Implementation teams should focus on the pain, gain, and cost of change for each maturity level.

SpiralUp™ implementation is an approach developed by The Adept Group. (See Figure 13.4.1.) It orchestrates setting up practices through one maturity level at a time. The Adept Group has detailed and fine-tuned the approach through research and many roll-outs. Also, product line work projects should not stop during the SpiralUp™ implementation. The cost of stopping projects outright can make process implementation costs appear to skyrocket.

The Adept Group's change model details the maturity levels for the *PLuS Framework.* There are five levels, each with specific capabilities to be developed.

1. Baselining the Product Lines
2. Advancing Insights
3. Anchoring the Approach
4. Empowering Product Lines
5. Futurizing the Business

The SpiralUp™ approach divides implementation into six orientations. Each should focus on its own milestones and objectives. And milestones and objectives change for each maturity level. The approach divides the change into chewable bites. More on the SpiralUp™ approach is available at the online resource site.[63]

I advise implementation teams to adhere to a brief list of principles when setting up the framework. I base these principles on research, trial and error, experience, and sheer practicality. These factors guide good roll-outs and apply to the *PLuS Framework.* Together, the principles provide practical and productive guidance.

Strategy Lenses for Product Lines

Implementation teams must be smart about how they set up the approach. They must influence change across all maturity levels. Good practices also call for product line teams to carry out *Strategy Lenses.* The order and progression are as important as the work within each.

Implementation teams must address the *Strategy Lens* workflow and the information flow. The idea is to orchestrate the flows logically

63 SpiralUp™ implementation resources can be found at https://adept-plm.com/plus-resources/

and smoothly. The goal is to have product line teams use the *Strategy Lenses* reliably and consistently.

Most teams have available at least eighty percent of the information to assess and improve a product line strategy. But there are two key challenges each team carries out when conducting their first run-through of the strategizing and roadmap management. First, they must find the information and data needed. These items are the raw material from which they develop insights. Second, strategizing teams must create and refine methods for compiling and transforming information and data into good insights.

Sometimes the strategizing team may need to invest time and money to find new information. But this should be only when critical information is unavailable. During the first use of the approach, best guesses and estimates are normally enough. Capturing what to do and how to do it is most important during early iterations. Over time, however, product line teams must invest in creating better data and information.

Concurrent Implementation Goals

When product line teams work through the process, there are three goals they should strive to achieve. They are to form insights, to form the strategy, and to build commitment to the strategy and its execution. The quickest path to achieve these goals is to start with a generic flow. That's why the previous chapter shared the generic flow and discussed several *Strategy Lenses*.

But implementation teams should go beyond generic flows. Instead, they should work with product line teams to customize the flow and the lenses. Implementation is as much about improving lens use and flow as it is about improving strategies. Getting top management to embrace a decision flow is the most critical factor in implementation. When teams anchor a decision flow, the workflow and information flow become much easier to set up.

Improving product line strategies needs two key links to top management. First, it needs management backing. Top managers should agree this is a smart way to go forward. Second, top managers should agree on how other chain-links must align with the product line's strategy. It matters how well chain-links roll up into an overall business strategy. Just as in portfolio management, the roll-up often presents trade-offs across product lines and other chain-links. Recognizing and resolving these trade-offs are key to good product line strategy.

Product line teams must decide how to gain support for their strategies and roadmaps. This is especially difficult when top managers do not understand the Strategy-Essence or roadmap. Therefore, a good implementation will also address management learning.

Executive briefings and whitepapers can help a great deal. However, expert coaching also aids top managers in learning about product line strategies. It enables executives to gain an understanding of topics before delving into strategies.

Capability Maturity Level and Implementation Category

In SpiralUp™ implementations, an organization conducts work within the process while setting it up. It uses a "Capability Maturity Model" to direct activities. In approaches like product line strategizing, it's helpful for organizations to advance their capability and skills one level at a time This is much easier and more sensible than trying to rise to a best-practice final state all at once. The SpiralUp™ helps teams focus on specific work within each maturity level.

Table 13.4.1: Six Categories of Implementation Versus Five Capability Maturity Levels

Category of Implementation		Capability Maturity Level
1. **Implementation Emphasis**		CM 1: Baselining the Product Lines
2. **Content Building**		CM 2: Advancing Insights
3. **Strategy Contribution**	**Versus**	CM 3: Anchoring the Process
4. **Roadmap Contribution**		CM 4: Empowering Product Line Strategies
5. **Process Integration**		
6. **Supports and Enables**		CM 5: Futurizing the Business

The approach is to facilitate the organization to:

1. Carry out the mechanics and achieve the milestones of each category.
2. Gain organizational learning and experience about the mechanics of each component.
3. Set up "consistency-in-use" toward the mechanics of each category.

Teams should apply the change equation (see Chapter 7) to one maturity level at a time. This keeps a focus on the pain, gain, and cost of change for what is important at that point in the implementation. Throughout implementations, teams should keep a sharp focus on critical milestones within each capability maturity level. (See table 13.4.2.)

Table 13.4.2

Capability Maturity Level	Key Implementation Goals
1	The baseline strategy and baseline roadmap for each product line
2	Fine-tuned *Strategy Lenses / PLuS Lenses*™. Gather strategy and roadmap insights. Advance the Strategy-Essence and roadmap. Conduct top-management reviews of product line strategies and roadmaps.
3	Top-management review of product line strategies with PID portfolio management. Top-management review of chain-link alignment and the business-growth portfolio (including all growth activities).
4	Use of software systems to support real-time dashboards and roadmap creation. Real-time strategy opportunity and issue tracking.
5	Futurizing analyses (5, 7, 10 years) of product lines and business unit strategy

Starting Up Implementation

The startup of an implementation differs from advancing each maturity level. Seldom do companies start at absolute capability maturity level zero. Usually, one category or another will be at a higher level. No matter the case, perceptions of the whole process must cause the change to begin.

Organizations should consider a few notable activities to start an implementation. Unlike moving from one capability to the next, most startups need help. The two biggest challenges deal with top management. The first is to gain approval for setting up the framework, which needs to come from a business unit's governance board. The second is participation in the implementation by top managers across functions or chain-links.

Here are hints to get going.

- Have an outside expert assess your business unit's product lines. Have them focus on strategies and roadmaps. Make sure their diagnostic looks at alignment between product lines and other chain-links.
- Create a value proposition for the business unit's governance team. This is a calculation about the change. It states how much value the organization will realize if the approach is set up. It also communicates lost opportunities inefficiencies if no change occurs. Convert the value proposition into a presentation using the change equation.
- Conduct introductory training to communicate what product line strategies are about. Explain how organizations gain value from good strategies.
- Create a "straw man" Strategy-Essence. Add to this with an example master roadmap. Use both to engage people in discussion about the product line.
- Describe how product development relates to product line strategy. Explain how your most recent portfolio prioritization reflects the product line strategy.
- Gain top management involvement before the implementation's start. It's always helpful for top management to take part in upfront work. This may be by kicking off meetings or by offering statements of support. But such support should not substitute for involvement during each capability maturity level rollout.

Role of Top Management

Top management involvement throughout an implementation is important. Just as implementation changes across capability maturity levels, so too does the role of top management. It starts by someone in top management expressing interest in improving product line strategies. This then should resolve into conducting a product line strategy diagnostic. From here, a value proposition, directed at business unit governance, should lay out why the benefits of change exceed the cost of change.

Table 13.4.3

Capability Maturity Level	Top Management's Role and Involvement
1	Emphasize repeated communication of the "pain" and the "gain." Strongly encourage conducting a thorough job with each product line strategy lens. Underscore that the output quality is important to the business's well-being.
2	Deep involvement in the review of individual strategies and roadmaps
3	Deep involvement in the full roll-up review
4	Review of improvement to the process
5	Involvement in the review of futurizing analyses

Behavior, Metrics, and Competencies

Successful implementations are as much about changing behaviors as they are about setting up new practices. Good implementations keep focus on this change and help people do work and think in new ways. Implementation teams may also add measures and metrics to intensify the focus. Metrics influence behaviors because, when set up correctly, they will tie tightly to implicit or explicit rewards (and punishments).

When seeking to change behaviors and build competencies, implementation teams should consider the use of measures and metrics that address:

1. The quality and thoroughness of insights.
2. The quality and intelligence of the strategies and roadmaps.

Both measures reflect qualitative judgments, like giving a score to beauty or elegance. In maturity levels one and two, it's helpful to have some metrics focus on the thoroughness by which strategizing teams conduct each strategy lens. Such metrics should also address the quality of the insights being generated. A good approach to this is to couple the product line team's self-evaluation to the implementation team's evaluation of the same. It's helpful and also motivating to inform teams, before they do work, that management will be reviewing these measures. This sets an implicit reward or chastisement associated with the measure.

As capabilities improve, so too should information, data, and content quality. This should lead to teams gaining better and more relevant insights about both their strategies and Execution Roadmaps. Implementation teams should consider measures or metrics such as:

- Scoring: *PLuS Lens* Use and Thoroughness
- Scoring: Quality of Insights from *PLuS Lenses*
- Scoring: Quality of Strategy-Essence
- Scoring: Quality of Roadmap

Timing and Duration

Implementations that go too fast or last too long can be problematic. The correct speed is as quickly as possible without disrupting either projects or the organization.

When planning an implementation, it's best to estimate the timeframe in which good implementations take place. From this estimate, implementation teams may add or subtract time to fit best the circumstances.

Table 13.4.4: Starting Point Duration for Settling an Implementation Timeline

Organization Size (people)	Median Time to Life cycle "Mature Stage"			
	2 Years	5 Years	10 Years	15+ Years
500-1000	12 months	18 months	24 months	30 months
1000 - 2500	18 months	24 months	30 months	36 months
2500 -7500	24 months	30 months	36 months	42 months
> 7500	30 months	36 months	42 months	48 months

As a rule, faster implementations are better than slower implementations. However, for organizations with over 500 employees, implementations will likely take longer than six months. For any organization larger than 7,500 employees, they may extend to several years.

Teams should first determine a timeframe to use as a baseline for the implementation. The duration may then be divided into capability levels. Tasks and milestones for each level are in table 13.4.5 below. The plan can be adjusted to be faster or slower and then assigned appropriate resources.

Table 13.4.5: Emphasis and Focus—SpiralUp™ Capability Maturity Versus Implementation Categories

	Rough timeline:	Year 1		Year 2		Year 3
		Baselining the Product Lines	Advancing Insights	Anchoring the Process	Empowering Product Strategies	Futurizing the Business
	Implementation Category Component	Capability Maturity Level 1	Capability Maturity Level 2	Capability Maturity Level 3	Capability Maturity Level 4	Capability Maturity Level 5
Implementation Emphasis	Imple-mentation Support & Focus	Individual PL team support	Deep top-management involvement in reviewing product lines	Clearly defined chain-link collaboration; key stakeholder involvement, top management review of all product lines, tie to business strategy	Full process and support systems optimization, new product line creation/targeting, new business model considerations	Futurizing; non-NPD actualization: venturing, partnering, co-development
	Orientation	Baseline creation (1 iteration only)	Key issue and opportunity clarification (1 iteration only)	Value-add (2 iterations in one year)	Leadership push (4 iterations per year); add platform-oriented envisioning	Leadership push (4 iterations per year); additive and dynamic
	Speed of Iteration	3 to 5 months	2 to 3 months	6 weeks	3-week sprints	3-week sprints, continuous dashboard management, biennial longwave envisioning
Content	Mindful Lenses (Use Focus)	Full use of preselected lenses; team customization of lenses	Use of customized lenses	Selective use of lenses; maximizing insights	Optimized use of insights, new mindful lens exploration	Streamlined, online support of mindfulness lenses, focus on new insights
	Insights Collection & Use	Team-focused only	Expanded team, add insights from people not on the team	Cross-organization (chain- link) insights, interactive to product lines	Outside-in derived insights from customers, suppliers, and competition; real-time insight interplay/building	Developing insights from envisioning, longwave insights
	Information & Data	Existing; identify Info needs	Improved, new info initiatives; determine and streamline key support analytics	World class, aggressive targeted info-data-insight initiatives, central repository	Leading edge, expansion and depth, quality analytics, info trends and long-wave impacts	

Rough timeline:		Year 1		Year 2		Year 3
		Baselining the Product Lines	Advancing Insights	Anchoring the Process	Empowering Product Strategies	Futurizing the Business
Implementation Category	Component	Capability Maturity Level 1	Capability Maturity Level 2	Capability Maturity Level 3	Capability Maturity Level 4	Capability Maturity Level 5
Strategy	Strategy Dynamics & Actions	Existing, as-Is state	Exploratory, new dynamics; chain-link interplay	Proactive advancement	Aggressive - continuous mid-term, development of longwave focus, business model Considerations	Longwave sustained leadership, business model advancement
Strategy	Strategy-Essence	Current state; baseline creation	Desired state and actual state; gap focus; verb-based attribute positioning;	Clarity and proactive communication; recalculate as needed	Clarity and proactive communication; recalculate as needed	Clarity and proactive communication; recalculate as needed
Strategy	Strategy Rationale Story	The preliminary rationalizing story, top-line issues and opportunities; Potential recourse	Prioritize issues and opportunities; Life cycle status and influences, deep situational analysis, competitors analysis	Focus on "winning" customers and against competition; implications for the business	Future trends, changes, discontinuities in technologies and markets	Envisioning the future, needed transformation

	Rough timeline:	Year 1		Year 2		Year 3
		Baselining the Product Lines	Advancing Insights	Anchoring the Process	Empowering Product Strategies	Futurizing the Business
	Implementation Category Component	Capability Maturity Level 1	Capability Maturity Level 2	Capability Maturity Level 3	Capability Maturity Level 4	Capability Maturity Level 5
Roadmaps	Roadmap Details, Objects	Current-state baseline creation	Emphasis on immediate future state	Optimizing all immediate and future states	Roll-up of platforms and CTRs	Roll-up[of platforms and CTRs
	Platforms, Platform Advance-ments, PLCs	Early definition	Defined	Defined, new	Defined, new; future possibilities/envi-sioning	Defined, new; future possibilities, disruptions
	PIDs	Simple iden-tification and characterization	Economic and life cycle fore-casts	Optimal flow as per portfolio and CTR status	Optimal flow as per portfolio and CTR status	Optimal flow as per portfolio and CTR status
	PIMs	Simple iden-tification and characterization	Economic and life cycle forecasts; PIM and life cycle relationship	Economic and life cycle forecasts, PIM and life cycle relationship	Economic and life cycle forecasts, PIM and life cycle relationship	Economic and life cycle forecasts, PIM and life cycle relationship
	PICs	Simple identifica-tion & character-ization	Generate Poten-tial PICs, Screen, Invest in Rapid Experimentation	Economic and life cycle forecasts, improvements to PIC generation	Economic and life cycle forecasts, Improvement to PIC feasibility, rapid experimentation	Economic and life cycle forecasts
	TBBs	Simple identifica-tion & character-ization	Understanding TBB gaps and opportunities	Tech scouting per TBB, and TBB's from tech scouting; open Innovation	Network building, expansion, and depth of open inno-vation, Venturing	TBB portfolio management
	Market Segments, Market Opportuni-ty Charters (MOCs)	Simple identification & characterization	Restructur-ing market segmentation to enable strategic impact / away from industry standards	Situational analy-sis; VOC influenc-es, competitor changes; why CTR's regarding strategy; prioriti-zation	Market segment opportunity search, roll-up directional policy matrix, future envisioning	Market segment and MOC portfolio management
	CTRs	List possible CTRs	Why CTRs re-garding strategy; prioritization	Newly generated CTRs, emphasis on CTRs across chain-links	Newly generated CTRs, emphasis on CTRs across chain-links	Newly gen-erated CTRs, emphasis on CTRs across chain links, longwave insights
	Roadmap Data Struc-ture	Generic template	Customized to org. template	Specific stan-dardization across organi-zation	Specific standard-ization across organization	Specific standardiza-tion across organization
	Road-mapping Graphics	Excel, Power-Point, MS Visio: Straw man -> team refined	MS Visio: desired strategy reflec-tive	MS Visio: desired strategy reflec-tive	Integrated, custom-ize graphing	Integrated, customize graphing

Rough timeline:	Year 1		Year 2		Year 3
	Baselining the Product Lines	Advancing Insights	Anchoring the Process	Empowering Product Strategies	Futurizing the Business
Implementation Category Component	Capability Maturity Level 1	Capability Maturity Level 2	Capability Maturity Level 3	Capability Maturity Level 4	Capability Maturity Level 5
Process Integration					
Multiple Product Line Roll-up	Each product line in isolation	Initial roll-up view of all road-maps, issue and challenge identification, consideration of budget planning	Conflict resolu-tion / opportuni-ty between PLs management review of rull set; added budget planning	New product line creation/\possi-bilities	Added disruption platforms
Chain-Link Alignment	None or little	Understanding of key issues and opportunities	Establish conflict resolution mech-anism	Collaborative chain-link innovation/ new business model exploration	Influence to transform the links; business model trans-formation enablement
Portfo-lio- Man-agement Interface	PIDs only	PIDs and PICs, defunding non-roadmap projects; product line systemic risks & roadmap throughput	PIDs and PICs with separate analyses for TBBs, platforms, market segments, groupings	Future skills and resource forecast-ing; bottleneck forecasting	HR planning integration for future skills and resources
Inno-vation, Concept Gener-ation, Ideation, Feasibility Integra-tion	Current as is + develop PIC focus	PIC focused; rapid experi-mentation, fast learning loops	Full open inno-vation leverage strong feedback loop	Collaborative chain-link innovation	Integrated in-novation, rad-ical platform innovation

Rough timeline:		Year 1		Year 2		Year 3
		Baselining the Product Lines	Advancing Insights	Anchoring the Process	Empowering Product Strategies	Futurizing the Business
Implementation Category Component		Capability Maturity Level 1	Capability Maturity Level 2	Capability Maturity Level 3	Capability Maturity Level 4	Capability Maturity Level 5
Supports and Enablers	**Systems Support**	Generic roadmap data structure; point solutions for roadmap creation point solution (e.g. SharePoint) for information, data, insight aggregation	Mindful lens support + insight compilation and manipulation -> insights from insights object support	Customized, organization standard yet flexible roadmap data configuration; cross business enterprise support, central repository	Dashboards - live roadmap roll-up with drill-down functionality	Aggregate analytics, issues, opportunities, and optimizations
	Facilitation and Guidance	External to PL team facilitation expert; just-in-time training	External coach/ facilitator; broad strategy-innovation training	Value-add consulting; external content contributors	Self-supportive, plus optimization training, strategy dynamics consulting	Self-supportive, plus optimization training, strategy dynamics consulting
	Measures and Metrics	None	Initial measures on quality of info, predictive measures of future product line impact, associated implicit rewards	Cross-organization standardization of info quality measure, and future impact of the product line, associated explicit rewards	Add CTR timing success, internal product line comparative benchmarking	Explore futurizing metrics and rewards

13.5: The Value Proposition for Governance Attention

The most common starting point to improve product line strategies is to gain approval and support from your business unit's governance board. This means building a case for the *PLuS Framework*. The case combines an economic value proposition with a foundational understanding of what it is and why it works.

For many businesses, setting up and using the *PLuS Framework* can yield substantial value. For some, it's overwhelming. The gains come from the approach having a large impact on top-line revenue, earnings, and shareholder value.

When critical challenges are affecting one or more product lines, the value proposition of getting to good product strategies can be significant. For example, you may have platform-levers rapidly reaching maturity. Or you may see market segments in quick decline.

Countering these influences is not just important, it can be a key to survival. Consider how the framework's value is the sum of benefits gained directly and the costs avoided. When avoided cost comes from dodging bankruptcy or failure, the value approaches infinity. No matter how you approach cases with product line challenges, the value proposition is profound.

But how do you support such descriptors like "profound" to senior management and your business unit's governance board? Great question; let's look.

Benefits Outweigh Costs

Below, I offer a starting point for figuring out the value of the *PLuS Framework* to your organization. I do not mean for you to copy this and present it to your colleagues in top management. If you did, they would not understand it. And more troublesome, you may not be able to defend it.

The purpose here is to build a sensible dialogue about the value to be gained from the *PLuS Framework*. **You and your colleagues will need to recraft this format to fit your organization and your product lines. All situations are unique**. It must match your situation and use language everyone understands.

The value proposition lays out the reasons the gains outweigh the costs of implementing the framework. Specifically, it seeks a sweet spot of maximum gain and minimum cost. It's about the economics of organizational change. I discussed this in chapter 13.1.

The simplest of value propositions lays out benefits from the framework and then assigns expected gains to each. It's like saying how much boost do we expect from each benefit. Table 13.5.1 below is a list of the framework's top ten value generators.

Using the format, a team of knowledgeable managers reviews any diagnostics, and as a group, estimates what it feels the gains might be in each area. The dialogue is important. Here, the team can explore issues, concerns, and uncertainties.

Companies can find they have moribund platform-levers or competition is peeling off key market segments. When this is happening, top managers may not be interested in setting up the framework. All they want is the solution—the answer to their problems. Unfortunately, experience suggests that if there were quick solutions, they'd already be in development.

Executives can find themselves in a terrible quagmire. Things can be so bad there is no time for setting up an approach like the *PLuS Framework*. Implementation in such cases looks different. Here, near-term survival can be the highest priority, not fixing product lines for a better future. In such cases, avoiding failure in the near-term may be infinitely more valuable than future economic gains from the framework. The only recourse for a product line is to find new solutions at the same time there is a need to lean out (cutting costs) the whole line. This is exactly the situation the *PLuS Framework* seeks to avoid. It's also why detailing the value proposition before things turn south is so important.

Table 13.5.1: Example Economic Gains Template

Gain	Reason for Gain	Expected Boost %
1. **Clarity**	The clarity gained from product line strategies enables organizations to judge the work and investments to be important or not. This helps set clear priorities across multiple products, guiding product management and portfolio management.	5
2. **Synergy**	Coupling a good Strategy-Essence to a sharp roadmap fosters synergy between products. It empowers platform-levers to deliver products quicker and more cost effectively.	10
3. **Alignment**	A good Strategy-Essence enables alignment among a business unit's chain-links. This boosts the product line's impact related to cash flow, customer satisfaction, and cost-of-product delivery.	5
4. **Need Matching**	Good product line strategy links the outcomes desired by the customer with product specifications. This increases the odds of product success. It also decreases the cost of stumbling through forming product specifications and confirmation.	15
5. **Insights**	Good strategy and roadmap practices help create insights, the "Magic Sauce" of strategy. With sharp insights, strategies avoid being limp and ineffective.	10
6. **Gaps**	Rolling up, analyzing, and rationalizing multiple product line strategies and roadmaps highlight gaps within a business's offerings, and expose threats to current offerings. They can also reveal white space opportunities for new offerings. Most important, they give purpose to investments both within and outside each product line.	5

7. **Faster**	Smart product line strategizing moves up the start time of the innovation clock to when teams form insights. This helps minimize the largest latency in strategy. It also increases a product line's competitiveness and impact.	15
8. **Bigger, Better**	Smart strategies drive better projects into the product-development portfolio. Good roadmaps minimize the waste from projects not critical to strategy. This pushes a portfolio toward its optimal value.	15
9. **Plurality**	Good practices help teams form strategy and roadmaps for the full product line. This goes beyond just creating individual products. It does this by guiding teams to employ openness, creativity, and forward-thinking toward the full product line. This wider perspective increases a line's contribution to an overall business strategy.	25
10. **Targeted**	Product line strategizing and roadmapping directs teams to create targets for innovation that deliberately match and drive strategy. By investing in specific targets, organizations improve the chance of finding significant innovations.	20
	SUM	125
	LESS REDUNDANT	30
	TOTAL GAIN EXPECTED FROM CURRENT	95%

In the fictitious case above, without cost avoidance, the value proposition is roughly to double (95%) the product line's value. But this does not capture all value. We also must include those costs avoided because the framework can mitigate product line challenges. Then too, we need to calculate the cost of implementing the framework.

My preferred approach is to keep cost avoidance separate. Often, a focus on avoiding cost can be so great that attention is drawn away from other potential gains. Also, figuring out cost avoidance is situational. To do it, I recommend an iterative approach with key managers exploring a few questions. The first ones are "What if we don't implement the framework? Is there a better way to advance our product lines? Will the alternative approach yield positive or negative impact over three years? Over five years? And over seven years?" Another question is "Why will we see this negative impact?" Also, teams should explore the notion "If we don't pursue the *PLuS Framework*, what alternatives approaches can we take?"

The managers should share and explore their answers. Once discussions trail off, call for a second response to the same questions. See if the group normalizes around economic values.

The question is whether your product lines should double down on current methods or approaches, pursue the *PLuS Framework,* or create some other approach. But each alternative carries a rollout or implementation cost. So what's the implementation cost for the framework?

Cost of Implementation

There are several costs to consider that are related to implementation. As we'll see, the largest is associated with managers' and executives' time to implement and learn the framework. Therefore, it's wise to structure an implementation to shorten its duration and the total man-days of involvement. Along the way, costs may also accrue for expert help and consulting to speed efforts and avoid implementation mistakes.

Resourcing an implementation should follow a few basics rules. Doing so helps minimize costs and maximize gains.

- Use an outside expert to ease and streamline the implementation, to help organizations avoid wasted or misguided efforts.
- Don't disrupt projects underway unless there is a strong argument to do so. Disrupting projects can be costly.
- Contributors to implementations should come from many functions, not just one. Therefore costs will be spread across an organization.
- Don't overburden contributors. Keep contributors time to less than 20% per month. Otherwise, the time burden can be disruptive.

- Don't underuse people. But if a person's time commitment goes to less than 5% per month, they'll need to spend most of it getting up to speed.
- Keep at least one person (the implementation leader) focused on the implementation at between 50% and 75% of her time. Surround the leader with a staff of several managers who spend at least 50% of their time on the implementation.
- Advance through one SpiralUp™ capability maturity level at a time.
- Maintain implementation oversight by the business unit's governance body. Don't allow only one function to take over this role. If the governing body approved going forward with the implementation, it should also recognize its responsibility in helping to remove hindrances and obstacles to the implementation.

Summing up the implementation costs is straightforward but requires some work. Go to outside experts if you need help. Review each cost with knowledgeable and experienced managers. Refine them based on discussions, and then simply add up them up.

Calculating the Value Proposition

The value proposition is a simple calculation. It's a view of gains and cost avoidance compared to implementation costs. I share the calculation in Figure 13.5.1.

Figure 13.5.1: Calculating the Proposition Value

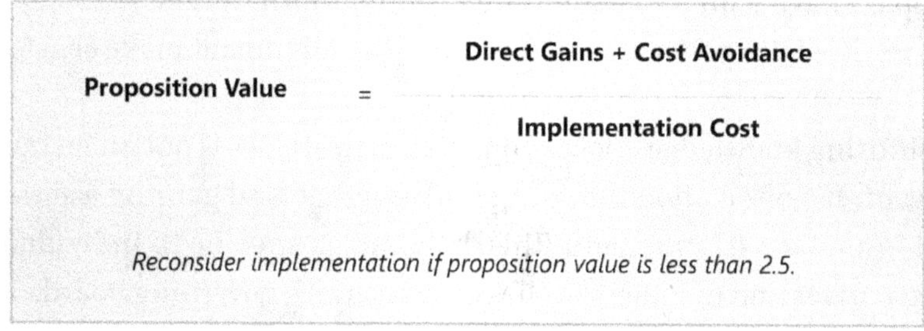
Direct Gains + Cost Avoidance
Proposition Value =
Implementation Cost
Reconsider implementation if proposition value is less than 2.5.

It's not wise to propose the framework when proposition values are less than one. No governance board would be attracted to such a proposition. With such values, product lines are probably not incurring much pain.

Direct gains from the framework often push this value to greater than three or four. When adding in cost avoidance, some teams may place a much greater value on implementation, approaching twenty to thirty times implementation costs. These values argue strongly to move forward with the framework. But I encourage teams to reconsider implementation if the proposition value is not at least two and one half.

Governance Understanding

One thing I've learned is that governing boards give no credence to value propositions if they don't understand the framework. In some businesses, this is the most difficult hurdle to overcome when seeking to improve product lines and their strategies. The value proposition is secondary to governance boards learning about the framework.

Several opportunities typically arise to share what product line strategies and the framework for getting them to good is all about. Such occasions pop up around annual operating plans and budgeting. Topics such as product development performance, innovation, and business-growth positioning often come to the forefront. In each topic, sharing an understanding about platform-levers, segmentation, attribute positioning, and chain-link alignment make sense.

Diffusing knowledge about product line strategies is not an instant event. It's often about building the language and gaining a series of "Aha, I get it" moments. This, however, is specific to individual executives and members of the business unit's governing board.

Good Implementations

Setting up the *PLuS Framework* and the process flows to carry it out demands that organizations change. Orchestrating change demands a deep knowledge of the framework. Plus, it calls for leadership and skills to aid change efforts.

Implementation teams must unfreeze their organization by working the change equation. They do this by influencing opinions. Implementation teams should drive awareness of the pain from poorly formed product line strategies. Teams should then add this to views about the gain realized from the new approach. The sum of the gain and the pain must offset the cost people sense toward making the change.

Well-conducted training and using outside experts also aid good roll-outs. Using independent experts to aid process design and implementation is best for most organizations. It boils down to a simple fact: Setting up the framework is as important as the strategies it produces. Doing so with an experienced and talented consultant can ramp up capability maturity levels faster and more effectively.

Implementing for Rapid Gains and Orchestrating the Flow

Smart Implementations

PRODUCT LINE STRATEGY: GETTING TO GOOD

Seek to:

Smartly implement your process.

- Good processes are more likely to yield good product line strategies.
- If good product line strategy is the golden egg, the process is the goose.

How you implement your process for forming, improving, and carrying out good product line strategies matters.

- Gain involvement when creating the process from those who will use the process. Those involved in creating the process are more likely to use it. Using it is the first step toward gaining benefit.

Avoid jumping to a "final" implementation state. Advance your organization's strategizing capabilities one maturity level at a time.

- Cross-organization capability maturity is key to gaining the benefits of good product line strategy.
- Capabilities should advance across the full architecture of product development and management, not just product line strategizing.

Match your timing of the product line strategizing process to other organizational processes. It must tie to creating annual operating plans, budgeting, portfolio reviews, and concept generation.

- Avoid leaving product line strategizing to hang on its own.
- Anchor product line strategizing to other organizational processes.

SECTION 6

RESOURCES AND SUPPORTS: Tools of the Trade and Finding Help

Guidance and Help to Form and Carry Out Good Product Line Strategy

Principles of Good Product Line Strategies

- Case Studies
- Glossary
- Index
- Online Resources

CHAPTER 14

Systems Thinking and the Principles of Good Product Line Strategies

I'VE TAUGHT PRODUCT line strategy to managers and executives for many years. Near the end of my classes, I ask participants to imagine they are about to take an old-fashioned blue book exam. Then I ask them to pick two numbers between one and twenty. Based on their numbers, I hand them two topics from a list of twenty. These include items like roadmap objects such as PICs, TBB, platform-levers, and PIDs. They are also broader topics like business strategy, organizational structure, and verb-based segments.

Their exam question is to describe how their two topics relate. I ask the class to consider what they'd write in three pages of a blue book to describe how their two topics relate to one another. This always produces groans and seat-squirming. But not to worry; no one writes a response. I do, however, ask class participants to talk about how they see the relationship between their two topics.

The point of the exercise is simple. It's that everything relates to everything else. If you see the relationship between the different topics, you probably understand what product line strategies are all about. But the insight goes a little deeper.

Getting people to see the relationships is another way of showing that product lines act as a system. From this perspective, principles that govern the strategies also guide interaction among the product line's parts. Somehow these principles must also consider internal and external forces. This is important because every product line has unique dynamics across its parts and with non-product line systems. It's the responsibility of product line teams to recognize these dynamics. It's also their responsibility to figure out how to manage the parts to deliver the best contribution to their business unit.

The System of Product Line Strategy

Seeing product line strategy as a system is powerful. By sharing what makes product line strategies good, I'm also stating key system principles. It's what makes the system impactful.

All organizational systems have basic forces and dimensions at play. Academics would say systems have "spatial and temporal" dimensions. This is the same as saying they have different parts and inputs are separated in time from outputs.

For product lines, we have many parts like platform-levers, innovation charters, and chain-links. Each is separate, yet all are related. Insights are system inputs, separated in time from outputs. In product line strategies, the system outputs are products, revenue, and customer satisfaction. What product line teams do and think today may take months or years to produce desired results.

The challenge in systems thinking is to recognize the parts of the system. It's seeing their spatial and temporal dimensions. And then it is figuring out smart principles to get the most out of the system.

First, let's look at a systems analysis of a problem-ladened stage-and-gate or waterfall type development process. MIT professor Nelson Repenning conducted the work. He calls his findings the "Tilting Effect."[64] It's not complicated, but it's spot on. Repenning's work homed in on what companies do when their development efforts are falling short on delivering successful products in terms of quality and economics.

Repenning shows there is a tendency for management to shift work efforts to late in the development process. The purpose is to fix problems happening within individual projects. Most of us know this as "firefighting." The problem is the resource shift removes resources from work being done early in the process. And it's early in development that quality and success determinants get formed. Management's firefighting response is under-resourcing work that prevents the problem. Over time, they'll need to tilt more resources to late in the development for more firefighting. The problem response keeps feeding the problem.

From a systems perspective, the Tilting Effect suggests that this firefighting response may be a mistake. It turns out that shifting resources to fix problems late in a product's development aggravates quality and success issues for subsequent projects. To make matters worse, some management teams reinforce the problem. They do so by rewarding the heroics of great firefighting. And they fail to recognize and reward the thoroughness and intelligence of early work that avoids the sparks that cause the fires.

If it's so logical, why does the Tilting Effect happen? It's because management is not thinking through the development system's space and time issues. Projects differ from one another. Stages and gates are also different. And ensuing projects are separated in

64 "Understanding Firefighting in New Product Development." Repenning, Nelson P. Journal of Product Innovation Management Vol. 18, No. 5 (2001): 285-300.

time from those with quality and success issues. From a systems perspective, management's seemingly "good" firefighting response to quality and success issues may not be so good. The solution is to stop the firefighting and shift resources to the front-end to make sure the problems don't happen. And yes, that means suffering through the near-term consequences of terminating or restarting the problem-laden projects.

The Product Line System

Now, let's think about the *PLuS Framework.* How do its parts act as a system? What are the system's constraints and desired outcomes? How are the parts separated by time? Table 14.1 lists some of the framework parts. Some are discrete items, others parts within larger parts. However, all parts relate to one another.

Table 14.1

Agile Development	Attributes of Product Offerings	Behavior & Culture	Business Growth Portfolio
Business Unit Strategy	Cash flow	Chain-links and their Alignment	Concept Generation
Customer Desired Outcomes	Customer Needs and Requirements	Customer Satisfaction	Decision Flow
Feasibility Assess-ments	Governance	Insights and insight Quality	Launch Schedules
Life Cycle Manage-ment	Measures and Metrics	Milestones	Noun-based Market Segments
Objectives	PICs- Product Innova-tion Charters	PIDs-Products in Development	PIMs-Products in the Market
Platform-levers	PLuS Lenses	Product Requirements	Product Specifications
Project Management Plans	Project Portfolio Management	Resource Use Effi-ciency	Resources
Roadmapping	Staged Development	Strategizing Process	Strategy-Essence
Prioritization	Product Retirement	Pivots	Roadmapping Recasts
TBBs	Verb-based Market Segments	Decision Rights	Risk and Uncertainty

The framework's four pillars, its process foundation, and its governance roof are groups of system parts. Recognizing the framework groups and their parts makes the systems view easier to understand. Our concern is how the parts interact with each other and how they might be separated by time.

For example, we know PICs can become PIMs. But the transition may take many months. And we know insights and customer-desired outcomes must combine to form good PICs. This too can take time. By managing the system, we must figure out how to guide the transition of insights into PIMs. The goal is to do this fast while gaining the most impact.

The systems view of product line strategies becomes powerful once you realize the interplay across the parts. What matters is whether the parts have a static or dynamic relationship influenced by outside or internal forces. These forces may come from the dynamics of technologies, customer needs, and chain-link strategies.

For example, no matter the situation, the Strategy-Essence relates the same to the roadmap. And technology building blocks always connect to verb-based segments through platform-levers. But timeline milestones for PICs and PIDs are situational. The same situation-specific nature is true for chain-link alignment and the decision flows.

The difference between statically and dynamically related systems parts suggests how best to address them.[65] For static relationships, a routine or waterfall-type approach is best. For dynamic relationships, an agile sprint approach is best. However, routine tasks

65 "Contingency Theory" is a principle that suggests the best way work to carry out work is match the approach with the situation's certainty or uncertainty. Research by many academics supports the theory. Gareth Morgan reviews the topic in his book *Images of Organization*, Sage Publication 2006. A caveat, however. This is a long book and not for the faint of heart.

may embed in agile work, and agile sprint-like work may embed in routine process work. Let me give an example. Forming or reforming a product line Strategy-Essence is best done through agile sprints using *PLuS Lenses* (as discussed in Chapter 11). But it's best to do the Strategy-Essence roll up to business unit strategy in a repeatable approach. This should be in cadence with an annual operating plan. Superb system performance requires teams to use these different approaches. The approaches must coexist.

Principles of Good Product Line Systems

From a systems view, we can then see several principles that help us get to good product line strategies.

1. Match how you work to the situation. Conduct agile sprints for dynamic and uncertain work. Conduct routinized or staged work for static tasks with little uncertainty.
2. Seek to maximize the Strategy-Essence with the product line master roadmap. Do this by iteratively adjusting the system parts within each. This calls for working the dynamics across platform-levers, attribute positioning, and chain-link alignment. Do this interactively with figuring out the best relationship of objects on the roadmap laid out across near-term and long-term time horizons.
3. Improvement of insights boosts system parts and drives major gains for the whole. Continually improving, capturing, and using insights is fundamental to getting the most from the product line system. Good product line strategy starts with intelligent, high-quality insights.
4. Objectives give a focus for advancing the product line system. Metrics reflect boundaries and limits to the system. Use both objectives and metrics to manage the product line system and its parts. They help drive product lines forward and keep them on track.

5. Product lines are part of a business unit. A product line system is part of a larger organizational system. A productive product line must tie into the larger organizational system. It cannot survive if isolated. The tie in happens though governance, chain-link alignment, and roll-up into the business unit strategy and business growth portfolio. Make sure these "tie-in" parts are in-place and strongly set into the larger organizational system.
6. Decision flows are as important to the product line system as are work flows and insight flows. A decision flow that fails to state clear decision rights will disrupt relations among product line system parts. Decision rights must be set by the business unit's governing body.

Correct the Tilt and Improve Results

From the systems perspective, good product line strategies work to offset the Tilting Effect mentioned above. Good product line strategy with smart execution improves the quality of objects on the roadmap. This focus on quality helps avoid the mindlessness of constant firefighting. It tilts resources to the front-end—to strategy and concept formation. This is important.

The system uses strategizing to create two key outputs. The first is a direction to follow. Teams capture this in their Strategy-Essence and roadmap. The second is to create innovation charters, the targets for innovation. The better the innovation charters, the healthier the offset to the Tilting Effect. But remember, this is about a <u>set</u> of charters. It's not about just one charter. It is about the plurality of the product line, not just a one-off new product.

A few things change when a company embraces product line strategy as a system. For example, project-portfolio management expands beyond just managing development projects. Now, it also includes product innovation charters. This is notable because it makes front-end work and products in development compete for resources. Plus, the notion of "portfolio balance" and "risk management" shift from project-portfolio management to the business growth portfolio. The project-portfolio management focus then zeros in on successfully carrying out the product line roadmap and ensuring the strategy's success. Let's face it, there is no point in "balancing" a project portfolio if it leads to ineffective product line strategies.

Guidelines to Good Product Line Strategy

The *PLuS Framework* works to push a product line system's performance. To do this, certain principles and rules are helpful.

1. Never jump ahead with a concept. Just because someone conjures up a product idea does not mean it should become part of the strategy, no matter how important the executive is doing the conjuring. Instead, teams should work to create innovation charters designed deliberately to advance the product line. They then shape the charter by using Strategy-Essence directives. At early stages, the relationship between product features and platform-levers is most important.
2. Smartly segmenting markets is a cornerstone of good product line strategy. Accepting off-the-shelf research reports' segment schemes is noun-based only. Noun-based segmentation is helpful, especially in finding segments offering growth. But noun-based segmenting is insufficient for laying out good product line strategies. It must be complemented by verb-based segmentation that spell out clusters of customer-desired outcomes.
3. Always position your full line of products with attributes that deliver outcomes customers want. It's about understanding and fulfilling a Job-to-be-Done. But do this in a coordinated manner across multiple segments yielding multiple attribute sets. Positioning products one at a time is a thing of the past.
4. Great platform-levers are requisite to good product line strategies. Less than stellar platform-levers can work but are never

as impactful as great ones. Figuring out new platform-levers and the renewal of old platform-levers are central to good product line strategies. This is an ongoing task.

5. Platform-levers are ineffectual without intense organizational focus. Teams gain such focus through well-defined fulcrums. Fulcrums are key parts of a product line system. If they are broken or don't work well, the whole system degrades.

6. Going around organizational norms is not as impactful as changing those norms. The problem with keeping old norms around forever is that, with time, they shift from being positive forces to being negative forces. Activities like Intrapreneurship and ring-fenced startups that sidestep the norms can be helpful. But for all the good they do, negative forces will continue to build on existing product lines. Although separated by time, avoiding changes to organizational norms will eventually weaken the product line system.

7. Use good roadmaps to present how a product line strategy will be carried out. Communicating expected work and milestones is key to keeping unison across system parts. Roadmaps should show how, over time, current and future products connect technologies to market segments using platform-levers. And when changes like pivots and recasts are made, all systems' parts need to adjust accordingly.

8. Do not focus solely on traditional time-to-market measures. Development speed is not helpful without also delivering strategic impact. Instead, focus on speed coupled to strategic impact, but also keep an eye on resource use efficiency. Keep this in mind as you work out your Strategy-Essence and its Execution Roadmap. Thinking that speed alone delivers strategic impact is a mistake many management teams have made. Do not repeat it.

9. Back off the old-school, unbending approach toward objectives. Yes, teams need them to have a deliberate focus.

Sometimes—and in my experience, more often than not—product line teams find they must change objectives.

10. Use metrics to influence behaviors and understand boundaries. Organizational culture is a collection of behavioral norms. Cultural forces are the underpinnings of how challenges get defined, work gets done, and decisions get made. These are internal forces on the product line system. Smart use of metrics helps guide and influence behaviors, so internal forces don't overwhelm the product line system. Good metrics also reveal where and how the system may be straying from desired outcomes.

Getting to Good

Good product line strategies have much to contribute to a business. But getting them to good requires knowledge and persistence. Through this book, I've tried to share the knowledge and show you what it takes to get it done in large organizations.

The *PLuS Framework,* described throughout the book, is a model that reveals that many parts and influences must come together to yield good product line strategies. When done well, the results can be profound. When done poorly, entire businesses can fail.

My hope is that you find the *PLuS Framework* as valuable as I know it to be. But I also recognize that product lines and their strategies will never be a finished topic. Practitioners need to use it and build from it. And academics need to analyze product lines as systems to better understand their parts and relations between the parts.

Moving from current single-product thinking to the plurality of product lines is a huge step for everybody—practitioners, consultants, and academics alike. To me, it's like employing calculus in a world where arithmetic and algebra are the common practice. With product line strategies, we see the need for multiple parts to change over different time horizons.

Getting to good product line strategies needs an organizational effort, not just heroics of individuals. This makes it a tough management challenge needing strong leadership and good facilitation. Simply pushing harder on old approaches won't gain much.

Welcome to the world of product line strategies!

CHAPTER 15

Case Histories—Understanding Product Line Strategy

I'VE PROVIDED SEVERAL examples of companies that ran into problems because they didn't have a good product line strategy. There are also a few examples of how companies succeeded because they continued to update strategies.

Here, I offer up four case studies on product line strategies. Three of the cases show how good product line strategies can help a company succeed and grow. The fourth describes how The Adept Group aided a client frustrated by having missed out to a great degree on an important market. Working with the client, we clearly showed how the company's pursuit of functional and operational excellence created a void in communicating insights about emerging markets and opportunities. The very thing driving its near-term business performance was also threatening the company's long-term growth.

Case History A: Dow Chemical

Dow Chemical's Product Line Strategy Pivot: Flipping a platform-lever to speed up market diffusion

Case History B: Rockwell

Why Rockwell Automation Missed a Market: Defining the need for product line strategizing and insight transfer

Case History C: US Gypsum

US Gypsum boldly invests in its next platform-lever: Moving the company ahead during a downturn

Case History D: Microsoft

Aging assumptions can wreak havoc with product line strategies. Purposely tackling assumptions is necessary to keeping product line strategies good.

Case History A:

Dow Chemical's Product Line Strategy Pivot

From Product Asset Platform-Lever to Design-to-Order Service Platform-Lever

In the movie *The Graduate*, someone leaned toward Dustin Hoffman and whispered the word "plastics." It was tongue-in-cheek. It was akin to saying, "go ahead and lose your soul" and become a proverbial "Organization Man"[66] in the new world of plastics.

Many smart people took advantage of the opportunity presented by plastics, but not all embraced the uncreative role of an Organization Man. Kurt Swogger, who joined Dow Chemical, didn't embrace the role. This case is about Kurt's out-of-the-box thinking at the product line strategy level.

Typically, people working on new products focus their creativity on coming up with concepts. They hope to turn a concept into a product and a product into a product line. However, it's less common to see managers focus their creative thoughts on recasting a product line strategy. Kurt Swogger and his team at Dow Chemical did this with their polyolefin line during the 1990s.

Polyolefins make up the largest plastics category. A handful of global producers like Dow and ExxonMobil Chemical pump out enormous volumes of polyolefin every year. They serve the needs of many tangible product producers, and to keep up with demand,

---

66 Whyte, William H. (1956). *The Organization Man*, Simon & Schuster, ISBN 978-0-671-54330-3. In this best-selling book, Whyte suggests large organizations seek to convince managers that organizations could make decisions and serve up creative ideas better than an individual. According to Whyte, many managers were trained mistakenly to serve the organization and not contribute individual creativity and critical thinking.

each producer invests in reactors that fit their offerings. Certain technology advances (most notably in catalysis and additives) have helped drive their performance. When Swogger joined Dow, user needs were advancing fast, and the competition was intense.

There are several polyolefin types. The two most significant are polyethylene and polypropylene. Within each polyolefin type, many molecule-related qualities control each polymer's performance features.

This is a blessing and a curse for the polymer industry. It's a blessing because it's possible to create unique polymers that outperform competitive alternatives. It's a curse because specialty performance runs counter to a commodity-oriented and capital-intensive business. Such businesses strive for leverage from scaling production asset platform-levers.

Plastics sold by producers like Dow and ExxonMobil are not an end-product. Rather, they are a material used in the customer's end-products. Introducing new polymers demands significant sales investment. In the 1990s, customers who wanted to take advantage of a new polymer had two choices. They could substitute the new polymer for a polymer already used. Or, customers could design a new end-product to take advantage of the new polymer's features.

Because Dow and Exxon's new polymers cost more than those already in use, the substitution approach was not likely to succeed. Somehow the customer would need to realize greater value from the new polymer's properties.

Customers needed to create new products exploiting the new polymer's uniqueness. The issue was that production volume depended on the customer's new product diffusing into its market. Building significant volumes could take years. Meanwhile, companies like Dow and Exxon had to keep their reactors at near capacity to gain scale and remain profitable. If production exceeded demand, the producer would then trade excess volume at an auction-like price. In effect, they would revert to the substitution approach. That wasn't good for profits.

The production challenge in polymer production is to reduce costs when cycling through polymer variants. The greater the polymer variation, the greater the waste and cost. The aim was to reduce waste while meeting customer demand for specific polymers. When new grades came in, production planning's job was to make sure the supply didn't get too far ahead of demand.

New polymers with new performance had margins greater than commodity polymers, but the challenge for producers was to have enough volume to reach break-even on their reactors. For most polymer product lines, the platform-lever was a production asset type, normally defined as a reactor combined with a catalyst.

Introducing new polymers could also cause notable time delays in filling a reactor. This was the case when Dow and Exxon went head-to-head in the 1990s. Both were introducing a new polyolefin made by using a new catalyst known as metallocene.

The new catalyst enabled a bimodal distribution of polymer chain lengths. The polymer could be tailored so each mode delivered properties of the polymer. This enabled producers to match performance properties to customer needs. Winning new customers for this new polyolefin type was critical to filling the new reactor-catalyst platform-lever capacity. The race to figure out how to do this was intense, with heated intellectual-property battles.

Both companies invested heavily in finding applications for their bimodal polymers. Dow had several solution-based reactors dedicated to their new plastic. Exxon, however, leveraged several large, commodity-scale gas-phase reactors. Dow's solution-based reactors were much smaller than Exxon's gas-phase reactors. This meant Dow could reach break-even more quickly than Exxon. Here's where Kurt Swogger steps in. The consummate polymer scientist, Swogger recognized the workload placed on development teams to tailor a polymer for each customer. He recognized how customers wanted unique performance from the polymer if they were to commit to buying it.

The challenge was that it could take up to six months to produce a unique polymer. Reasoning that challenge was no different for Exxon, Swogger realized that, if Dow wanted to win the metallocene war, it needed to reduce its sales cycle.

Figuring out how to produce the plastic with specific characteristics for each customer was difficult. First, researchers had to find out the polymer structure that gave the attributes. Up to that point, they used time-consuming and complex trial-and-error methods.

Next, Dow moved its prototype into a small pilot plant to refine production scale-up. Only after pilot plant work could its polymer begin production trials in Dow's full-scale reactor. Along the way, the company's customers would test the new polymer and provide comments on its use and performance.

However, what came out of Dow's lab was not easily transitioned to a pilot plant. And what came out of the pilot plant did not easily transition to full-scale production. The whole approach was more art than science.

That was where creative product line strategy took hold. Swogger figured Dow could win big if it delivered the new polymer to customers more quickly than Exxon. However, the industry's traditional focus was on gaining scale from production asset platforms.

The Pivot: Changing the Platform-Lever

Swogger realized that winning this new market would likely require a design-to-order service as a platform-lever, employing software models to determine polymer characteristics and the associated production settings. He believed that this type of platform-lever would allow development of a unique polymer, which could then be produced in half the time. He also reasoned Exxon would find it difficult to change its traditional approach to production, sales, and R&D because its gas-phase reactors and operating practices did not suit the design-to-order approach.

In design-to-order work, companies provide significant service before reaping any rewards. Typically, customers don't pay for that service directly. Instead, it's covered later by revenue from the sale of the product. Swogger had to decide if a service platform-lever would provide enough leverage to win in the market. After much thinking and exploration, he decided the strategy move was smart.

Dow's later investment into new polymer design and production scale-up modeling exceeded normal laboratory modeling. Much was done to link its laboratory to the pilot plant and to full-scale production. The company also shifted as a whole to support this new approach with key managers focusing directly on ensuring that they delivered on their speed promises.

Within two years, Swogger's novel platform-lever reduced the time between receiving customer requirements to delivering full production runs, cutting this time by 80%. The new service platform-lever gave Dow a big advantage in the polyolefin world.

This product line strategy move became known at Dow as "speed-based development." It enabled Dow to become the early leader in the metallocene-derived polymer market. Because of this, Dow won the Product Development and Management Association's prestigious "Innovator of the Year" award[67] in 2003.

And the Pivot Back

But as the bimodal polyolefins market matured, the speed of market diffusion faded in importance. So too did the need for keeping service at the center of Dow's polyolefin product line. By 2005, Dow abandoned its intense focus on its service platform-lever. Instead, it moved to a traditional production platform-lever and continued using that model to support production.

Large gas-phase reactors came to dominate the markets because of their advantages of scale and lower costs, allowing Exxon to gain market share. In the 2000s, Dow's top management saw the writing on the wall in the polymer industry and bought Union Carbide Corporation. Among the assets they gained were several large gas-phase polyolefin reactors, new platform-levers for new market dynamics.

Lessons from the Case

1. Good product line strategy is situational toward markets, customers, competition, and technologies.
2. When you change part of the Strategy-Essence, in this case the platform-lever, the move is called a "pivot." When one Strategy-Essence part changes, good product line management will look to adjust the other two parts. Here, Mr. Swogger changed the platform-lever from the large reactor-production asset to the rapid-modeling algorithm. For this to work in strategy, changes were needed for both the sales chain-link and the operations chain-link. Attribute

67 Dow Chemical received The PDMA 2003 Innovator of the Year award.

position also changed to emphasize speed—the time it takes a customer to profit from the new bimodal polymer.

3. Because an existing platform-lever is a notable investment does not mean it can't be relegated to being a technology building block. For Mr. Swogger, it made perfect sense to do so.
4. As markets change, evolve, or mature, so too must product line strategies. In this case, when the market for bimodal polymers matured, it was inevitable that the platform-lever would revert to the large reactor-production asset. This second "pivot" also brought with it changes to the other Strategy-Essence components.

Case History B:

Rockwell Automation Misses a Market by Being Siloed and Lean

This case shows the challenges large companies face in ensuring the flow of product information and insights across functions and hierarchies. Its focus is on how companies transfer knowledge and insights to drive new developments. The case addresses market changes, potential opportunities, and complex offerings when also using lean practices.

Background

Rockwell Automation is a large business-to-business, hard-goods producer. It engaged The Adept Group to analyze how it missed an emerging growth market that today we recognize as oil- and gas-well hydraulic fracking.

Rockwell was always number one or two in the markets it served. They had smart people with stellar track records. So it's not surprising that Rockwell's top management wondered why they were number six in the new hydraulic fracking market.

Oddly enough, many people in the company knew about the fracking market as it was emerging. Yet the company failed to develop a timely product to service it. Now management wanted answers to two key questions:

1. Why did Rockwell fail to act quickly to take advantage of the hydraulic fracking growth market?
2. How do other companies ensure a timely response to market changes and capitalize on emerging opportunities?

To answer these questions, The Adept Group's team undertook a thorough examination of Rockwell's approach and of the development systems of certain other companies. This secondary research included many interviews with key managers at other, noncompeting companies. The Group's findings were revealing.

Early in our engagement, we found that data on the emerging fracking market had been available. A young market research manager had compiled a report describing the market and detailing its relationship to two of the company's product lines.

Unfortunately, the company had no means to follow through on this information. No one acted on the information. This important market information had nowhere to go within the organization. No one used the information to form insights that could drive new product offerings.

What the Research Says

Our secondary research suggested these three points:

1. It's best practice if the person who could use information is also the person who discovers that information. This means that no transfer of knowledge is needed. Therefore, when creating new products and services, market research is best done by those who will use the information, provided they're trained to do so. In Rockwell's case, this would have been the engineering group.[68]
2. Proximity can be important for communication and sharing of information. When information providers and receivers

68 This is shown in research by Professor Abbie Griffin of The University of Utah. Prof. Griffin and her colleagues, Professor Emeritus Raymond Price, University of Illinois, and Professor Bruce Vojak University of Illinois, discuss this in their book *Serial Innovators: How Individuals Create and Deliver Breakthrough Innovations in Mature Firms*. It was published in 2012 by Stanford University Press.

locate near one another, the likelihood of informal "water cooler" discussions increase dramatically.

3. In complex settings, a process flow helps to ensure that information moves to the right people.

Rockwell's silo structure hampered the knowledge transfer needed to win in the fracking market. Separating offices, even on the same campus, also hindered communications.

Our benchmarking interviews with key managers at noncompeting companies were also revealing. We learned about the methods they use to promote information flow. Yet none considered themselves to be superb at transferring information into actions. The methods they used did help them in specific, one-off situations. But they did not work consistently across the board. The methods they cited are shown in Table 15.B.1 below:

Table 15.B.1 Analyses Methods Employed by Rockwell Automation Managers

Competitive analysis	Customer feedback (general)	Customer trends - system and product
Economic analysis	Sales and partner feedback	Project feedback (lessons learned)
Geographic analysis	Technology trends	Country/Political risk
Market access analysis	Regulatory/certification/ government trends	Customer usability feedback
Customer commitments	Performance measures (e.g., unit/$ shipments)	Customer loss feedback

However, it wasn't enough for us just to discover the company's need to develop cross-organizational knowledge transfer and communication processes. That was part of the solution. The Adept Group also needed to create an insight flow for Rockwell based on what was working at other firms. As with all processes, this needed three critical components: a workflow, an information/data flow, and a decision flow.

The first task was to map a simple insight flow. Therefore, The Adept Group team created a construct of the insight flow to show how data and information should translate into actions and value realization. The flow divided into three phases (see Figure 15.B.1).

Figure 15.B.1: Insight Flow

This is the basic flow of how insights move from their raw state to realizing

Figure 15.B.1: Insight Flow

This is the basic flow of how insights move from their raw state to realizing value.

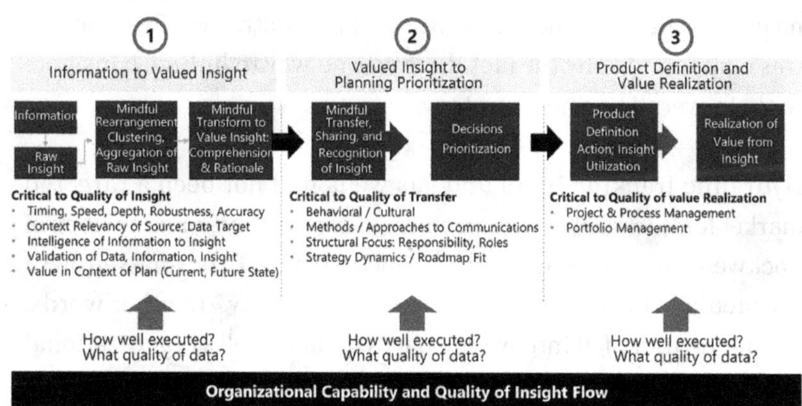

Rockwell's challenge was that they failed to translate information about the fracking market into insights and so move it forward. The transfer between Phase 1 and 2 in the flow shown in Figure 15.B.1 wasn't happening. Without realizing it, Rockwell depended on the proximity of people to induce information transfer, and, unfortunately, this was not effective.

Rockwell's size and product complexity created a need for better information flow, and a deliberate process would have facilitated that. It would have helped development efforts by connecting raw information and insight creation to value-realization work.

The market research and the intellectual property teams within the company were collecting much information. Working independently, each compiled information and converted it into insights. Some insights were deep and meaningful, while others were seemingly random. However, the two teams were not unifying their insights. Instead, they would separately present their findings at planning meetings within each business unit. There was no formal, forward-looking process that integrated their thinking.

Product development portfolio management wasn't a mature skill within the organization. Stage-and-gate practices and project management were well founded at Rockwell. However, there were no product line roadmaps in which to roll up activities. This problem was compounded by the fact there was no way to link such insights to their overall business strategy.

Hydraulic fracking in oil and gas wells had not been a targeted market for Rockwell. It was an emerging opportunity, and so none of Rockwell's product managers were focused on it. In business-growth vernacular, this was a "white space opportunity." In other words, the opportunity fell into white spaces on Rockwell's organizational chart, landing somewhere between the boxes, and so was almost invisible.

Previously, Rockwell had successfully addressed white space opportunities. Top management had to merely mandate the work. What made the difference? The organization had undergone several years of "leaning out" at Rockwell, a smart response to the downturn in the economy. There was little breathing room to undertake thinking about new endeavors or new markets.

The Adept Group team showed Rockwell's leadership how its quality of work affected its results. Rockwell's flow in Phases 1 and 3 in Figure 15.B.1 was good, but our diagnostic suggested the Phase 2 flow wasn't. Insights were not being recognized as important or prioritized for product planning.

Rockwell's offerings were complex at the time and still are. However, the company lacked "process proximity" among its key players. It needed to add a process to enable the flow of insights from their origination through to the value realization associated with them. The critical parts missing were product line strategizing and roadmap management.

More important, Rockwell also needed to roll up its product strategies and roadmaps. The process flow pictured in Figure 15.B.2 would enable all white space opportunities to be highlighted. The hydraulic fracking market would have been one of those.

Figure 15.B.2: Process Flow of Insights to Value Realization

Product line strategizing is a process. It connects information and insights to commercialization and value realization.

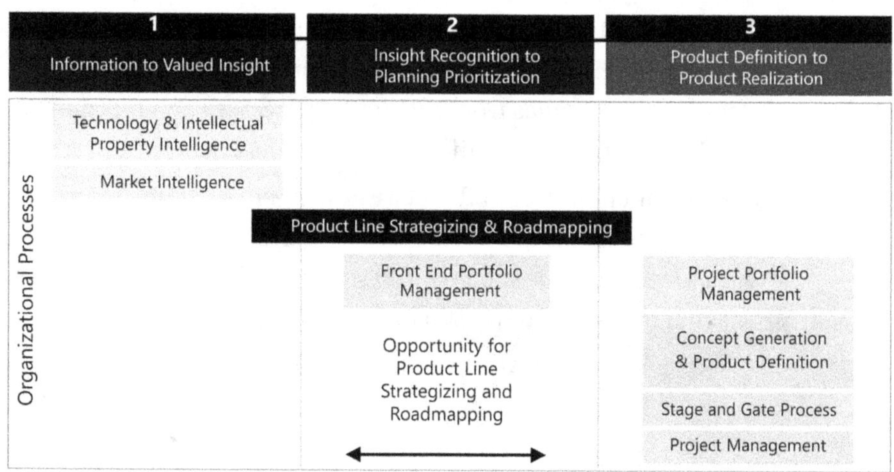

RA implemented our advice. They customized elements of product line strategizing and roadmap management to match their practices. Plus, they added two situational methods observed in our Adept Group research of other companies. After three years targeting the hydraulic fracking market, their market position went from number six to number four. But unfortunately, the entire fracking market went into decline.

The Flow of Information and Insights

Well-functioning organizations, especially those with lean practices, need to proactively guide information flows. This is especially true when the core goal of the business strategy is to create greater value from new offerings. The flow will be unique to the company and built on current organizational practices. Companies in situations like Rockwell's should work to customize a process flow specific to improving their product line strategies and roadmaps.

Lesson Learned

1. Insight flow is critical to gaining benefits from any opportunity. For product lines to flourish over time, organizations must facilitate the flow. The larger the organization, the more important the facilitation.
2. The time between information being available and key insights forming is the most crucial period for any product. Good strategy comes from setting up processes and mechanisms to aid the flow of information and insights.
3. Leaning out practices and processes that aid gathering information and forming insights can be dangerous to product lines. Organizations should build such practices into organizational behaviors and tie them directly to business strategy.

Case History C:

US Gypsum Boldly Introduces New Platform-lever

(When the world seemed to be crashing in)

In a few industries, platform-lever life cycles can have a long duration that can last decades. In fact, some managers may only ever experience one platform-lever, albeit mature, throughout their entire careers. Consequently, for the product line strategist, exiting a mature platform-lever and investing in a new one can be challenging. An organization's inertia can crush that thinking from the outset. This case explores a mature platform-lever strategy move and how leadership encouraged smart execution of this move.

Background

Maintaining a long-term focus is difficult for most organizational leaders. But a long-term orientation can pay off. However, this takes a deep understanding of markets, technologies, and products. Plus, it takes a whole lot of "corporate courage."

The 2009 Great Recession was more depression than recession for the building materials industry. New housing construction peaked in early 2006 and then dropped by over 75%. Builder after builder succumbed to the fall, as shown in Figure 15.C.1. Holding their breath collectively, materials suppliers did everything they could to cut costs. "Lean" and "downsizing" were the mantras of those industries.

Product strategists in the building materials industry are familiar with working on mature platform-levers. It's common for some products in that industry to have life cycles extending well over 50 years.

Good product line strategies will always be sensitive to the life cycle stage of their underlying platform-levers. When a platform-lever enters the mature stage, a strategist has two key questions to answer:

1. Should the company extend it by instituting minor incremental enhancements?
2. Should organizational investment and focus move to create a new platform-lever?

Mature organizations with mature platform-levers can find themselves in quite a predicament. In that situation, organizations are often lean and keep a concerted focus on leveraging their existing platforms. They typically make each chain-link in their strategy as lean as possible. Unfortunately, when taken to the extreme, leanness can create an environment where it's impossible to create or recast platform-levers for product line strategy purposes. There is just not enough organizational capacity to do so.

Figure 15.C.1: Housing Market Index and Single-Family Starts

This chart shows combined data of the "Housing Market Index" and "Single-Family Starts" (new construction for the period starting in 1985 and ending in 2014.)

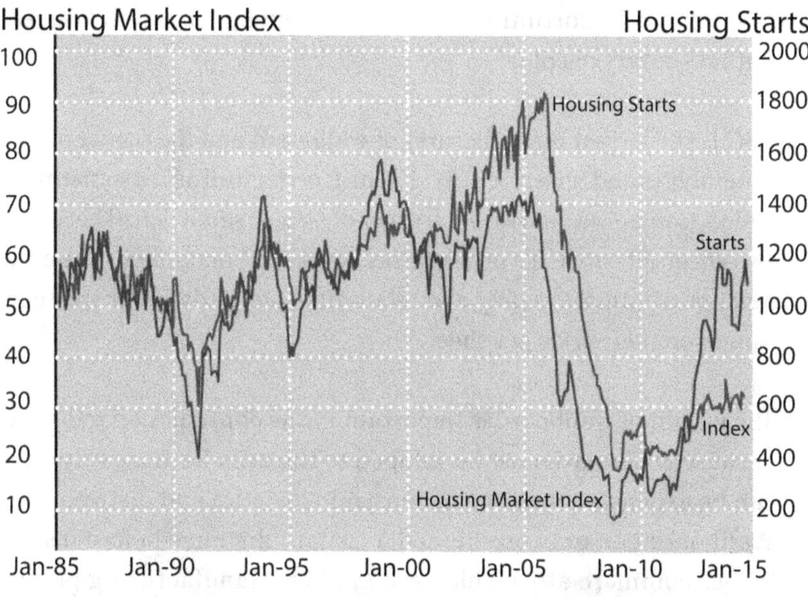

Source: NHAB/ Wells Fargo Housing Market Index, US Census Bureau

Leading the Product Strategy

The product line platform-lever of choice in the materials supply industry is a manufacturing process. It's been that way for several decades. To win market share, players must "out-leverage" their competition and achieve lower cost positions.

USG Corporation provides an example of a mature organization in the materials supply industry with a mature platform-lever. James Metcalf became the CEO of USG prior to the Great Recession, another difficult time for the company. USG was just coming out of bankruptcy caused by asbestos claims. During that transition, James Metcalf and USG developed an important business relationship.

Part of USG's exit from bankruptcy was the "purchase guarantee" of a stock issuance by Berkshire Hathaway. Warren Buffett was taking a position in USG. Buffett is not only CEO of Berkshire Hathaway but is also an investor and business leader known for his business acumen. Buffett's purchase guarantee made it certain that USG's equity would remain above water. In addition, James Metcalf now had the opportunity for one-on-one mentoring from Warren Buffett—a very big plus.

USG is the largest manufacturer of wallboard and the owner of the venerable brand Sheetrock®. Wallboard, or drywall as it's sometimes called, is merely a quarter-inch sheet of plaster sandwiched between two sheets of paper. It's pretty basic. Wallboard manufacturers only must pass minimal safety and reliability standards. Their strategy hinges on their price per sheet.

The weight of wallboard is important in the construction industry because wallboard must be shipped to the user. Because shipping can be expensive, weight can constrain logistics and distribution. Wallboard can only be shipped a certain distance before it's no longer commercially viable for a market. Manufacturing plants producing heavy boards have geographical markets smaller than those for plants manufacturing lightweight boards.

Weight also affects the laborers who must lift and install wallboards. Lifting a couple of tons of the product every week is normal. Cutting this weight could be attractive to an installer, if the price is right.

A major innovation project known as "Project Avalanche" had gotten underway at USG before the Great Recession took hold. Its goal was to reformulate and recraft the standard wallboard. The objective was to create a wallboard that was at least 33% lighter than its current wallboard and as strong, if not stronger.

Other product characteristics like fire, water, and moisture resistance had to remain the same. The project's aim was to recast USG's key platform-lever. The question was whether resulting products with higher price could find a market niche to warrant the investment.

When the Great Recession hit, firms like USG had some serious soul-searching to do, but that soul-searching was not done among its middle managers. It fell to USG's leadership. When times are tough, the easiest business move to make is to cut overhead and eliminate expenses. Project Avalanche was an easy target for elimination, or as some might say to be "put on the shelf"—temporarily.

But a cost-cutting orientation usually reflects a desire for improved short-term results. Warren Buffett, on the other hand, emphasizes long-term over short-term objectives. He also stresses the need for companies he invests in to create competitive advantage. He thinks management teams should create an "economic moat"[69] around their business to protect it and enable them to grow it further. (For more on the value of Buffett's concept of "economic moats," go back to Chapter 3.) Buffett believes that investors must identify and understand the economic moats that businesses have created and their importance to the company's ongoing performance.

Buffett gave James Metcalf strong advice, to double down on Project Avalanche, even though the near-term market was dismal. The reason? Buffett understood intuitively that strong product line platform-levers are key to building an economic moat. Thus, to Warren Buffett, supporting Project Avalanche was "a no-brainer," since it was aimed at developing a new platform-lever for the company.

---

69 For a definition of "economic moat," a term coined by Warren Buffett, please see http://www.investopedia.com/ask/answers/05/economicmoat.asp

Positive Results

As a result, USG developed the new product—Sheetrock® UltraLight.[70] Now, several years after its launch, the product accounts for over two-thirds of the company's revenue. Meanwhile, their top two competitors—Certainteed and Georgia-Pacific—have struggled. James Metcalf's leadership and bet on Project Avalanche paid off handsomely.

Lesson Learned

1. During tough times, the best move in product strategy might be unconventional and even counter-intuitive. While cutting expenses, especially for new developments, may save money in the short run, focusing on the long run with new or reformed platform-levers can prove to be a smart strategy move. New platform-levers can prevail when they are well thought out and yield products that match customer needs at a lower cost than otherwise. During bad economic times, value in performance can be powerful. In such cases, not going forward with such a strategy move is much riskier.
2. Deliberate decisions, especially in tough economic times, demand leadership involvement. The product line move to build a new platform-lever could only have survived with Mr. Metcalf's involvement. Here, the product line strategy and the business strategy were closely united.
3. Once again, while USG's product line strategy move was to create a new platform-lever, the benefits would only be realized by also changing the other two Strategy-Essence components: attribute positioning and chain-link alignment. USG knew the desired customer outcome—easier-to-lift wallboard and installing more sheets per day. This made attribute positioning a straightforward task in directly guiding the new

70 Sheetrock® UltraLight is a trademark of USG Corporation.

platform-lever development. Then, to reap the benefits from the new platform-lever, changes were needed. Sales needed to recast its pitch. Distribution needed to expand regions. Production levels at key plants needed to increase. And the supply chain needed to shift to address the new demand.

Case History D:

Microsoft and Aging Assumptions

(The Good, the Bad, and the Ugly)

Microsoft is an interesting case study on product line strategy dynamics. As it turns out, assumptions play a critical role.

Assumptions and Platform-Lever Maturity

In 1985, Microsoft introduced Windows as the personal computer operating system platform-lever of the future. Windows was radically different from the disk operating system (DOS). It introduced many programmers and end-users to the concept of clicking on objects in different "windows." That was a radical advance from typing in code. The windows operating platform-lever notably improved the user-friendliness of personal computers.

Some argue the Windows operating platform-lever was the "Wintel" platform-lever (i.e., a combination of Microsoft's Windows software and Intel's CPU chips). That makes sense in product line strategy. When technologies always combine in a platform, they should be considered part of that platform. But "Wintel" didn't make sense from the viewpoint that the platforms are managed by two different organizations.

For the next two decades, Microsoft and Intel both advanced their platforms following Moore's Law. They believed computer processing speed would double every two years. That led Microsoft to two critical challenges. One damaged its position in the personal computer market. The other made the company an also-ran in handheld devices.

"Moore's Law says that with time, processors get both faster and cheaper. Processor cycles are cheap. Code software accordingly—for power rather than for efficiency. That was how Microsoft programmed both Vista and Windows Mobile. Both OSs were designed to run decently on the processors of the day, but optimally on faster processors of the future."

"Microsoft made the dangerous assumption that PC and hand-held manufacturers would keep choosing the fastest affordable chips. That's happened with desktop CPUs but not with hand-held CPUs or graphics hardware. And with Vista relying so much on graphical "wow," even a fast CPU doesn't cut it when paired with slow graphics."

"Microsoft thought it was safe with its near-monopoly position in desktop PCs. Intel keeps churning out faster desktop processors, and NVIDIA and AMD are following suit with faster graphics cards. But these faster components actually have to make it into mainstream PCs (the majority of market segments) for Microsoft's strategy to work."[71]

71 "Microsoft's Mobile Speed Trap," by Sascha Segan May 2, 2008, © *PC Magazine*.

Figure 15D.1: Microsoft Windows Multi-Generational Platform-Lever Evolution

This is a multi-generational view of Microsoft's Windows operating system platform-lever. It is a compilation of data and information from various sources. Adapted from Reuters.

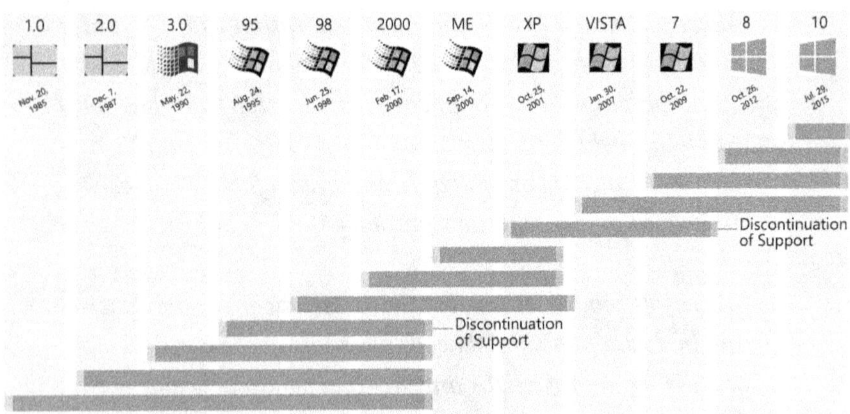

During the mid-2000s, personal computing saw major market changes. While a few market segments sought ever-increasing systems speed, other segments demanded other attributes. Speed was in a trade-off with lower cost, lighter weight, and longer battery life. At the same time, the use of hand-held devices like iPhones and Kindles took off.

Microsoft also supported a version of the Windows platform-lever for the mobile and hand-held device market. First created as a lightweight version of Windows known as Windows CE, it quickly evolved into "Pocket PC." Then in 2003, it advanced to become "Windows Mobile."

The idea was to enable the Windows platform-lever to pull its massive developer network and applications to all things mobile. At first, that platform-lever extension approach worked. At one time,

Windows Mobile was the market leader. Then Google ratcheted up its Android operating system, and Apple focused on iOS.

By 2010, Microsoft had all but abandoned Windows Mobile. Instead, it focused on Windows Phone, an operating system developed from scratch. But Windows Phone was at the bottom of all market share reports for mobile operating systems. By the end of 2015, Microsoft's mobile platform-lever was near death. It held less than 2% of the smartphone market and only 10% of the tablet market.

For far too long, Microsoft assumed that Intel and the PC manufacturers would stay the course with Moore's Law. They believed industry players would not cut corners to keep prices down, nor would they embrace underpowered integrated graphics in PCs. But market demands were a much greater force on platforms than Moore's Law. While science and engineering might progress in lockstep with Moore's Law, consumer behavior is totally independent.

Intel cut costs by developing computer motherboards not tied to the graphics approach in Windows Vista. Microsoft was forced to move forward with a mismatch between Window Vista and PC graphics.

Reforming the Platform-lever

In January 2015, Microsoft announced the impending launch of its Windows 10 operating system platform. This platform-lever addresses all devices, whether PC or mobile, gaming, or the Internet of Things. Plus, Windows 10 doesn't have life cycle beginning and endpoints for different versions. Instead, Windows 10 provides continuous upgrades. It's more like a service than a defined application. Microsoft was quick to point out that Windows 10 is not just recasting its platform-lever as it had done in the past. It was reforming it from the ground up.

Terry Myerson, Executive Vice President of Microsoft's Windows and Devices Group, explained it this way:

> *"We'll deliver new features when they're ready, not waiting for the next major release. We think of Windows as a service -- in fact, one could reasonably think of Windows in the next couple of years as one of the largest Internet services on the planet. And just like any Internet service, the idea of asking 'What version are you on?' will cease to make sense... With universal Windows apps that work across the entire device family, developers can build one app that targets the broadest range of devices – including the PC, tablet, phone, Xbox, the Internet of Things, and more."*[72]

Equally important for the Windows 10 platform-lever was Microsoft coordinating its development and fundamental architecture with Intel. Microsoft's Windows 10 and Intel's CPU, code-named Skylake, were "designed together." Kirk Skaugen, Senior Vice President, General Manager PC Client Group at Intel, explained that in an interview with Verge. He stated:

> *"There's a symmetry of purpose between Intel's efforts and Microsoft's. One wants its software to be ubiquitous and running on everything; the other wants its chips to be omnipresent and powering everything."*[73]

Skaugen articulates Intel's mission as "a continuum of performance, from servers to wearables." He also sees Intel's role as evolving toward being a "communications and connectivity company as much as an IT company." A decade ago, Intel was "a PC company

72 Terry Myerson, Executive Vice President, Windows and Devices Group, Microsoft, Windows Blog, January 21, 2015.

73 "An interview with Intel's general manager of the future of connected computing," by Vlad Savov on September 1, 2015, The Verge.

aspiring to sell PCs and servers." The new vision for the future is one where "if it consumes electricity, it computes; and if it computes, it connects; and if it's smart and connected, it will be best to have Intel."

Compared to previous platform-lever roll-outs, Windows 10 is more focused on the future than on shoring up weaknesses of the past. It's a reformation of the operating system platform, not an improvement and extension of past systems. Two years after its launch, Microsoft declared it would cease support for previous Windows operating systems.

The key to Windows 10 is its focus on operating system needs in the future. It doesn't hold onto or support old operating requirements. Many customers may have voiced their need to maintain legacy operating platforms. But Microsoft concluded that approach would be dangerous to its business. The dynamics suggested that Microsoft had to focus much more on the future and not be weighed down by the past.

Will It Work?

The product line strategy dynamics of Microsoft's Windows provides an interesting history for practitioners to observe. Not all moves like Vista and Mobile were stellar, but many like Windows 98 and 2007 were.

Just how it will turn out for Windows 10 in the years ahead is only conjecture. But it's obvious that Microsoft is relying on a common platform-lever to serve all devices. Much will depend on how well the company executes that strategy. Moreover, as platforms change, so too must its Strategy-Essence. The Windows 10 strategy choice and how Microsoft changes to facilitate its chain-link alignment will matter.

In the mobile market, Microsoft missed the boat. Windows powered less than 2% of the smartphones sold in 2015. Also, Microsoft's share of the tablet market hovers at a mere 10%. The Windows domination that served Microsoft so well in the age of the PC has been rendered increasingly irrelevant. The move to mobile has created great pressure on Microsoft.

Key Lessons

1. The dynamics impacting product lines and key assumption teams use to guide their work will eventually turn against a strategy. The challenge is to figure out which dynamics and assumptions will change ... when, and how.
2. Strategy dynamics should encourage the recognition of past mistakes but require platforms to "reform" for the future. Glance back at the past, but look and cast toward the future.

All platform-lever changes affect the product line Strategy-Essence, and some may impact business model. It's important to work through the details about how changes to platform-levers may affect the attribute positioning, chain-link alignment, and the business model. Understanding these impacts is critical to forming good product line strategies.

Glossary of Key Terms

Term	Definition
Agile	Agile is the term given to a set of product development principles to guide cross-functional teams as they incrementally develop new products and adapt to change. The aim is to get new or enhanced products to market quickly and cost effectively. Many companies combine agile practices with waterfall (staged) development processes
Attribute Positioning	The targeting and development of product or service attributes to secure a place within a specific market segment. The match of attributes to the needs and wants of customers within a market segment.
Balanced Scorecard	A performance measurement tool used to support the implementation of a business strategy or operational activities. The balance recognizes trade-offs between and among metrics.
Business-Growth Portfolio	All investments, projects, and ventures contributing to or taking away from the business unit's top-line revenue growth. All of a business unit's product lines are included.
Business Model	How an organization creates, delivers, or captures value.

Business Model Transformation	When an organization purposely changes how it creates, delivers, or captures value. This always involves changes to product line strategies.
Chain-Link	Different functional links in an organization's business strategy, e.g., production, sales, marketing, product, intellectual property, etc.
Chain-Link Strategy	A construct for thinking about business strategy in which many sub strategies are just one link in the chain. For example, supply chain, finance, and human resource strategies. Product line strategy or the roll-up of all product line strategies is just one link within the chain-link business strategy.
Concept Feasibility	The subprocess or set of activities to evaluate the feasibility of a new-product concept. Feasible concepts may progress to the stage/phase-gate or agile development process.
Concept Generation	Creating or otherwise generating new-product concepts.
Critical-to-Success (CTS)	A project or activity on a roadmap that is so significant that if it fails, it will compromise achieving one or more of the strategy objectives.
Culture (in large organizations)	The summation of behaviors affecting work and decisions, which are guided and influenced by beliefs, principles, and prevailing assumptions.
Cultural Inertia	A force internal to an organization that works against desired outcomes. It arises from cumulative behaviors and judgments across an organization and up and down its organizational structure. It is an artifact of an organization's culture.

Customer-desired Outcome	This is the verb-oriented statement of a customer need. It is the fulfillment or achievement of a customer's desired end result from buying and using a product or service.
Ecosystem Platform	Powerful marketplace levers carried out by business models and whole business strategy. Companies gain leverage externally in the marketplace, not internally to the product line. Examples include Google, Apple, and Facebook. Leverage comes from external players, independent of the company. Without external players, ecosystem platforms realize no leverage.
Expected Value	The risk-adjusted value of a project.
Front-end	A term for an initial portion of the new-product development process, in front of stage-and-gate development. It is often referred to as the "fuzzy front-end" to indicate the uncertainty that often exists before final product specifications can be determined.
Fulcrum	The combination of organizational structure, software systems, cross-organizational processes, practices, and methods that enable a management team to focus on and gain leverage from a specific platform-lever.
Full Process Architecture	A set of organizational processes that integrate into a full approach for conducting new-product development.
Growth Portfolio	The set of all growth activities and initiatives within a business unit, including, but not limited to, those for all product lines.

Jobs-to-be-Done Theory	This is a concept that give insight toward understanding customer needs based on fulfilling customer-desired outcomes. The theory credited to Harvard Professor Clayton Christensen and builds on Outcome Driving Innovation developed by Tony Ulwick.
Leverage	An advantage derived from a platform-lever. This has a major influence on the likelihood of the product line succeeding in the marketplace against competitive alternatives.
Market Segments	Defined parts or slices of a larger market. In product line strategizing, market segments must be prioritized or otherwise ranked against one another.
Master Product Line Roadmap	A roadmap that is more comprehensive than the traditional roadmap. In the case of a product line strategy, the master roadmap will contain additional information related to product line strategy and its execution, making it more useful to the team.
Pillar	A support for *PLuS Framework*. There are four pillars in the *PLuS Framework*: The Strategy-Essence; Master Roadmap and Sub-Roadmaps; Objectives, Measures, and Scorecards; and Rationale and Roll-up.
Pivot	The type of change that changes the Strategy-Essence, and how the functional chain-links interface or work with one another. It is one step up from a strategy move.

Platform-Lever — A common factor that cuts across multiple products in the product line. It enables leverage in the creation, production, use and/or sale of related product offerings. There are several types of platform-levers used in product line strategies. They may be used by themselves (singly) or in combination with other platform-levers.

Platform-Lever Life cycle — Just like products, platform-levers progress through four life cycle stages: introduction, growth, maturity, and decline. Platform-lever actions and strategies will be different for these four different life cycle stages.

Product Innovation charter (PIC) — A target for a product innovation. A PIC communicates the innovation target's objective and purpose in product line strategy. It also includes a set of guidelines to provide focus toward the target and a rough estimate of the economic value of "hitting" the target.

Product Line Strategizing and Roadmap Management — The complete planning of specific product line platform-levers at a strategic and a tactical level, that is, during project planning. Key to this planning is linking value-adding technology building blocks to the platform-lever, as well as to the critical drivers in the marketplace.

PLuS Framework™ — A framework developed by The Adept Group for creating and improving product line strategies. PLuS stands for Product Line Strategy. It is flexible and adaptable. The objectives of this framework include driving greater cash flows, ensuring that resources are used more effectively, and increasing overall customer satisfaction. *PLuS Framework* is a tradename of The Adept Group Limited, Inc.

Product in Development (PID)	A defined product development project with resources assigned to it, currently under development within the stage/phase-gate and/or agile development process.
Product in the Market (PIM)	A product currently being sold or marketed.
Portfolio Management	The management of a full set of new-product development projects into which resources are invested. Key aspects of portfolio management include mix management to ensure alignment with a defined strategy, and pipeline management to allocate appropriate human, physical assets, and financial resources.
Ring-fence	To separate an activity such as developing a potential component of a product line or a full line from the core business and its functional and cross-functional chain-links. The notion is to protect or insulate the activity from the standard behaviors and procedures of the organization.
Roadmap	A visualization of execution of a strategy that includes times and dates for the completion of key tasks.
Roadmap Entropy	The accumulation of changes to a strategy and its Execution Roadmap. When left unmanaged (lack of governance), the changes lead to deeply rooted chaos. Corrections may require major changes a product line's Strategy-Essence and Execution Roadmap.
Roadmap Management	The oversight and ongoing synchronization of master roadmaps and subordinate roadmaps across product line and in concert with project management and portfolio management.

Roadmap Recast	A change to a project on the master roadmap, without change to the strategy. For example, a recast may require changes in completion dates or product attributes being delivered. The main characteristic of this type of change is that it does not alter the Strategy-Essence. There is no change to market positioning, platform-levers, or chain-link alignment.
Roadmap Synchronization	To create a timing for delivery of individual components and attributes specific to an offering or platform-lever. Ideally, all parts come together on time and as quickly as possible.
Roll-up (Noun) **Roll up, to (Verb)**	**N.** The result of combining various strategies such as the product line strategy to examine under the overall umbrella of the business strategy. The roll-up can be described either in words or illustrated in a graphic. **V.** To effectively combine each product line strategy within the business strategy and illustrate the relationship either in words or in a graphic.
SpiralUp™ Implementation	An approach toward implementation that proceeds one capability maturity level at a time. During such implementations, the team focuses on specific objectives for each maturity level and minimizes impact on projects underway.
Stage-and-gate development process	An approach to carry out development of a new product after its conceptualization and feasibility assessment. Predetermined work is carried out in "stages" that precede and deliver output to predetermined decision "gates."

Strategy Move An action notable enough to cause a change to a platform-lever, positioning, or a chain-link. This, by definition, is a change to the Strategy-Essence. However, it does not change the relationship between the Strategy-Essence parts.

Strategy-Essence Pillar #1 of the *PLuS Framework*. It has three parts: Chain-link alignment and synergy, segmentation and positioning, and platform-levers. Each of these parts can build upon and add value to each other.

Strategy Pivot A major change to the product line and its strategy that changes the Strategy-Essence. It also changes how the functional chain-links interface or work with one another. Ideally, the pivot should be proactive and done in anticipation of (or as an early response to) changing conditions. If it is done reactively or made too long after conditions changed, it may be less effective or even made too late.

Subordinate Roadmap (sub-roadmap) Roadmaps that supplement a master roadmap with important information about key areas related to the product line strategy.

Success Trap A conundrum in which companies can find themselves. Companies get "trapped" by overemphasizing the very practices, behaviors, and strategy that made them successful.

Systematic Risk The uncertainty that is inherent across a large set of projects due to common factors such as market, technology, and industry changes.

Technology Building block A technology that augments or adds value to the platform-lever. Good product line strategies often organize technologies by grouping them. A common grouping is to create sets of technology building blocks that focus on the same verb-base segment or common jobs-to-be-done. Those responsible for the group then seek new technology building blocks to advance their set.

ONLINE RESOURCES

Please sign up for Adept Group's online *PLuS Resources*™. There is a small fee to gain access.

Go to: https://adept-plm.com/plus-resources/

Here are some articles, whitepapers, blog posts, and videos you'll find in the *PLuS Resources.*™

- ✓ Product Development and Governance: What Business Schools Don't Teach: Guidelines for Successful Implementations
- ✓ Potential Metrics
- ✓ Understanding Platform-Levers and Their Fulcrums: The Key to Great Product Line Strategy
- ✓ Verb-based Segmentation and Creating Outcome-driven Product Specifications
- ✓ *PLuS Lenses*™ & Process Templates
- ✓ Systems and Solutions as Offerings
- ✓ Visio Template for Master Product Line Roadmaps
- ✓ Tools & Techniques for Peering into a Product Line's Future
- ✓ SpiralUp™ Implementation of the *PLuS Framework*™
- ✓ The History of Product Innovation Charters and Why You Need Them

- ✓ Governing Product Line Strategy – What Top Managers Need to Know
- ✓ Clustering Technology Building Blocks: Jobs-to-be-Done Value Centers
- ✓ The Management Art of Product Line Roadmapping
- ✓ Project-portfolio Management and Product Line Strategies
- ✓ Decision Flows in Product Development and Management
- ✓ Product Line Roadmapping: Tricks of the Trade
- ✓ The Many Religions of Product Development
- ✓ Winning The Red Queen's Race (in Product Development)

About the Author

Paul O'Connor founded The Adept Group in 1984 with a single focus: improving innovation and product management in large companies. Today, his clients include a long list of global companies across nearly every industry.

O'Connor began his career with a leading innovation and strategy "Think Tank," using original open innovation methods. Paul led and simplified innovation initiatives at major companies like Exxon and Procter & Gamble. He worked with pioneers in practices such as project screening, staged development, portfolio management, and intrapreneurship.

From 1990 to 1992, O'Connor served as president of the Product Development and Management Association, a leading proponent of best practices in innovation and product management. Paul played a key role in shaping PDMA's first certification test for professional recognition. He also helped set up foundational research on best practices and measuring new product success.

Paul has published in peer-reviewed journals and business publications. He was among the original contributors to PDMA's Handbook of Product Development in 1996 and 2008. He also wrote for PDMA's 2004 ToolBook and was a contributing editor to *R&D Magazine.* His work also appeared in the respected *Journal of Product Innovation Management.*

O'Connor teaches master courses in product line strategy and is a frequent speaker at corporate meetings and seminars. His topics include Product Line Strategy, Roadmapping, Portfolio Analytics, and Innovation Productivity … focused on large organizations.

O'Connor earned a Bachelor of Engineering degree from Stevens Institute of Technology and a Master of Business Administration degree from Babson College.

At Babson, Paul supported the faculty in creating the first Entrepreneurship curriculum. Paul's job was to find, organize, and deliver articles and books professors requested from the Harvard Business School Baker Library and other locations around Boston. He was selected for this job because he owned a car, a strategic advantage the other two candidates, both foreign, could not match. More than once, Paul says, his advantage won him the right to empty the garbage which the Finance group frequently overproduced. Today, outside his professional activities, Paul spends much of his free time involved with family, music, and dogs.

www.ingramcontent.com/pod-product-compliance
Lightning Source LLC
Chambersburg PA
CBHW061009220326
41599CB00023B/3883

* 9 7 8 0 9 9 9 7 3 8 1 0 8 *